KABIR LEGENDS

and Ananta-das's *Kabir Parachai*

Sri Garib Dass Oriental Series No. 140

KABIR LEGENDS

and Ananta-das's *Kabir Parachai*

With a translation of the *Kabir Parachai* prepared in collaboration with Jagdish Kumar and Uma Thukral and with an edition of the Niranjani Panthi recension of this work

David N. Lorenzen

Sri Satguru Publications
A Division of
Indian Books Centre
Delhi-India

Published by :
SRI SATGURU PUBLICATIONS
Indological and Oriental Publishers
A Division of
Indian Books Centre
40/5, Shakti Nagar,
Delhi-110007
(INDIA)

First Indian Edition : Delhi, 1992

ISBN 81-7030-316-8

Printed at :
D.K. Fine Art Press,
Delhi

Printed in India

CONTENTS

A NOTE ON TRANSLITERATION

In this work, diacritics are used only for transliterated generic words in Hindi and Sanskrit that are italicized. Diacritics are not used for proper nouns, book titles, or generic words in nonitalicized Roman. The standard transliteration system employed for Sanskrit is used, except for a few modifications introduced to bring the spelling closer to Hindi and English pronunciation.

In the case of Hindi words, a mute *a* at the end of a word or before a hyphen is usually dropped. A final *a* is usually kept when it is preceded by two consonants (including nasals and semivowels). Nasal consonants written with an *anusvāra* are changed into the appropriate class nasal, except before *s* and *h*, and when it seems important to indicate the original spelling. In such cases, and in the case of nasalized vowels (*anunāsik*), the nasal sound is indicated by an *ṃ*. Urdu phonemes are not distinguished from their closest Hindi equivalents, except for *f* and *z*. The word "*pad*" (poem) is arbitrarily distinguished from "pada" (quarter verse). Hindi and Sanskrit words commonly used in English are not italicized.

Other changes include the following:

ऋ	and	रि	=	"ri"
च	and	छ	=	"cha" and "chha" respectively
ड	and	ड़	=	"da" or "*ḍa*"
श	and	ष	=	"sha"

PREFACE

I first heard the name Ananta-das in 1976 when I was just beginning my research on the Kabir Panth. In a series of interviews with Gangasharan Shastri, the administrative head of the Kabir Chaura monastery in Varanasi, he read to me portions of a book on Kabir's life that he was writing and would soon publish as the *Kabir Jivanacharitra*. In this book and his comments on it, he often referred to Ananta-das's *Kabir Parachai*. The only manuscript of this text he knew of was in the library of the nearby Nagari Pracharini Sabha. Since the library was (and continues to be) quite jealous of its manuscripts, he was not allowed to copy more than two pages, but he worked around this obstacle by sending, one by one, a dozen or so sadhus to the library. Each sadhu copied another two pages until the text was complete. Gangasharan Shastri himself was reluctant to share his handwritten copy and only gave me a chance to glance through it. At the time, my chief research interest was the monastery and not Ananta-das in any case. Nonetheless, my curiosity was aroused, and the idea of working more closely with this text stayed with me.

My chance to do so came in October 1982 when I stopped in London en route back to Mexico from India in order to look at a manuscript of the *Kabir Parachai* [A 12] that I had learned was in the India Office library. After examining the manuscript, I ordered a photocopy of a microfilm of it from the library. This photocopy was kept mostly filed away until 1985 when Professor Jagdish Kumar of the University of Delhi joined the Center of Asian and African Studies of El Colegio de México as a visiting professor of Hindi. He began the task of teaching me to read the text. With very little help from me, he prepared a tentative translation of the text into modern Hindi. The work was complicated by the fact that we had only one manuscript to work with. In addition, since this India Office manuscript is bound as a thick book, the letters nearest the spine are either out of focus or simply blacked out in the photocopies of the microfilm. To make matters worse, the parts of the original manuscript written in red ink are virtually invisible since the photographer failed to use a green filter. Nonetheless, with the help of a number of what later proved to be remarkably accurate guesses, Professor Kumar managed to fill in most of the missing letters.

I finally set about getting copies of some additional manuscripts in 1986 during a one month visit to India. With the help of Dr. Shukdev Singh of Banaras Hindu University, I managed to get permission from the director of the Nagari Parcharini Sabha Library to look at the *Kabir Parachai* manuscript [no. 877] that the sadhus of the Kabir Chaura monastery had copied several years before. I was allowed to compare it to my transcription of the India Office manuscript and to note down any differences in the readings. The two texts proved to be remarkably similar. Both are in fact important manuscripts of what I eventually came to call the Niranjani Panthi recension of the text because of its association with the religious sect known as the Niranjani Panth or Niranjani Sampraday (see below, chapter four).

About this time, I also learned that Professor Ram Kumar Varma of Allahabad University had published in 1983 a text of Ananta-das's *Kabir Parachai* as an appendix to his book, *Kabir: Ek Anushilan.* In the company of Dr. Shukdev Singh, I then went to Allahabad to ask Professor Varma about the manuscript he had used. Professor Varma claimed that he had lent the single manuscript used for his published text to a student who hever returned it. On this same visit to Allahabad, we had somewhat better luck in the Hindi Sahitya Sammelan. The authorities of the Sammelan kindly gave us permission to photograph their sole manuscript of the *Kabir Parachai* [HSS 1900] and promised that after the electricity came back on they would make a xerox copy of it and mail it to me, which they did.

A few days later, I set off for Rajasthan and Gujarat to visit some of the Kabir Panth monasteries in that region in the company of *sant* Vichar Das, an influential young sadhu and fine scholar from the Kabir Chaura monastery. Professor John S. Hawley of Columbia University had previously suggested to me that there might be copies of the *Kabir Parachai* in the manuscript collections of the Rajasthani Shodh Samsthan [RSS] and the Rajasthan Prachyavidya Pratishthan [RPP] in Jodhpur. We made Jodhpur our first stop. In the libraries of these two institutes we found numerous manuscripts of Ananta-das's *parachaī*s of various *sant*s including Kabir. With the kind permission of Dr. N. S. Bhati of the Rajasthani Shodh Samsthan and Dr. Padmadhar Pathak of the Rajasthan Prachyavidya Pratishthan, I was allowed to photograph several *Kabir Parachai*s found in these manuscripts. Unfortunately, in the latter institute the guardian of a room containing several other manuscripts was on vacation, and we were unable to examine those kept in this room. I was finally able to see these manuscripts on a subsequent visit in 1990. In 1986, after my visit, Dr. Pathak sent me a photocopy of the *Kabir Parachai* found in the 1693 V. S. manuscript [RPP 11583] via the Mexican ambassador in Delhi, Professor Graciela de la Lama, who sent it on to me in Mexico City. This appears to be the oldest extant manuscript of the *Kabir Parachai.*

Early in 1987, I met Dr. Winand Callewaert of the Catholic University of Leuven at a Sikh Studies conference in Berkeley, California. He was working on the preparation of a critical edition of a number of the *parachaī*s attributed to Ananta-das, mainly on the basis of manuscripts found in the library of the Dadu Mahavidyalay. We were naturally very interested in each other's projects and agreed to try to collaborate. I lent him copies of the manuscript photographs and photocopies I had collected in London and India and later sent him a draft copy of the English translation of the *Kabir Parachai* text. He sent me transcriptions of several of the manuscripts he was working with as well as drafts of his own critical edition of the *Kabir Parachai* text. Unfortunately, this collaboration did not work out quite as well as we had hoped because of the difficulties of working together by mail and because of a purely scholarly disagreement about the relative values of what turned out to be the two principal recensions of the text (what I have called here the "Niranjani Panthi and Dadu Panthi recensions" respectively). In any case, it should be clear that both Callewaert and I have benefited from each other's work.

In September of 1987, Dr. Uma Thukral arrived in Mexico to join the staff of the Center of Asian and African Studies of El Colegio de México to become professor of Hindi, Professor Jagdish Kumar having returned to Delhi in December of 1986. Professor Thukral and I then set about preparing a full English translation of the *Kabir Parachai* with the help of the various manuscripts at our disposal as well as Callewaert's transcriptions and a draft of his critical edition. We chose as our basic text a "corrected edition" of the Niranjani Panthi recension of the text that I prepared on the basis of the India Office library manuscript [A 12] and other manuscripts of this recension (see the discussion in chapter four). We also consulted and translated the alternate readings of the Dadu Panthi recension of the text as given in the 1693 V. S. manuscript [RPP 11583] and in the draft of Callewaert's critical text.

The first three chapters of this book represent a considerably revised and expanded version of an unpublished article on "Kabir Legends" that I wrote early in 1986. In the first chapter, I have discussed the importance of the Baghel dynasty and King Virasimha Baghel in determining the date of Kabir and in helping to explain the spread of the Kabir Panth. I have argued that it can now be taken as almost certain that Kabir flourished in the last years of the fifteenth century and first years of the sixteenth. I have also argued that it is quite probable that Kabir was a disciple of Ramananda as tradition claims and that Ramananda flourished in the second half of the fifteenth century.

Chapters two and three summarize and discuss the various versions of each important Kabir legend. Chapter two examines those legends first found in Ananta-das's *Kabir Parachai*, while chapter three examines those first found in various other texts. Almost all these legends clearly reflect the socio-economic as well as the religious concerns of their authors. I regard the transmission of these various "ideological messages" as playing a pivotal role in the creation, presevation and continuing popularity of the legends. Some of these messages are relatively self-evident, others much less so.

Chapter four is essentially an introduction to the translation and the corrected edition of Ananta-das's *Kabir Parachai* which follow. In this chapter I have given my reasons for associating the 1693 V. S. and related manuscripts with the Dadu Panth and for associating the India Office and related manuscripts with the Niranjani Panth.

This chapter also explains why Uma Thukral and I have preferred to take the Niranjani Panthi recension of Ananta-das's *Kabir Parachai* as the basis for our translation, and why I have chosen this recension for my corrected edition of the text. It is worth reiterating here that our preference is not based on the relative antiquity of the two recensions. The oldest surviving manuscript of the *Kabir Parachai*, that of A.D. 1636, belongs to the Dadu Panthi recension. The oldest manuscript of the Niranjani Panthi recension is dated in a year equivalent to A.D. 1665. We have preferred the Niranjani Panthi recension of the *Kabir Parachai* mostly because of its greater logical and linguistic coherence, as well as because of the later historical importance of the somewhat disputed first section, generally found only in manuscripts of the Niranjani Panthi recension of the text. In our opinion, neither the Dadu Panthi recension nor the Niranjani Panthi recension can be convincingly identified as being closer to a supposed original version of the text. Indeed, the traditional oral style of the composition suggests that no fixed original version may ever have existed.

About the translation and corrected edition of Ananta-das's *Kabir Parachai* contained in chapters five and six, little need be said here. As noted above, the translation was a collaborative effort by Jagdish Kumar, Uma Thukral, and myself. The corrected edition is my own, although the choice of correct readings, when it varies from the India Office library manuscript, owes much to our joint effort of translation. The translation itself aims to be accurate and understandable before being elegant. The original text is written in narrative verse rather than in an elaborate poetic style. Nonetheless, the text is often quite elliptical, and the minimal inflections and ambiguous syntax of the *sadhukkaḍī* Hindi dialect in which it is written often make it still more difficult to decipher. We have often added phrases to complete the sense. These additions are put in brackets only when they are somewhat debatable.

Many people have offered help and encouragement during the preparation of this project. I especially want to thank my colleagues Jagdish Kumar and Uma Thukral. They not only collaborated on the translation but also offered much good advice about the rest of the book. Jagdish Kumar died unexpectedly early in 1988. He was a good friend as well as a collaborator and teacher. His many friends in Mexico and I all miss him.

Particular thanks are also due to Dr. Shukdev Singh of Banaras Hindu University, Dr. Winand Callewaert of the Catholic University of Leuven, and *sant* Vichar Das of the Kabir Chaura monastery in Varanasi. As has already been partly noted in this preface, they all helped immensely in obtaining the materials used in the preparation of this book. My correspondence back and forth with Winand Callewaert about the different readings of Ananta-das's text amounts to a small book in itself. Other persons who have contributed helpful comments and advice include Professors Susana Devalle of El Colegio de México, John S. Hawley of Columbia University, Linda Hess of the University of California Berkeley, Philip Lutgendorf of the University of Iowa, W. H. McLeod of Otago University in New Zealand, and Charlotte Vaudeville of the Sorbonne. Financial assistance during various stages of this project has been generously supplied by the Government of India (through the Mexico-India cultural exchange agreement), the American Institute of Indian Studies, and El Colegio de México.

But at last she said, "I didn't expect to see you again."
"Didn't you? Any particular reason?"
"When someone goes away they become legendary."
"I don't understand."
"You became a legend, Ian."
"Is legend what you mean? It seems the wrong word to me."
She said, "I think it's the right word."
"Fantasy with its roots in fact."
"Yes."

Paul Scott, *A Male Child.*

PART I

THE LEGENDS

CHAPTER 1

LEGENDS AND HISTORY

In India, as elsewhere, the appearance of legends about saints and heroes is a mysterious event. It is not just that there rarely exists much independent historical evidence against which to compare the legends. Even in the few cases where such evidence is available, it helps very little to explain how and why the legends have arisen. Most legends contain more fantasy than history, more dreams than everyday reality. Often it is only the embarrassing or inconsequential details of the legends —the warts and blemishes that the process of converting the legends and their heroes into idealized archetypes has been unable to remove— that preserve some memory of what really happened. The rest is imagination.

But imagination takes many forms. Legends do not gather around saints and heroes completely at random. Legends arise from the rich treasury of themes and motifs that history makes available to each particular society, but for each individual saint or hero the creative process is selective. Certain themes and motifs are conserved and others are discarded. The usually unknown authors of the legends, whether individual or collective, construct the legends on the basis of their own and their listeners' or readers' needs, tastes, hopes, and desires. Any episode, fact or fiction, that fails to serve these ends tends in time to be forgotten. Any episode that does serve them is preserved in popular memory like a favorite melody that new singers may reinterpret but not omit from their repertoire.

Simply to trace the evolution of the many retellings of legends is an exacting task, rather like the excavations of the archaeologist who unveils the many reconstructions of the multilayered Mexican pyramids.

This task has its own charms and rewards, but I prefer to pay more attention to two related questions: What are the social and psychological needs, tastes, hopes, and desires that helped create and popularize the legends? And how did these motivations, as they evolved and sometimes mutated in later historical environments, influence the evolution of the legends? One should, as Alan Dundes insists, try to keep the folk in folklore [Dundes 1980: viii].

Unlike myths and fairy tales, which often share similar motivations, legends claim to recount the deeds of *historical* persons in *historical* time [Dundes 1980:231]. In cases where some historical substratum to the legends about a particular saint or hero seems to exist, scholars have often struggled to reconstruct his or her "true" history. Since in most cases the legends provide virtually the only source material on which to base such historical reconstructions, the choice of criteria to determine what is history and what is not is by no means an easy one. Most scholars would agree that miracles and divine or supernatural interventions must be discarded and that the embarrassing events and inconsequential details of the legends are most likely to be true. In between these two extremes, however, one finds a vast amount of material that cannot be clearly classified as either "fact" or "fiction." Just how far should we go in "demythologizing" our saints and heroes?

Unfortunately, answering this sort of question helps very little to explain why legends about saints and religious founders, hagiographies, play such a key role in the beliefs and practices of nearly all sects and major religions. Whether these legends are based on historical fact or not, they claim to offer historical explanations of how these religious movements arose and how their traditions were preserved, often in the face of adversity, in later years. The legends take the form of stories that the members of the community tell about and for themselves. They are reflexive commentaries that define the imagined shared past of the community, its historical identity, as well as normalize its religious, social, moral, political, and even economic values [Oberoi 1987:26-28; Geertz 1973:448-53].

At the same time, legends can and do serve either to justify or to protest against the asymmetrical relations of power that prevail in the larger societies of which the communities that tell the legends form a greater or lesser part. In other words, the legends embody a socio-religious ideology. By the term ideology, I refer specifically to what John B. Thompson [1984:4] has called a "*critical conception*" of ideology, one that directly links ideology to the exercise of social power. Nonetheless whereas Thompson regards ideologies exclusively as instruments of domination—"the ways in which meaning (or signification) serves to sustain relations of domination"—I prefer to also regard the various sorts of discourse that protest against such social domination as forms of ideology. Indeed, in the case of the social meanings that are implicit and explicit in the Kabir legends, their primary intention is to protest against social discrimination and economic exploitation rather than any legitimation of existing institutions of domination. The Kabir legends manifest the ideology of the poor and powerless, not the rich and powerful.

Myths—in the folklorist sense of narratives about how things first came to be as they are [Dundes 1980:224]—also embody ideological messages. In the case of myths, however, these messages are mostly concerned with the basic conceptual, social, and psychological structures that define the communities and their members. Legends, on the other hand, are generally more directly concerned with the specific socio-economic and political situations faced by the communities in the course of their historical development. As a result, legends often require, and permit, less "depth" analysis than myths do. It is no accident that both structuralist anthropologists like Claude Lévi-Strauss and religious psychologists such as Mircea Eliade have preferred to work with myths rather than with legends.

This does not mean, however, that legends can be simply left to speak for themselves. Their ideological messages may not have the same character as those of myths, nor are legends as subject to the psychological condensations and distortions typical of myths. Nonetheless, the messages that legends contain are often subtle ones and may be disguised or left implicit rather than openly specified. In the case of the legends about Kabir, the audience of low class peasants, laborers, and artisans for whom—and to some extent by whom—the legends were composed may have tended to absorb the ideological messages more subliminally than discursively. Outsider intellectuals may be better able to analyze and articulate the messages, but they are confronted with an immense historical and psychological gap between themselves and the original creators of the legends. A sympathetic leap of the imagination can help to bridge this gap, but such intellectuals can never have direct or complete access to the original historical and psychological context of the legends. As a result, many of the social, political and psychological implications of the legends are simply beyond the grasp of imaginative reconstruction.

The legends about Kabir have attracted comparatively little attention from academic scholars. Mostly such scholars have been content to try to somehow derive from the legends a historical "biography" of Kabir.[1] As might be expected, this approach does not lead very far. The rigorous historical criteria used by Charlotte Vaudeville, for instance, cast doubt on all but a few basic "facts" of Kabir's historical biography. Apart from extracting this historical residue, Vaudeville has little interest in the Kabir legends. For the most part, she is content to observe that "the legendary life of Kabir follows well-known patterns of Indian hagiography" [Vaudeville 1974:46]. The same may be said of most other academic scholars. The only partial exceptions are David Scott and a few scholars such as G. H. Wescott, F. E. Keay, Parashuram Chaturvedi, Kedaranath Dvivedi, and K. K. Bhatta (see note 1), who have been interested in the Kabir Panth as well as in Kabir himself. Even these scholars tend to be more interested in extracting a historical biography than in discussing the legends as manifestations of socio-religious ideology.

In the present study, I will discuss only a few specific historical questions about Kabir's life, namely, his dates, his relation to Ramananda, and his family situation. I shall not discuss in any detail what might be called the "prehistory or archaeology of these legends," that is, the identification of the sources of the stories before they were appropriated by the authors of the Kabir legends. Nor will I attempt to make a detailed classification of the specific folkloric motifs found in the legends. It is, however, necessary to at least outline the main broad narrative themes that characterize most of the legends.

When one begins to compare the main narrative themes of the Kabir legends, it quickly becomes apparent that almost all the legends fall into two or three related categories. Moreover, it can be shown that their themes are characteristic not of Indian hagiography in general, as Vaudeville tends to suggest (see above), but that they are themes particularly emphasized in the hagiographies of the saintly heroes of low-class persons.

The main narrative theme of most of the Kabir legends is a direct test of Kabir by a powerful political, economic, or religious figure: by a king, a sultan, a merchant, a Brahman, a Muslim *kāzī*, a god or a goddess. Not surprisingly, it is the low-class underdog, Kabir, who invariably ends up prevailing over all these figures, who attempt to

1. The more serious attempts to reconstruct Kabir's biography include those of C. Vaudeville [1974: 27-48], David Scott [1985], R. K. Varma [1966, 1971, 1977], K. N. Dvivedi [1965], K. K. Bhatta [1975], P. Chaturvedi [1964: 132-79], H. P. Dvivedi [1971], P. D. Barthwal [1946: 79-127], Mohan Singh [1934], F. E. Keay [1931: 26-50], and G. H. Wescott [1953 1-27].

discredit or to harm him by either trickery, magic, or brute force. In the legend of Sikandar testing Kabir, Kabir prevails over the attempt of the sultan, inspired by Brahmans and *kāzī*s, to drown, burn, and trample him to death. In the legend of Kabir's wife and the libidinous merchant, Kabir prevails over the efforts of the merchant to sexually exploit Kabir's wife. In the legends of the Brahmans demanding food and the unexpected feast, Kabir prevails over the greed and jealousy of the Brahmans. In the legends of Kabir's encounters with the Brahman devotees Tatva and Jiva, the Brahman scholar Sarvajit, the yogi Gorakhanath, and the Muslim *kāzī*, sheikh Taki, Kabir manifests his spiritual superiority by a display of miraculous powers. Kabir prevails even in a test of his generosity made by God disguised as a beggar of Kabir's cloth and a test of his chastity by a goddess or an *apsarā*.

In several other legends, Kabir abandons the somewhat passive role of the would-be victim (who ends up turning the tables against his more powerful examiners). In these legends, Kabir himself takes on the role of a sort of trickster figure who initiates his own test of the politically and religiously powerful. In the legend of his initiation, Kabir tricks the Brahman guru Ramananda into giving him a mantra of initiation and later proves his spiritual worth to his reluctant guru. In the legend of the visit to Kabir of the Muslim holy man Jahan-gasta, Kabir ties up a pig in front of his own house and uses it to turn the tables on his orthoprax visitor. In the legend of the prostitute, the *paṇḍā* and the king, Kabir tricks the king into doubting Kabir's moral character and magical powers. When Kabir's claims are proven correct, the king is forced to repent and humble himself before Kabir. Even the legend of Kabir's death at Magahar is in part the story of how Kabir uses his supernatural power to "trick" his royal disciples, Bijali Khan and Virasimha, into abandoning their quarrel over the possession of Kabir's corpse.

A few legends, which do not directly concern any test of Kabir's virtues and powers, nonetheless are also intended to reveal his innate, though hidden superiority. Most important in this regard are the various versions of the legend of Kabir's birth. These attempt to show that Kabir was not really a low-caste Muslim by birth. Rather they claim that he was either adopted by Muslims (who in some versions are said to be fallen Brahmans), that he was himself a Brahman in a former life, or that he was a direct incarnation of God.

What all these two or three general narrative themes have in common is a fantasized revenge by the weak against the powerful, by the poor against the rich, by the scorned against the scorners. The legends are in large part typical dreams of glory, wealth, and power dreamed by low-class persons such as those who became the followers of Kabir.

The narrative themes of the Kabir legends may be profitably compared with those about Mahatma Gandhi discussed in a fascinating article by Shahid Amin [Amin 1988:288-348]. These Gandhi legends were told mostly by poor peasants in the Gorakhpur region of Uttar Pradesh in the early 1920s. Amin identifies four basic themes in the stories [Ibid., 314]: "Testing the power of the Mahatma. . . . Opposing the Mahatma. . . . Opposing the Gandhian creed. . . . Boons granted and/or miracles performed." The similarity to the Kabir legends extends even to quite specific thematic motifs such as the hero's causing a dry stick to sprout leaves [Ibid., 328-30] (above, p. 57) and his ability to produce or otherwise control water and fire [Ibid., 315, 330-33] (see index). Both these specific motifs and the broader narrative themes may arise out of a common storehouse of the building blocks of Indian legends and myths, but they are selected and emphasized on the basis of the social and psychological needs of those who tell and listen to the stories.

The lack of any factual historical basis for the Kabir legends does not mean that they have no historical importance. Quite the contrary. These legends are themselves active historical forces, dynamic manifestations of the evolving values of the community that created them and has been their principal audience. From this point of view, it is clearly a mistake to limit the role of history to that of providing a "background" or "context" in which to locate the legends. History is not a scenic backdrop to the stage on which the legends are performed. History is the play itself, and the legends are important actors in it. However dependent these legends may be, in the last instance, on the economic and political factors that molded the mentalities of their authors and audience, they have also served to create the imagined shared past and the social, moral, and religious values that have defined the historical community and its relation to other constituent groups of society.

For Kabir's followers within and without the Kabir Panth, these legends have been a vital source and part of their religious faith, of their communal and personal identities, and of their socio-religious ideology. The legends provide the fullest expression of this faith, identity, and ideology at the same time that they serve to inculcate them in the minds and hearts of these followers. Without these legends the Kabir Panth would, in fact, not exist, just as Vaishnavism would be inconceivable without the legends of Rama and Krishna, Christianity without the legends of Jesus, Buddhism without those of Buddha, Islam without those of Muhammad.

The Early Texts

Two texts compete for the honor of being the oldest to contain a coherent set of legends about Kabir: the *Kabir Parachai* of Ananta-das and the *Nirbhayajnan*. The latter has not been published. I did briefly examine a manuscript of the *Nirbhayajnan* found in the Hindi Sahitya Sammelan library in Allahabad [catalogue no. 3-75/1443], but I was unable to secure a copy or study it in any detail. Kedaranath Dvivedi [1965:3-4] gives a short summary of the text in his *Kabir aur Kabir-pantha*. He also claims that the Nagari Pracharini Sabha library in Varanasi has a manuscript of the *Nirbhayajnan* dated V. S. 1633 (A.D. 1576). I was unable to locate this text in the Nagari Pracharini library in 1985. Dvivedi himself was only able to examine another manuscript of this text copied in V. S. 1856 (A.D. 1799). Dvivedi says that the *Nirbhayajnan* takes the form of a conversation between Kabir and his disciple Dharma-das. This shows that the text must belong to the Dharma-das branch of the Kabir Panth. This fact also puts in doubt the early date attributed to it since Dvivedi himself has shown that Dharma-das probably lived at least a hundred years after Kabir. Unless clearer proof of its early date can be found, I strongly suspect that the *Nirbhayajnan* is more likely a composition of the eighteenth century.

Ananta-das's *Kabir Parachai* is a much better known work and one whose early date is not in doubt. A version of Ananta-das's text based on a single, now lost manuscript was published as an appendix to a book on Kabir by Ram Kumar Varma [1983:95-107].[2] W. M. Callewaert is about to publish a critical edition of most of the *parachai*s attributed to Ananta-das including the *Kabir Parachai* as well as those of Nam-dev, Pipa, Dhana, Trilochan, and Ravi-das. The corrected edition and translation of Ananta-das's *Kabir Parachai* included in the present book is based on a different manuscript tradition from that used by Callewaert for his base text (See chapter six below for further details).

Ramananda's and Kabir's Dates

In his *Pipa Parachai*, Ananta-das lists his own spiritual genealogy as follows: Ramananda, his disciple Anantananda, his disciple Krishna-

2. See R. K. Varma [1983:95-107]. In an interview with Varma in 1985, he claimed that he had loaned his manuscript to a student who had never returned it to him.

das, his disciple Agra-das, his disciple Vinodi, and his disciple Ananta [-das].[3] If this spiritual genealogy is combined with that given by Nabha-das in his *Bhaktamal*, it yields the genealogical tree given in figure one. Nabha-das mentions all the names except that of Ananta-das himself. Ananta-das's *Kabir Parachai*, in both its two main recensions, supports Nabha-das's claim that Kabir was a direct disciple of Ramananda. According to J. N. Farquhar [1967:317], Nabha-das flourished between A.D. 1585 and 1623. The most prominent present-day authority, R. D. Gupta [1969:64], seems to accept A.D. 1624 as the latest possible date for Nabha-das's *Bhaktamal*. Since Ananta-das and Nabha-das are separated by only one spiritual generation (Nabha-das is Ananta-das's spiritual uncle) and could easily have been contemporaries, a floruit for Nabha-das of about 1600, or even 1625, agrees quite well with the 1588 A.D. date Ananta-das himself gives for the composition of his own *Nam-dev Parachai*.

Figure One

The guru genealogies of Ananta-das and Nabha-das

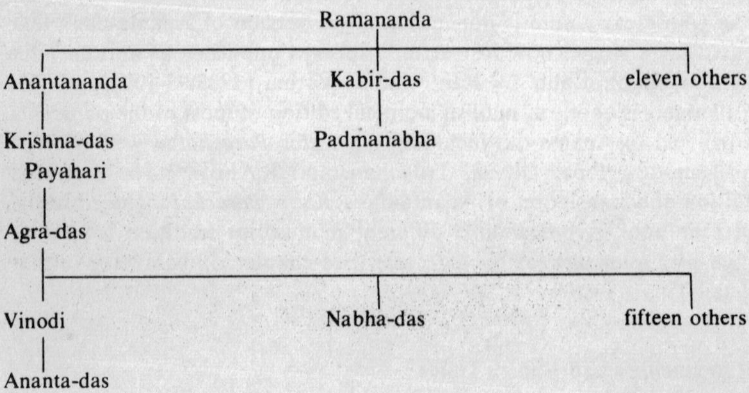

All this leads directly to the vexing and much discussed questions of the historical relation between Kabir and Ramananda and the dates

3. This verse is quoted by L. P. Dube [1968:30-31] in two different versions, one of which omits the names of Krishna-das and Vinodi.

of both. A detailed review of the extensive scholarly arguments on these questions is fortunately not necessary. This has been ably done by P. Chaturvedi [1964: 845-70] in Hindi, and the major points of his long discussion have been well summarized in English by Charlotte Vaudeville [1974: 36-39, 110-17]. Nonetheless, Chaturvedi's and Vaudeville's tentative conclusion—that Kabir probably died about the middle of the fifteenth century—is no longer tenable in the light of the data from Ananta-das's *parachaīs*. Although Chaturvedi and Vaudeville had access to most of this data, they did not make adequate use of it, particularly the historical synchronism of Kabir and Virasimha Baghel.

The question of the guru-disciple relation of Ramananda and Kabir cannot be separated from that of their respective dates since several scholars have claimed that Ramananda died too early to have been Kabir's guru. Some scholars have argued that the connection between Ramananda and Kabir (and other *sants* such as Pipa and Dhanna) was invented in order to legitimize, and also to tame, Kabir and the other *sants* by giving them a learned Brahman as their guru. It has also been claimed that this connection served to establish a hypothetical historical link between the *sants* and the important Ramanandi Sampraday reputedly organized by Ramananda's more orthodox Brahman disciples [see B. P. Simha 1957; B. N. Shrivastav 1957; Burghart 1978]. Tradition in fact associates both Nabha-das and Ananta-das with this Ramanandi Sampraday. The modern scholars C. Vaudeville [1974: 30-31, 37-40] and W. H. McLeod [1976: 155-56], in particular, are quite skeptical about the guru-disciple relation between Kabir and Ramananda.

What is the main evidence that *supports* the existence of this guru-disciple relation? Quite simply, it is the unanimous claim of tradition that Kabir was a disciple of Ramananda. The exact correspondence of the names in the genealogies of Ramananda's pupils found independently in the works of Ananta-das and Nabha-das (figure one) is one strong argument in favor of the historicity of the Ramananda-Kabir connection. Both these works were written within about a hundred years of Kabir's probable death. This entire genealogy, minus only the name of Ananta-das himself, is still accepted in the traditions of the Ramanandi Sampraday [B.P. Simha 1957:333-34, 352]. Other early texts that affirm this connection include the *Nirbhayajnan* [K. N. Dvivedi 1965:3-4], Hariram Vyas's (died A.D. 1612) songs [L. P. Dube 1968:31-38; Chaturvedi 1964:134-35], and Raghav-das's [1965:51-55] *Bhaktamal* (A.D. ?1720). The associated legend of Kabir's tricking Ramananda into giving him the "Ram" mantra, first told in the first section or chapter of Ananta-das's *Kabir Parachai*, is undoubtedly a pious fiction. Its presence in this first section is in fact one of the principal reasons for doubting that this section formed part of the "original" text of the *Kabir Parachai.* Nonetheless, the guru-disciple relation between Ramananda and Kabir is reaffirmed in the very first verse of the second section of the *Kabir Parachai*, and the story of Kabir tricking Ramananda is already found in Priya-das's A.D. 1712 commentary on Nabha-das's verse about Kabir. This commentary is almost certainly based on a recension of Ananta-das's work that included the controversial first section (see below, pp. 78-79).

On the other hand, it must be acknowledged that none of the three oldest collections of Kabir's works (the Sikh *Adi Granth*, the Rajasthani *Kabir Granthavali* and the Kabir Panthi *Kabir Bijak*) refer to Ramananda as Kabir's guru. Where Kabir's verses refer to a guru, it usually seems to be a divine rather than a human guru. Nonetheless, one verse of the *Bijak* (*shabda* 77.4) does seem to mention Ramananda, and at least one verse from the less authentic collections mentions Ramananda as Kabir's guru [H. P. Dvivedi 1971:260 (no. 29)]. Since most of the other early *sant* poets rarely refer to their human gurus by name, this objection does not seem to me to be a particularly important one.

At first sight, a more serious objection to Kabir's having been a disciple of Ramananda is that Kabir's verses radically break with the Brahmanic orthodoxy that Ramananda supposedly represents. This objection is also of little weight, however, since almost nothing is in fact known about what religious and social doctrines the historical Ramananda actually espoused. Apart from a few short compositions in Hindi and Sanskrit somewhat dubiously attributed to him [Ramananda 1955], he remains a historical enigma. In one of his Hindi songs, he rejects both the Vedas and *smriti* and claims that God is immanent in all things, especially in one's heart [Barthwal 1978:69]. This religious stance is obviously closer to Kabir than to Brahmanic orthodoxy. The real question, then, is still that of the dates of Ramananda and Kabir.

The attempts to establish a date of Ramananda without relying on the date of Kabir are, I think, basically futile. Nonetheless, they deserve to be reviewed if only to show that they can in fact be better used to establish a late date for Ramananda than an early one. The only significant evidence for an early date of Ramananda is the A.D. 1299 birth date of Ramananda said to be given in the *Agastya-samhita.*[4] Since this date is incompatible with most other evidence, it is curious that several

---

4. There are discussions of the dates of Ramananda in the works cited in note 1 above. See also P. D. Barthwal [1978: 197], R. G. Bhandarkar [1965:66-67], B. N. Shrivastav [1957: 69-98], Nabha-das [1969:281-96], Farquhar [1967:323], and Shrikrishna Lal [in Ramananda 1955:33-50].

important modern scholars have accepted it. C. Vaudeville, P. Chaturvedi, and P. D. Barthwal all favor an early date for Ramananda. R. K. Varma, J. N. Farquhar, G. H. Westcott, and other scholars prefer later dates.[5] In what follows, I will argue that the attempts to assign early dates to both Ramananda and Kabir are almost certainly mistaken.

The main arguments for dating Ramananda independently from Kabir and from Ramananda's other spiritual descendants center on Ramananda's supposed inclusion in the spiritual genealogy of the famous South Indian theologian Ramanuja. Ramanuja's traditional dates, themselves the subject of controversy, are from A.D. 1017 to 1137. If we give Ramanuja a floruit of about A.D. 1125 and assign an average of twenty-five years to each following spiritual generation up to Ramananda [see Trautmann 1969:564-77], what do we get? It all depends on which traditional genealogy we use.

In somewhat ambiguous fashion, Nabha-das [1969:281-316, 949-54] mentions the names of three gurus between Ramanuja and Ramananda. This cannot be a complete list. Another text, the *Ramarchana Paddhati* attributed to Ramananda, lists twelve, thirteen, or nineteen names *between* Ramanuja and Ramananda, depending upon the edition or manuscript consulted.[6] If we count forward from the proposed A.D. 1125 floruit of Ramanuja, assigning twenty-five years to each generation, we get the following three possible floruits for Ramananda: A.D. 1450, 1475, and 1625. The first two dates are both compatible with the probable dates of Kabir. Nonetheless, it should be clear that the whole procedure of dating Ramananda on the basis of his spiritual descent from Ramanuja is a house of cards of little real value.

In reality the only reasonable way of dating Ramananda is to count backward from the better known dates of Kabir, Ananta-das and Nabha-das. If Ananta-das is given a floruit of A.D. 1600 (on the basis of the A.D. 1588 date of the composition of the *Nam-dev Parachai*), then Ramananda's floruit would be about A.D. 1475. If we give Nabha-das the same floruit of about A.D. 1600, then Ramananda's floruit would be pushed back to about A.D. 1450. Both these dates are again perfectly compatible with the probable dates of Kabir, as we shall see, and also with the more doubtful date of A.D. 1425 often given as the birth date of Ramananda's reputed disciple Pipa [Farquhar 1967:323; Chaturvedi 1964:235-36].

---

5. See note 1 above.

6. See B. N. Shrivastav [1957:155-57], R. Burghart [1978:121-39], and R. K. Varma [1977:10-15]. Burghart bases much of his article on B. P. Simha [1957]. Burghart and Simha both prefer the genealogical list with twelve intervening names.

Despite the fact that the dates of Kabir have provoked so much discussion and disagreement, I think it is now possible to establish his approximate floruit with considerable confidence. Although different traditional verses give different dates for Kabir's death and birth [Chaturvedi 1964:846], the dates now accepted by most followers of the Kabir Panth assign him a life span of 120 years, from 1455 V. S. (A.D. 1398) to 1575 V. S. (A.D. 1518). This long life-span is obviously a pious invention, and these dates cannot be independently confirmed in any case. What we are left with are essentially four independent tests: (1) the genealogical count back from Ananta-das, (2) the similar count back from Nabha-das, (3) the legendary synchronism with Sikandar Lodi (ruled A.D. 1488-1512), and (4) the legendary synchronism with king Virasimha Baghel. Both these last two synchronisms are found in Ananta-das and most early and later legendary texts. The synchronism with Virasimha Baghel is particularly interesting since no modern Kabir scholar seems to have noted that Virasimha Baghel was in fact a historical person whose approximate dates are known.

Before giving the results of these four texts, it is necessary to review what is known about king Virasimha Baghel. In Ananta-das's *Kabir Parachai* [6.1], Virasimhadev Baghel is identified as the king who does penance before Kabir during the episode of the *paṇḍā* of Jagannath Puri (below, pp. 29-32). Virasimhadev Baghel is apparently the king of Varanasi although Ananta-das's text never directly says so. Later legends also associate Virasimha Baghel (as well as an otherwise unknown Muslim named Bijali Khan) with the events of Kabir's death at Magahar. This death legend is also found in Ananta-das's *Kabir Parachai*, but this text does not mention the presence of any king at Kabir's death, much less Bijali Khan or Virasimha Baghel.

The Baghel dynasty is historically associated with the Baghelkhand region of northern Madhya Pradesh (centered in Satna, Rewa, and Shadol Districts) and not with Varanasi. A verse chronicle of the dynasty in Sanskrit, the *Virabhanudayakavyam*, was written in A.D. 1540 by a Madhava, son of Abhayachandra [1938; H. Shastri 1925]. Another historical chronicle of the Baghel dynasty, the *Baghelavamshavarnan*, was published as an appendix to the A.D. 1906 Venkateshvar Press edition of the *Kabir Bijak* [Kabir 1906:659-731]. This text was written in Hindi by Yugal-das at the behest of the Baghel king Raghurajasimha (A.D. 1823-1879).[7]

---

7. I would like to thank Shukdev Singh and Linda Hess for making their copy of this Venkateshvar Press edition available to me.

Madhava's [1938; H. Shastri 1-14] *Virabhanudayakavyam* contains no mention of Kabir, but the text does make Virasimha Baghel a contemporary of the Mughal emperor Babur (ruled A.D. 1526-1530). Virasimha Baghel is also mentioned in Babur's own memoirs [Babur 1970:521, 562, 639]. Madhava further claims that Virasimha's son Virabhanu, the hero of the *Virabhanudayakavyam*, was a contemporary and friend of the Mughal emperor Humayun (ruled A.D. 1531-1540, 1555-56). Hirananda Shastri [1925] claims that Virabhanu must have died in 1540, the year in which Madhava's text was composed, but historians generally place his death a few years later [Srivastav 1964: 97-98]. It seems likely that Virasimha died in about A.D. 1530. Some Persian historians seem to claim that Bir Singh (alias Nar Singh) died after an unsuccessful battle against Sikandar Lodi in about A.D. 1494. Apparently, however, this claim confuses him with his cousin (uncle's son) Vahararaya [A. B. Pandey 1956:126-27]. In Madhava's *Virabhanudayakavyam*, Virasimha is said to have ruled from his capital at Gahora, a still unidentified site in the Baghelkhand region [Madhava 1938; H. Shastri 1925:12]. He should not be confused with king Virasimhadev of Bundelkhand who was responsible for the death of Akbar's famous minister Abu'l Fazl in A.D. 1602 [Rizvi 1975:487-91]. Nor is he the same as the hero of Keshav-das's *Virasimhadev-charitra* [D. Varma 1986:107, 389-90, 577].

Yugal-das's *Baghelavamshavarnan* does connect Virasimha Baghel and other kings of the dynasty with Kabir. The text is in fact couched in the form of a dialogue between Kabir and his reputed direct disciple Dharma-das (despite its references to kings later than both). The text makes all the kings of the Baghel dynasty followers of Kabir. Virasimha Baghel is said to have lived first at Prayag (Allahabad) and then to have been given control of the fort of Bandhogadh (Shadol District) by the *bādashāh* of Delhi. This *bādashāh* must be Babur although Yugal-das does not identify him by name [Kabir 1906:672-77] as Madhava does in the *Virabhanudayakavyam.* Yugal-das [Ibid., 677-80] does describe Virasimha's son Virabhanu as the contemporary and friend of Babur's son Humayun as does Madhava.

The Baghel dynasty and region have many historical ties with the Kabir Panth [Lorenzen 1981:277]. The ethnographers R. V. Russell and Hira Lal [1969: vol. 4, pp. 434-35] reported in 1916 that the members of the ruling Baghel family of Rewa State were traditionally Kabir Panthis. According to Gangasharan Shastri [1976: 153-57], not only king Virasimha Baghel but also king Ramasimha Baghel of Bandhogadh became direct disciples of Kabir. Yugal-das's *Baghelavamshavarnan* [Kabir 1906:677-81] identifies this latter king as the grandson of Virasimha Baghel and son of Virabhanu. All three are said to be direct disciples of Kabir, however chronologically unlikely this may be.

Madhava's *Virabhanudayakavyam*, although it does not connect the dynasty with Kabir, also notes [Madhava 1938; H. Shastri 1925:10] that Udayakarna, Virasimha Baghel's brother, went and settled in Orissa (Utkala). In Puri there is still a small but well-known monastery of the Kabir Panth that claims to house samadhis of Kabir, Dharma-das, and several other important Kabir Panthi saints [K. N. Dvivedi 1965: 178-79]. This samadhi of Kabir is already mentioned in Abu'l Fazl's *'Ain-i-Akbari* (A.D. 1598) [Vaudeville 1974:33-34]. Two important legends also connect Kabir with Puri and the Jagannath temple (below, pp. 29-32, 48-49). My guess is that the original responsibility for this connection between the Kabir Panth and Puri may well lie with Virasimha Baghel's brother.

A much later Baghel king of Rewa named Vishvanathasimha (A.D. 1789-1854) wrote the well-known *Pakhanda khandini* commentary on the *Kabir Bijak*. This commentary was included with the earliest published text of the *Kabir Bijak*, lithographed in A.D. 1868 [Vaudeville 1974:333; Sadhusaran Gosvami 1978:255-70]. Vishvanathasimha's grandson Ramanujaprasadasimha financed the 1906 Venkateshvar Press edition of the *Kabir Bijak* that includes this commentary and the *Baghelavamshavarnan* appendix [Kabir 1906].

The Baghel dynasty is also associated with other leaders of the *sant* movement. Legend claims that Kabir's fellow disciple Sen, although a barber by caste, became the guru of king Rajaram of Bandhogadh [Chaturvedi 1964:232-35; Garg 1963:316]. Yugal-das's *Baghelavamsha-varnan* [Kabir 1906:677-81] seems to make Rajaram and Ramasimha alternate names of the same king, the son of Virabhanu and grandson of Virasimha. This text claims that the barber (*nāpita*) Sen treated the wounds of king Ramasimha after an attack that took place previous to an interview with Akbar. This text does not, however, have Sen replace Kabir as the king's guru. Another Baghel king, Raghurajasimha of Rewa (A.D. 1823-1879), the son of the *Kabir Bijak* commentator Vishvanathasimha, wrote an important commentary on Nabha-das's *Bhaktamal* [D. Varmà 1986:575].

Although no historical source directly associates king Virasimha Baghel with Varanasi, Madhava's *Virabhanudayakavyam* does claim that Virasimha's grandfather Bhaidachandra had conquered Gaya, Varanasi, and Prayag [Madhava 1938; H. Shastri 1925:6]. The Baghel-khand city of Rewa is located only about 190 kilometers (in a straight line) to the southwest of Varanasi. There is little doubt that the Vira-simhadev Baghel mentioned in Ananta-das's *Kabir Parachai* is the same as the Virasimha Baghel of the *Virabhanudayakavyam*. However unhistorical the *paṇḍā* of Jagannath legend may be, the indicated historical synchronism of Kabir and Virasimha Baghel is still important.

The situation with regard to the synchronism between Kabir and the Muslim Sultan Sikandar Lodi (ruled A.D. 1488-1512) is similar. In this case, Sikandar *is* known to have visited Jaunpur and possibly Varanasi in about A.D. 1495, but there is no independent mention of his having met Kabir [Vaudeville 1974:38]. Many scholars have justifiably doubted the historicity of the legends of Kabir's persecution by Sikandar. Nonetheless, I cannot agree with the statement by Vaudeville [1974:38] that "there is no historical evidence—not even any probability—that Kabir was Sikandar Lodi's contemporary, as is shown by Mohan Singh, [P. D.] Barthwal, and Parashuram Chaturvedi." Whether or not the legends are historical in any strict sense, the chronological synchronism is still of value.

Two other points need to be mentioned before summing up the results of the four tests of Kabir's probable floruit. First is the claim by A. Führer [1891: vol. 2, 224] that the Muslim tomb (*rauzā*) of Kabir at Magahar in Basti District near the city of Gorakhpur was "erected in A.D. 1450 by Bijli Khan and restored in 1576 by Nawab Fidai Khan." This of course implies that Kabir died in 1450 or shortly before. Unfortunately it is not clear on what evidence Führer based his statement. I visited Magahar in 1976 and 1985 but was unable to find any information to support it. The Muslim caretaker of the tomb did tell me that several land grants relative to the tomb at Magahar were preserved in the Sunni Vaqf Board in Lucknow. My then assistant, Mr. Anand Ghildayal, was able to examine the documents and make a summary of their contents. The oldest is a Mughal grant from the reign of Alamgir (Aurangzeb). It bears the date 1110 *hijrī* (A.D. 1698-1699). The grant registers the gift of the village Kabirapur Karmua for the upkeep of the Muslim tomb of Shah Kabir. Three later grants have to do with law suits between various persons and the managers of the lands and the tomb. The managers claim to be descendants of Kabir. None of the documents can be used to either confirm or deny Führer's statement about Bijali Khan having built the tomb in A.D. 1450. Given the strength of opposing evidence, I prefer to reject Führer's claim.

The second point that should be mentioned is the supposed contemporaneity of Kabir and Guru Nanak. This claim is not found in the early legends about Kabir. It *is* found in some of the early Sikh *janam sākhīs*. W. H. McLeod, the academic authority on these texts, argues [McLeod 1968:85-86] that "as they stand the *Miharban* and the B40 accounts can certainly be rejected. They are completely different, they are vague as far as location is concerned, they offer no recognizably genuine information concerning Kabir, and their obvious purpose is to exalt Guru Nanak by having Kabir acknowledge his superiority." Later Kabir Panthi texts also mention the meeting of Kabir and Guru Nanak, but of course make Guru Nanak acknowledge *Kabir*'s superiority (below, pp. 68-69). Guru Nanak's dates are known (A.D. 1469-1538) and are in fact quite compatible with a possible meeting between him and Kabir, but in this case the legends are so late and so obviously tendentious that it is difficult to assign much importance even to the synchronism they assume between Kabir and Guru Nanak.

What, then, can we conclude from the four proposed tests of Kabir's date? The first test, counting back from a floruit of about A.D. 1600 for Ananta-das, gives Kabir a floruit of about A.D. 1500. The second test, counting back from an approximate 1600 floruit for Nabha-das, gives Kabir a floruit of about 1525. The third test, the synchronism with Sikandar Lodi (ruled A.D. 1488-1512), gives Kabir a floruit of about 1500. The fourth test, the synchronism with Virasimha Baghel (died *c.* A.D. 1530) and Babur (ruled A.D. 1526-1530), gives Kabir a floruit in the first quarter of the sixteenth century. Taken together these tests give Kabir a floruit of between about A.D. 1500 and 1525. Although this floruit goes against the early death date proposed by C. Vaudeville and Parashuram Chaturvedi, it does agree quite well with Kabir's traditional death date of A.D. 1518. Common sense in fact would suggest that tradition is more likely to be correct about Kabir's approximate death date than his traditional birth date of A.D. 1398. If we also suppose that Kabir had a relatively long life (although not the 120 years traditionally assigned to him), we can date his birth to sometime around the middle of the fifteenth century.

Kabir's Family

Did Kabir have a wife and children? This question would be of comparatively minor importance except for the fact that it has become a matter of controversy between the sadhus of the Kabir Panth and academic scholars. For most Kabir Panthi sadhus, the idea that Kabir could have had a wife and children is an anathema. For them, Kabir was a celibate sadhu like themselves.

Nonetheless, the balance of historical evidence clearly suggests that Kabir had a wife and children. This evidence includes the text of Ananta-das's *Kabir Parachai* and of Priya-das's commentary on Nabhā-das, several "autobiographical" songs and verses attributed to Kabir found in the Sikh *Guru Granth Sahib* or *Adi Granth* and the Rajasthani *Kabir Granthavali* collections, and verses attributed to Kabir's son

Kamal. The Kabir Panth *Kabir Bijak* collection, not surprisingly, omits all such references.

C. Vaudeville [1974: 39-48] has ably discussed the autobiographical material found in texts attributed to Kabir. These texts mention Kabir's mother, his father, a wife perhaps named Dhania, and his son Kamal.[8] Kamal was apparently a religious figure of some importance in his own right. There still exist a number of verses attributed to Kamal in which the signature line (*bhaṇitā*) identifies him as the "son of Kabir" [see K. K. Bhatta 1975: 12, 29-30, 36-47]. Kamal is not mentioned by name in Ananta-das's *Kabir Parachai*, Priya-das's commentary on Nabha-das's *Bhaktamal*, nor other earlier versions of the Kabir legends, but he does appear in later Kabir Panthi versions. Kabir Panthi texts also mention a daughter named Kamali. These texts, however, claim that Kamal and Kamali were *adopted* by Kabir after he had miraculously raised them from the dead and were not his natural children (below, pp. 50-51).

The strongest evidence in favor of Kabir's having had a wife and children comes from Ananta-das's *Kabir Parachai*. Verse 6.12 mentions the quarrels of Kabir's mother and her daughter-in-law (*bahū*). Verse 1.7 mentions Kabir's father-in-law. Verse 2.5 mentions the children in Kabir's house who cried because they had to go hungry. The corresponding verse in Priya-das's commentary on Nabha-das, which is here mostly based on Ananta-das's text, refers specifically to Kabir's "wife, child(?ren) and mother" (*tiyā suta māta*) [Nabha-das 1969: 483]. Similarly, several Sikh legends collected by Macauliffe [1963: vol. 6] refer to the wives and mother of Kabir. There is also an interesting legend about Kabir and his wife in Muhsin Fani's *Dabistan-i-Mazahib* and in the *Bhaktavijay* of the Varakari author Mahipati (below, pp. 49-50).

Given all this evidence, one has little choice but to accept that Kabir probably married and had children including a son named Kamal. To argue otherwise obviously takes special pleading similar to that of Roman Catholic scholars who would deny the existence of Jesus's brothers and sisters.

The Later Texts

Since Ananta-das's *Kabir Parachai* is apparently the oldest existing collection of legends about Kabir, the legends it contains have a certain

---

8. As Vaudeville [1974: 43-44] points out, the word *loī* in Kabir's works probably means "people" and is not the name of a wife of Kabir as Sikh tradition claims. Similarly, the term *Rām janīā* is probably a generic one meaning "Ram's handmaid."

priority over those that are found only in later sources. Likewise, its *versions* of legends that are also found in later texts are particularly interesting. This does not mean, however, that the legends of Ananta-das's collection are necessarily those that are most important to the present-day followers of the Kabir Panth. Since Ananta-das's text is now virtually unknown to the sadhus of the Kabir Panth, its *versions* of the Kabir legends are to them much less important than the versions found in popular texts such as the *Kabir Manshur*.

Ananta-das's *Kabir Parachai* is of particular interest from several points of view. It is, first of all, the oldest collection of Kabir legends, and as such it brings us closest to the historical epoch of Kabir. Nonetheless, its contents are clearly only minimally useful for any attempt at reconstructing a historical biography of Kabir. Ananta-das's text *can* be used to reveal the ideological messages its author wanted to convey to his listeners. Nonetheless, Ananta-das's text cannot be used to reveal some hypothetical timeless "essence" of the legends any more than any other versions of the legends can be used for the same purpose. Every version of each legend must be located and analyzed in its own social and historical context.

For me the primary importance of Ananta-das's text lies rather in the fact that the Kabir legends it contains can help us to trace the historical evolution or "genealogy" [Foucault 1984: 78-79] of the Kabir legends over a long time span. As a result, we can get a much more complete idea of the changes in the ideological messages of the legends as conveyed in different historical epochs by different authors for different audiences. From the point of view of the historical and sociological impact that the legends have had, however, it must be kept in mind that the most important legends and versions of those legends are those that have been most popular and not those that are the oldest.

In the following chapters, I shall discuss first the cycle of legends found in Ananta-das's *Kabir Parachai* and then the legends found only in later sources. Wherever possible, I shall trace the more significant changes in the different versions of each legend. The later legend collections to be discussed in some detail include Priya-das's *Bhaktirasabodhini* commentary (A.D. 1712) in Hindi on Nabha-das's [1969] *Bhaktamal*; the *Dabistan-i-Mazahib* (A.D. *c.* 1650) in Persian attributed to Muhsin Fani [1843]; Raghav-das's [1965; 1969] *Bhaktamal* (A.D. ?1720) in Hindi;[9] Mahipati's [1982] *Bhaktavijay* (A.D. 1762) in Marathi;

9. Callewaert [1988: 14] argues quite persuasively that this work was most likely compiled in A.D. 1720 instead of the date A.D. 1660 preferred by other scholars.

Paramananda-das's *Kabir-i-manshur* (A.D. 1887) in its translation from Urdu to Hindi;[10] Chandradatta's [1926] *Samskrita-bhaktamala* (A.D. *c.* 1850) in Sanskrit; Brahmalinamuni's [1960] *Sadguru-shrikavira-charitam* in Sanskrit with his own Hindi commentary; and Gangasharan Shastri's [1976] *Kabir Jivanacharitra* in Hindi.

I shall not discuss in detail a number of other texts that were either not available to me or whose versions of the legends are not significantly different from those found in the texts just mentioned. One work not available to me was Mukunda Gugli's *Kabir Charit*, a Gujarati text reputedly written in A.D. 1651 [Sethi 1984: 5, 14; Bhatta 1975: 21]. Also unavailable to me were a number of the post-Priya-das commentaries on Nabha-das's *Bhaktamal*. For the verse hagiography of Kabir written by Garib-das (A.D. 1717-1778), I had access only to those parts that are quoted at considerable length in Paramananda-das's [1956, 1984] *Kabir Manshur* and in the *Kabir-charitra-bodh* [Yugalananda 1953: vol. 11].

Of the texts that I did have access to but have used only sparingly, the most important is a collection of mostly verse texts in Hindi edited by *svāmī* Yugalananda Bihari [1953] and published in eleven small volumes under the general title of the *Kabir Sagar*.[11] Most of these texts seem to date from the eighteenth and nineteenth centuries. Several of them recount various Kabir legends. Particularly important in this regard is the *Kabir-charitra-bodh*, a work in mixed prose and verse (including many of Garib-das's verses) that may in fact have been written by Yugalananda himself in about the early 1930s [P. D. Barthwal 1978: 281]. A quite popular work collected in the *Kabir Sagar* that contain versions of several of the Kabir legends (unfortunately mostly legends about Kabir's previous lives) is the *Anurag Sagar* [Yugalananda 1953: vol. 2]. This text has been recently translated into English [*Anurag Sagar* 1984].

Most of the works collected in the *Kabir Sagar* are texts of the Dharmadasi branch of the Kabir Panth. Their versions of the Kabir legends generally closely follow those of the *Kabir Manshur* and Brahmalinamuni's *Sadguru-shrikavira-charitam*, two texts that I do discuss

---

10. Paramananda-das's work has two versions, one long and one short, both of which have been translated into Hindi. In this book I will use the short version translation unless otherwise indicated. The short version translation [1956] is by Sudhadasaji Saheb "Sukavi." The long version translation [1984] is by Madhavacharyya.

11. This collection seems to have been first published in the early 1930s. Some of the texts included in it are summarized in K. N. Dvivedi [1965], P. D. Barthwal [1978], F. E. Keay [1931], and G. H. Wescott [1953]. See also U. Thukral [1979].

in some detail. The same may be said about two other Dharmadasi texts, the *Kabir Kasauti* (A.D. 1885) of Laihana Simha alias Haridas [1962][12] and *shrī* Tapasvi's [1976] *Satya Prakash Satik*. Similarly, Ramananda-das's [1974] *Shri Sadguru Kabir*, a work of the Kabir Chaura branch of the Kabir Panth, contains versions of the legends that do not significantly differ from those found in Gangasharan Shastri's [1976] *Kabir Jivanacharitra*. An interesting but somewhat anomalous life of Kabir from the smaller Jagu-das branch of the Kabir Panth, Shankar-das's *Shri Kabir Charitamrit* [1955], will be discussed only in passing. This verse text claims, rather dubiously, to be based in part on a lost manuscript of *shrī* Hamsa Sahab copied in V. S. 1582 (A.D. 1525).

12. The introduction to this work claims that it was written in the year 1942, evidently of the Vikrama era [= A.D. 1885]. M. A. Macauliffe [1963: vol. 6, p. 123], in a work first published in 1909, refers to the "*Kabir Kasauti* of the late Lahina Singh of Panjor in the Patiala State." G. H. Wescott [1953: 3], in a work first published in 1907, mentions "a Hindi pamphlet entitled *Kabir Kasauti* published at Bombay in 1885," which was "the joint production of five members of the Kabir Panth." The legend about Kabir that Westcott seems to attribute to this *Kabir Kasauti* does not occur in the 1962 edition.

CHAPTER 2

THE *KABIR PARACHAI* CYCLE

The *Kabir Parachai* of Ananta-das contains thirteen sections or chapters (*kaḍavak*) of about sixteen or seventeen verses each (fifteen or sixteen *chaupāī*s plus one *dohā*). Insofar as he can, Ananta-das attempts to weave the legends into a continuous narrative. The narrative divisions between the legends do not always correspond to the section divisions. The following legends may be distinguished: (1) Kabir's initiation by Ramananda [section 1]; (2) God begs cloth [section 2]; (3) the Brahmans demand food [3.1-4.8]; (4) the prostitute, the *paṇḍā* and the king [4.9-6.6]; (5) Sikandar tests Kabir [6.14-9.10]; (6) the unexpected feast [9.11-10.11]; (7) the *apsarā* and Hari [10.12-12.16]; (8) Kabir's death at Magahar [13.2-13.10]. All these legends are retold in most of the major later collections of Kabir legends. The more important additional legends found in these texts will be discussed in the next chapter.

The present chapter will summarize and discuss each of the legends narrated in the *Kabir Parachai* as well as the more significant variations on them that appear in the later collections. The discussion will center on the socio-religious ideology implicit in these *Kabir Parachai* legends and on the changes in this ideology implicit in the narrative variations found in their later versions. A few specific textual and historical problems will also be analyzed.

Kabir's Initiation by Ramananda

This legend is included in almost all manuscripts of the Niranjani Panthi recension of the *Kabir Parachai*, but is not found in most manuscripts of the Dadhu Panthi recension.[1] The legend is also found in almost all later collections of Kabir legends.[2] Ananta-das's version begins with the claim that the weaver from Kashi spent many days among the worshippers of the Goddess (Shaktas) before receiving a divine message from God (Vidhi). God offers to give Kabir a divine vision if he will put on the Vaishnava forehead mark and prayer beads. When Kabir protests that he belongs to a Muslim caste, the divine voice tells him to take his initiation (*dīkshā*) from Ramananda. Kabir again protests that Ramananda will not consent even to look at him. The voice tells Kabir to go at night to the lane where Ramananda will come walking and wait for him. Ramananda trips over the waiting Kabir and as he does so exclaims the word "Ram." Taking this to be his mantra of initation, Kabir returns home, puts on the forehead mark and prayer beads, and begins to sing the praises of Ram. Kabir's Muslim family angrily ask him why he has abandoned his family religion. Ramananda is also informed about Kabir's activities. Kabir is brought before Ramananda. From behind a curtain (evidently placed to avoid Ramananda having to look at a person of so low a caste), Ramananda asks [vs. 1.11]: "Tell me! When did I give you prayer beads? Why do you say you are acting in my name?" Kabir reminds Ramananda about what had happened in the lane at night. Kabir then convinces Ramananda of his sincerity and the depth of his wisdom and asks Ramananda to reveal himself. Ramananda opens the curtain and gives Kabir a proper initiation.

---

1. This and other differences between these two major recensions of Ananta-das's *Kabir Parachai* will be discussed in more detail in chapter 4 below. Here it will suffice to again note that the absence of the initiation legend in the Dadhu Panthi recension cannot be taken to suggest that the legend of Kabir's relation with Ramananda was a later invention since this relation is affirmed in both manuscript traditions, and is also mentioned by Ananta-das's spiritual uncle, Nabha-das (above, pp. 9-13). The initiation legend itself is also found in Priya-das's A.D. 1727 *Bhaktamal* commentary. In chapter four, I shall argue that the differences in the two *Kabir Parachai* manuscript traditions most likely represent the differences of two different sectarian versions of the text, neither one of which can be confidently said to be closer to Ananta-das's original composition.

2. Nabha-das [1969:282 (verse 36)] and Raghav-das [1965:51 (verse 122)] both make Kabir a disciple of Ramananda, but they do not mention the legend. This is perhaps simply because their discussions of Kabir are so short. Nabha-das has only one verse [1969:479 (verse 60)] dedicated to Kabir. Raghav-das has about eleven verses [1965:52-55, 177-78 (verses 125-30, 349-53)]. The legend *is* found in Nabha-das's commentator Priya-das [Nabha-das 1969:480-82] and in Raghav-das's commentator Chatur-das [Raghav-das 1965:53]. Other versions are found in Muhsin Fani [1843:vol. 2, pp. 187-88], in Mahipati [1982:vol. 1, pp. 112-17], in Paramananda-das [1956:108-11], in Brahmalinamuni [1960: 95-125], in Chandradatta [1926:chap. 82, vss. 1-41], in Gangasharan Shastri [1976:17-28].

The later versions of this legend add relatively little to it. Several specify that Ramananda was on his way to bathe in the Ganges in the early morning darkness when he stepped on Kabir, an element already present in at least one manuscript [RSS 95] of Ananta-das's *Kabir Parachai* and in Priya-das's *Bhaktamal* commentary [Nabha-das 1969: 480-82]. Some versions also specify the place of this "initiation" as being on the steps (*ghāṭ*) leading down to the river. Several texts also make it clear that Kabir had proclaimed to everyone that Ramananda had initiated him and state that this is what provoked his interrogation by Ramananda. A few versions also mention how Ramananda's other disciples wholeheartedly accepted Kabir into their brotherhood after Ramananda had formally initiated him.

One interesting detail mentioned in several of the later versions of the legend is the claim that Kabir was only a child when Ramananda stepped on him. Brahmalinamuni and one or two other authors offer a variant on this motif in which Kabir magically takes the form of a small child before lying down to wait for Ramananda.

One manuscript of Ananta-das's text [RSS 95] and a few later versions of the legend such as the *Kabir Charitra Bodh* [Yugalananda 1953: vol. 11, pp. 15-27] add a miraculous element to the confrontation of Kabir with Ramananda behind the curtain. Ramananda is said to be dressing an idol of God, but cannot figure out how to put on the God's garland. Without being able to see what Ramananda is doing, Kabir tells him to untie the string of the garland before putting it around the God's neck. In one or two texts, this event is separated from the story of Kabir's and Ramananda's first real meeting and is said to have occurred at some later date.

The most obvious aim of the Ramananda legend is to affirm a genealogical link between Ramananda and Kabir. Whether or not this link was in fact a historical one (above, pp. 9-18), the question of why it should be so emphasized has no such obvious an answer. Ananta-das and Nabha-das, the earliest authors to affirm the link, are associated by tradition with the early Ramanandi Sampraday [B. P. Simha 1957]. In their case, the emphasis on the relation between Ramananda and Kabir may reflect both a wish to show Ramananda to have been senior, and hence in one sense superior to Kabir, and a wish to "cash in" on some of the popularity of Kabir and in this way attract some of Kabir's followers to the Ramanandi Sampraday. Considering that both Ananta-das and Nabha-das were obviously quite favorably disposed toward the more radical *sant* tradition, they also may have emphasized the relation between Ramananda and *sant*s such as Kabir in order to counter the trend toward greater religious and social conservatism within the early

Ramanandi Sampraday.

In the case of later versions of the initiation legend found in Kabir Panthi collections, the likely motives for emphasizing the relation between Ramananda and Kabir are in large part the inverse of the motives of Ramanandis such as Ananta-das and Nabha-das. Many Kabir Panthi authors evidently felt that they could Hinduize Kabir and neutralize some of his religious and social radicalism by making him a disciple of a supposedly orthodox Brahman guru. I have elsewhere [Lorenzen 1981] discussed such efforts to use these legends to "legitimize" Kabir in terms of Srinivas's concept of Sanskritization, but this concept now seems to me to unfairly ignore the presence in the legends of elements of both a more radical egalitarian ideology and a reactionary anti-Muslim communalism.

The motif of Kabir having been a child at the time of his initial meeting with Ramananda—in one or two cases expressed in terms of his having magically disguised himself as a child—possibly reflects in part an attempt to resolve the lack of agreement between the traditional dates of Ramananda and Kabir, or perhaps even an actual historical disparity in their ages. The motif may also simply be intended to simultaneously emphasize the precocious greatness of Kabir and the superior truth of the various sorts of *sant* Vaishnavism that Ananta-das and the other authors wish to promote. Why Kabir should magically take on a child's form is not so easy to understand. This legend variant—found only in two or three texts that consider Kabir to be an avatar of God—may intend to show that Kabir took this child's form *voluntarily* in order to give Ramananda the honor of becoming his guru.

However inaccurate may be Ananta-das's appreciation of the respective socio-religious ideologies of Ramananda and of Kabir, it is important to note that the initiation is in effect a reciprocal one. Ramananda is portrayed as a caste-conscious orthoprax Brahman, who agrees to abandon his orthopraxy after receiving Kabir's religious teaching. Kabir, in return, receives the right to call Ramananda his guru and wear the Vaishnava paraphernalia. In some later Kabir Panthi versions of the legend, the authors take pains to assert that Kabir was a disciple of Ramananda only in name; in reality it was Ramananda who was Kabir's disciple.

One significant detail found only in Ananta-das's version of the legend is his reference [1.1] to Kabir having earlier followed the customs of the worshippers of the Goddess or Shaktas. It offers striking evidence in favor of the theory—first put forward in 1930 by P. D. Barthwal [1946: 54-78] and later reaffirmed by H. P. Dvivedi [1971: 17-36], C. Vaudeville [1974: 24-25, 81-89] and other scholars—to the effect that Kabir's Muslim family may have been only recently and partially converted to Islam from an original association the Naths, a yogic sect distinct from but related to the Shaktas.

God Begs Cloth

This legend is not today one of the more popular legends about Kabir, but it fills the whole second section of Ananta-das's *Kabir Parachai* (forming the first section of the Dadu Panthi recension) and is included in several of the longer Kabir Panthi collections.[3] According to Ananta-das, Kabir continues to weave and sell cloth after becoming a devotee of Ram. One day God disguises himself in human form and begs cloth from Kabir. Kabir first offers to give him half a measure of cloth, but the beggar demands a whole measure. Kabir gives it to him, leaving himself with nothing. Kabir does not return home empty-handed. He goes off and hides himself somewhere. For three days the people of his house go hungry while "the children cry" [2.5]. Hari, in human disguise, then arrives at Kabir's house with a bullock load (*bālad*) of food. Hari tells Kabir's mother not to worry, that Ram had given the food, but she protests anyway. Kabir, she says, has never begged for anything. Hari then tells her that the food was a gift from a king who had come to Kashi to have a darshan of Lord Vishvanath and that Kabir had accepted the king's gift in order to hold a public feast. Then Hari disappears. Kabir finally returns home and asks where the food had come from. His mother tells him what the diguised Hari had said, but Kabir intuitively knows the truth of what happened.

Most later versions of this legend do not differ greatly from that of the *Kabir Parachai.* Although Ananta-das and most other sources claim that Hari comes to beg from Kabir only once, Mahapati says that Hari appears to Kabir twice: first as an aged and poor Brahman and then as a Muslim fakir. Each one begs half of Kabir's cloth, leaving him with nothing.

The evident aim of this legend is to praise Kabir's extreme generosity. The motif of the poor but generous layman who gives away everything he has is common to much Hindu religious literature. The recipient of his charity is often a learned Brahman or sannyasi guest. Mahipati's

3. The legend is found in Priya-das [Nabha-das 1969: 483-84], Chatur-das [Raghav-das 1965: 53], Mahipati [1982: 84-90], Chandradatta [1926: chap. 82, vss. 42-51], Gangasharan Shastri [1976: 32-34]. The legend is possibly alluded to by Raghav-das [1965: 177 (vs. 350)]. A verse attributed to Mirabai also seems to refer to it [see Gangasharan Shastri 1976: 33n].

ecumenical version, where Kabir gives cloth to both a Hindu and a Muslim, shows how Kabir's generosity rises even above communal sectarianism. Gangasharan Shastri identifies God's beggar disguise as that of a poor *sant*, a term that implies a non-orthodox, lower caste Vaishnav sadhu such as those of the Kabir Panth. The need for the sadhu authors of these texts to foster lay charity to themselves hardly requires comment.

One curious feature of this legend and of two others also found in Ananta-das's text—those of the Brahmans demanding food and the unexpected feast—is the motif of Kabir going off to hide after his generosity had left him unable to feed his family in this case, to feed the Brahmans and sannyasis in the legend of the Brahmans demanding food, and to feed his many guests in the legend of the unexpected feast. What exactly this going off to hide is meant to indicate about Kabir's character is not clear. It *seems* to suggest that Kabir is very timid, even cowardly. For this reason, the modern Kabir Panthi author Gangasharan Shastri makes a special effort to excuse Kabir's behavior. In his version, after Kabir has given away all his cloth, he goes to ask credit from a merchant who refuses to give it. Only then does Kabir go off, not to hide but to pray on the bank of the Ganges where he falls into a meditative trance (*samādhi*).

Considering that these texts are hagiographies—stories meant to praise their saintly hero—it is unlikely that Ananta-das or the any of the other authors would consciously include anything derogatory about Kabir. In any case, fearlessness is in fact one of Kabir's most notable virtues. Both his own verses and the explicit statement of Nabha-das [1969: 479 (vs. 60)] testify to his amazing courage. Similarly, his fearlessness is a major theme of several of the legends, most notably that of Sikandar testing Kabir (below, pp. 32-35). Given all this, the hiding motif of these two legends remains something of an enigma.

The Brahmans Demand Food

Most sources consider this legend to be a continuation of the previous one.[4] Ananta-das says that Kabir decides to hold a public feast for the devotees (*bhagat*), presumably with the bullock load of food left by Hari. Kabir gives everything away. This angers "the

4. See Priya-das [Nabha-das 1969: 483-84], Chatur-das [Raghav-das 1965: 53], Chandradatta [1926: chap. 82, vss. 52-64]; Gangasharan Shastri [1976: 34-42]. Mahipati [1982] omits this legend but not the previous one.

Brahmans and the sannyasis" [3.1], who complain that Kabir has "given everything to the Shudras." The Brahmans and sannyasis go to Kabir and demand to be fed. Kabir says he has nothing to offer them but agrees to go and purchase some food for them. Kabir leaves and again hides himself somewhere. Then Hari himself assumes the task of feeding the Brahmans. He again appears in human disguise, this time as Kabir himself, and gives flour, rice, sugar, and ghee to the Brahmans. Each Brahman receives two and one half sers of food. Each is then given a rolled pan. At least for the time being, they go away pleased with Kabir.

This legend expresses quite clearly the social and religious antagonism between the followers of Kabir, the low-caste *sant*s and *bhagat*s, and the upper caste, orthodox Brahmans and sannyasis. This legend is altered in some later versions to soften the evidence of social conflict. In his *Samskrita-bhaktamala*, for example, Chandradatta claims that Kabir "gave everything to the sadhus," rather than to the Shudras. Those who then come to demand food are simply "the Brahmans and all the others." On the other hand, Gangasharan Shastri's modern *Kabir Jivanacharitra*, which often displays a tendency toward Sanskritization, bases its version in large part on Ananta-das and clearly indicts the Brahmans and sannyasis. Brahmalinamuni's *Sadguru-shrikavira-charitam* and Paramananda-das's *Kabir Manshur* omit this and the preceding legend altogether. In at least Brahmalinamuni's case, it can be assumed that he found the anti-Brahman and anti-orthodoxy message of the legend inappropriate.

The Prostitute, the *Paṇḍā* and the King

Ananta-das states that as Kabir's fame grows, more and more people flock to his place. In order to rid himself of this fame and the crowds of visitors, Kabir goes early one day to the house of a prostitute. He puts his arm around her neck and grabs a vessel filled with holy water (*charaṇodak*). Pretending that this water is liquor, he and the prostitute go to the market "as if all his wisdom had been forgotten" [4.9-4.11]. All the town begins to laugh at Kabir. The devotees of Hari can say nothing to defend him, while the Brahmans and Baniyas revile him, saying: "Everyone wants to perform bhakti, but how can low-caste persons do it? Kabir performed bhakti for about ten days. Now look! He has taken up with a prostitute." [4.12-4.13].

Kabir then goes to where the "king of the town was sitting" [4.14]. Formerly the king always got up from his throne to greet Kabir, but now he pays him no respect. Everyone is astonished that Kabir has so degraded himself. At this moment, Kabir pours the water he had been pretending to be liquor on his own feet. When the king asks Kabir why he has done this, Kabir explains that he has just saved from being burned the feet of a *paṇḍā* (priest) of the temple of Jagannath in far away Puri (Orissa). Everyone is astonished. The king sends two men to Jagannath Puri to verify the miracle. After ten days they arrive at Puri and ask the *paṇḍā* what had happened. The *paṇḍā* explains that he had broken a pot of boiling rice over his feet, and Kabir, a visiting weaver from Kashi, had come running up and poured (cool) water on the *paṇḍā*'s burning feet. Ten days later, the two men arrive again in Kashi and tell the king what they had seen and been told.

This confirmation of the truth of Kabir's miraculous story greatly worries the king. He asks the queen what they should do. She tells him: "Don't delay! Run and fall at Kabir's feet!" The king puts an axe on his shoulder and a load of straw on his head and goes with his family to Kabir [5. *dohā*].[5] At this point in the story [6.1], the king is named as Barasinghade (i.e. Virasimhadev) Baghel (above, pp. 14-18). Kabir gets up to greet the king and tells him: "Throw down the bundle on your head. There is no anger in my heart. For me there is no question of either hatred or love, nor any difference between king and commoner." [6.2]. The king prostrates himself before Kabir, and Kabir embraces him. Kabir says: "You have done something good. Your coming here has honored me. Whoever gives greatness to others is himself great. A great person is one who consumes wealth by sharing it with others." [6.5]. The king and queen happily return home.

Other versions of this legend are similar.[6] In some modern versions the *paṇḍā* is given the name Ramaharsha. Brahmalinamuni prefaces the legend with another one about Rai-das (i.e., Ravi-das). He says that Kabir warns Ramananda that many Untouchables (*antyaj*) such as the Chamars were becoming Muslims. Kabir tells Ramananda to reconvert (*shuddha karanā*) them by means of the *mantra* "Ram." Ramananda accepts this reconversion effort as an emergency expedient (*āpad-dharma*). Among the Chamars, Rai-das was a great devotee of Ram. One day Rai-das sends a fruit offering to the Ganges River by the hand

---

5. This penance is not mentioned in law books, but an identical penance is found in Tulasi-das's *Ram-charit-manas* 6.29.4. The basic idea is that the noble person should assume the role of a common laborer.

6. See Priya-das [Nabha-das 1969: 484-87], Chatur-das [Raghav-das 1965: 53-54], Chandra-datta [1926: chap. 83, vss. 1-21], Brahmalinamuni [1960: 481-96], Gangasharan Shastri [1976: 70-81]. Jan Gopal's seventeenth century *Dadu Janma Lila* briefly alludes to it [Callewaert 1988: verse 4.5.3] as does Raghav-das [1965: 177 (vs. 350)].

of his Brahman neighbor. When the Brahman offers the fruit, the Ganges gives back a gold bracelet. The Brahman gives the bracelet to his own wife instead of to Rai-das. The wife then refuses to eat unless her husband gives her a mate to the bracelet. The Brahman asks the Ganges to give it, but the Ganges refuses. In desperation the Brahman tells Rai-das what had happened. Rai-das reaches into the wetting tub he uses for tanning, pulls out the mate to the bracelet, and gives it to the Brahman (evidently Brahmalinamuni feels the Brahman thief somehow deserves it!). Brahmalinamuni here notes that Rai-das had received his mantra from Ramananda, but Kabir was Rai-das's real teacher. King Virasimha Baghel of Varanasi is said to have not approved of the reconversion campaign for Untouchables sponsored by Ramananda and Kabir. For this reason, the king's faith in Kabir lessens (here Brahmalinamuni prudishly substitutes this explanation for the omitted episode of Kabir and the prostitute). Nonetheless, the king still greets Kabir with respect when he comes to the court and pours water on his own feet to cool the burning feet of the *paṇḍā* of Jagannath.

Various versions of this legend are still popular among the followers of Rai-das. It would take us too far afield, however, to compare these different versions. In Brahmalinamuni's retelling, the message of the legend seems rather confused. The main purpose is clearly to show how the religious merit of the Untouchable Rai-das could induce the goddess Ganga to bestow a gift, even from within an impure tanning tub. But why should this gift be turned over to a rather dishonest Brahman, and what has it all to do with the reconversion of the Chamars from Islam, with Ramananda cast in the role of a precursor of the Arya Samaj leader Dayananda Sarasvati? Brahmalinamuni's pro-Brahman and anti-Muslim sentiments seem to have introduced several illogical and contradictory elements into the story.

The main legend of the encounters of Kabir with the prostitute, the *paṇḍā* of Jagannath, and the king as it is narrated in the *Kabir Parachai* embodies a complex ideological message. The legend contrasts Kabir's relations with representatives of three radically different social classes and illustrates three different "signs" of Kabir's religious greatness. In each case, the social roles of Kabir and his interlocutor are partially inverted.

Kabir's association with the prostitute is said to be motivated by his desire to cast off the bothersome nuisance, and perhaps the pride of worldly fame. It also involves a bit of trickery since Kabir does not *really* make love to the prostitute nor does he drink liquor. This is somewhat reminiscent of the Pashupata practice of courting dishonor by disreputable behavior during the "unmarked" stage of spiritual training of the Pashupata adept [Lorenzen 1972: 187-88]. In the Pashupata case, the aim of the practice aims both to induce humility in the adept as well as to surreptitiously transfer his bad karma to his revilers and transfer their good karma to himself. In this *paṇḍā* legend, the prostitute in a sense behaves as a chaste woman, while Kabir, however good his ultimate motives, acts as a trickster.

Kabir's encounter with the *paṇḍā* of Jagannath also portrays him as eager to serve a representative of Brahmanic orthodoxy. At the same time, it bestows on Kabir miraculous powers far superior to those of the presumably good but clumsy *paṇḍā*.[7] The hostility of the Brahmans toward Kabir coupled with his somewhat ambiguous behavior toward them is typical of several Kabir legends such as those of the Brahmans demanding food and the unexpected feast. In this *paṇḍā* legend, it is Kabir who bestows *prasād* (grace) on the *paṇḍā*, not the *paṇḍā* who bestows *prasād* (rice offering) on Kabir.

Kabir's adamant refusal to bow down before political authority in the person of the king is another important element in the ideological message of both this legend and the Sikandar legend. Ananta-das emphasizes this theme more than the authors of most later versions of the legend, but the theme is in any case central to all versions. Kabir's attitude is summed up in his assertion that for him there is "no difference between king and commoner" [6.2]. This is both a cry of defiance against oppression by the powerful and a plea for the equal dignity of all men (and perhaps even of women as well). At the same time, Kabir's gracious and forgiving behavior toward the repentant king shows again Kabir's great generosity and nobility. In this legend, it is the king who is the humble petitioner, while Kabir is the noble bestower of favors.

Sikandar Tests Kabir

This is one of the most famous and popular of the Kabir legends. Two songs attributed to Kabir in the *Kabir Granthavali* and the *Guru Granth Sahib* seem to refer to the ordeals that Sikandar is said to have imposed on Kabir, although neither of these songs refers to Sikandar by name.[8] Likewise, no chronicle of Sikandar Lodi's reign mentions

---

7. Why the *paṇḍā* should be from Jagannath is a difficult question. Kabir and the Kabir Panth do have several traditional associations with both Puri and the Jagannath temple that may date back to the migration to Orissa of Virasimha Baghel's brother (above, pp. 15-16).

8. Kabir 1969: 349-50 (*bhairūṃ* 341/16), 363-64 (*bilāval* 365/4); Kabir 1966: 225 (*bhairau* 18), 167 (*gauṇḍa* 4).

anything about his having met Kabir. Ananta-das says that Shah Sikandar's visit to Kashi pleased Kabir's enemies among the *kāzīs*, mullahs, Brahmans, and Baniyas. They and Kabir's own mother gathered to petition Sikandar to put a stop to Kabir's activities. Sikandar asks them: "What has happened, brothers? Has he snatched away a village or a district?" The crowd of petitioners then gives a remarkable answer that reflects Ananta-das's sharp awareness of and support for the original radical character of Kabir's movement:

> No, he hasn't taken a village or a district. Instead, this Julaha has done an unconventional thing. He has abandoned the customs of the Muslims and has broken the touchability rules of the Hindus. He has scorned the sacred bathing places and the Vedas. He has scorned the nine planets, the sun and the moon. He has scorned Shankar and the Mother. He has scorned Sharada and Ganapati. He has scorned the rites of the eleventh day of the fortnight, the sacrificial oblations of ghee and the ceremonies for the dead. He has scorned the Brahmans, whom the whole world worships. He has scorned service to one's mother and father, sisters, nieces, and all the gods. He has scorned the hope of all religions, the six systems of metaphysics and the rites of the twelve months. In this way he has corrupted everyone. He has separated himself from both the Hindus and the Muslims. For this reason no one respects us as long as this Julaha remains in Kashi [7.2-7.5].

Sikandar orders that Kabir be brought immediately to answer the charges. When Kabir arrives, the *kāzī* says to him: "Offer obeisance in the royal court, brother."[9] Kabir replies: "What do I know about offering obeisance?" Sikandar then threatens to send Kabir to hell, saying: "You have abandoned the true path and taken a bad path. Why is this, Julaha? Who has misled you? One gets salvation by following one's own traditional path. Ask both the Hindus and the Turks." Kabir replies: "The Hindus and the Turks are the ones who will fall into hell. The *kāzīs* and the mullahs are clumsy fools. I have found salvation through bhakti. I have sung about the virtues of Ram through the guru's grace. I am faithful to Ram alone." [7.12-7.16].

The Brahmans then demand that Kabir be stripped of his garland and forehead mark and be stoned to death. Instead, the enraged Sikandar orders that Kabir be bound with chains and thrown into the Ganges.

---

9. The phrase *kari tasalīma* can also mean: "Make a confession." Priya-das's commentary on Nabha-das [1969: 488] uses the word *salāma* in place of *tasalīma:* "'You must salaam to the *bādashāh.*'" Kabir replies: "'I don't understand salaam, I understand only Ram.'" Chatur-das's commentary on Raghav-das [1965: 54] and Gangasharan Shastri [1976: 89] also use the word *salāma.*

As soon as Kabir enters the water, the chains fall off and he floats unharmed. Next he is tied and thrown into a house that is then set on fire. The fire becomes as cool as water, and the Gandharvas send a rain of flowers from heaven. The *kāzīs* and Brahmans protest that Kabir has used magic to save himself. Sikandar then sends for a wild elephant to trample Kabir to death. When the mahout goads the elephant to attack Kabir, Hari takes the form of a great lion and stands in front of the elephant. The elephant refuses to attack. Sikandar has to accept Kabir's victory: "Kabir, your Ram is the true God. Just this once, please save my life. The *kāzīs* and the mullahs do not understand the inner truth. The Creator has accepted your word." Kabir agrees not to call down the wrath of God on Sikandar, and Sikandar offers him gold, silver, cloth, villages, districts, whatever he would like. Kabir, of course, refuses to request any worldly reward. Sikandar bows to Kabir, and Kabir returns home.

The later versions of this encounter between Sikandar and Kabir add several additional ordeals.[10] Also, while Ananta-das makes it clear that Kabir has offended both the religion of the Brahmans and Baniyas and the religion of the *kāzīs* and mullahs, later sources tend to make the conflict one between a Hindu Kabir and his fanatic Muslim opponents. Brahmalinamuni's *Sadguru-shrikavira-charitam* in particular displays this anti-Muslim bias quite systematically.

Another added episode of the post-Ananta-das versions of this legend is that of Sikandar's fever. In Paramananda-das's *Kabir Manshur* [1956: 112-18], Sikandar Lodhi (*sic*) is said to have arrived in Banaras in V. S. 1545 (A.D. 1488) suffering from a terrible fever. He asks the townspeople who might able to cure him. They suggest Kabir, hoping that he will fail and be punished by Sikandar. As soon as Sikandar sees Kabir, his fever vanishes. Sikandar is pleased with Kabir, but Kabir's enemies among "the pandits and *kāzīs*" complain to Sikandar that Kabir is a heretic (*nāstik*): "He goes against the religious rules both of the Hindus and the Muslims. He goes about screaming 'I am the Godhead (*khudā*) and the sole Lord (*prabhu*) of the whole world.'" Kabir defiantly confirms the accusation: "Yes, I am the Lord, Creator of the whole universe." This version preserves the joint Hindu-Muslim opposition to Kabir but makes the accusation against him that of claiming to be God (a charge often made against mystical Sufis) rather than that of turning

10. See Priya-das [Nabha-das 1969: 487-90], Chatur-das [Raghav-das 1965: 54], Paramananda-das [1956: 112-20], Brahmalinamuni [1960: 126-216], Chandradatta [1926: chap. 83, vv. 22-41], and Gangasharan Shastri [1976: 85-98]. Mahipati [1982] omits the Sikandar legend altogether. The legend is twice referred to by Raghav-das [1965: 54 (vs. 127), 177 (vs. 350)].

people against the observance of both Muslim and Hindu customs and rites.

According to Paramananda-das, Sikandar then has a cow brought and killed in front of everyone. He says to Kabir: "If you are really the Godhead, then revive this cow." Kabir snaps his fingers. The cow revives and gives milk enough for everyone. At this point sheikh Taki, the chief *pīr* (Muslim preceptor) of Sikandar enters the story. Sheikh Taki is naturally jealous of the attention Kabir is getting from Sikandar. He becomes the ringleader of the Brahmans and mullahs opposed to Kabir and eventually convinces Sikandar to submit Kabir to no less than fifty-two ordeals. These ordeals take the place of the mere three ordeals found in Ananta-das's version of the legend. In most Kabir Panthi versions, sheikh Taki plays the role of Kabir's principal opponent. This sheikh also figures prominently in the legends of Kabir's "son" and "daughter," Kamal and Kamali (below, pp. 50-52).

The Unexpected Feast

This is another of the more popular legends about Kabir. According to Ananta-das, as more and more people come to see Kabir, the Brahmans again plot against him. Four Brahmans have their heads shaved and put on forehead marks and prayer beads like those of the *sants*. The four are then sent out in four directions to invite people to a great feast they say will be given by Kabir. The Niranjani Panthi recension of the text claims that the Brahmans leave on the ninth day of the first half of the month of Magh (January-February) and that the feast is to be held on the festival day of Basant Panchami (the fifth day of the light or waxing moon half of the same month). No one discovers the ruse, and great crowds arrive at Kabir's hut on the appointed day. As he had done before (above, pp. 27-28), Kabir leaves and hides himself somewhere. As before, Hari appears, this time evidently in the disguise of many Kabirs, and greets all the guests. Whatever anyone asks for is given. After five days of festivities, Hari gives cloth to all the *sants*. The real Kabir then returns and mixes with the guests and feels that his life has been made worthwhile.

Ananta-das's version of this story clearly intends to illustrate the conflict between Kabir and the Brahmans. In other versions Kabir's opponents are not so clearly identified.[11] In Mahipati's *Bhaktavijay*

11. Priya-das [Nabha-das 1969:490], Chatur-das [Raghav-das 1965:54], Mahipati [1982: vol. 1, pp. 117-21], Chandradatta [1926:chap. 84, vv. 2-19], Paramananda-das [1956: 120-21], Brahmalinamuni [1960: 451-64], Gangasharan Shastri [1976: 180-84]. Raghav-das [1965: 177 (vs. 350)] briefly alludes to the legend.

(A.D. 1762), for instance, they are described simply as "evil-minded persons." Since this text was written by a Brahman follower of the relatively orthodox Varkari tradition, the change is not surprising. Brahmalinamuni's modern *Sadguru-shrikavira-charitam* describes Kabir's opponents in this legend simply as "proponents of violence" (*hiṃsāvādī*) and "meat eaters" (*māṃsāhārī*). Other Kabir Panthi works such as Paramananda-das's *Kabir Manshur* and Gangasharan Shastri's *Kabir Jivanacharitra* follow Ananta-das's version more closely. Chandradatta's Sanskrit *Bhaktamala*, not a Kabir Panthi text, calls Kabir's enemies in this legend simply "bad people" (*durjana*).

There are certain chronological problems surrounding the date of the feast. If the Brahmans disguised as *sant*s left on the ninth day of the first fortnight of Magh and the feast began on Basant Panchami (the fifth day of the light fortnight), they must have left in the dark fortnight and had only about nine days to distribute their invitations. The text also claims that they were told to do so "in all the villages up to a radius of eighty *kos*" and that the guests kept arriving for "about twenty days." Unless these latter two statements are simply poetic hyperbole, the nine days given for the Brahmans to deliver the invitations is clearly insufficient. This nine day gap also depends on the use of the Samvat calendar that puts the dark (waning moon) half of the month before the light (waxing moon) half. The Vikrami calendar reverses this order. The Samvat system is the more common one in northern India.

On the other hand, the old 1693 V. S. (A.D. 1636) manuscript [text *f*] and two other of the manuscripts used in Callewaert's edition of the text give the date of the feast as the eleventh day of the first half of Magh and do not specify when the Brahmans first set off. This at least creates no chronological difficulties, except that the feast day must be the eleventh day of the *light* (waxing moon) half of the month since, in the days before electricity, no five day feast could be held toward the end of the dark fortnight. Since the text specifies that it is the eleventh day of the "first half" of Magh, it must be using the Vikrami calendar in which the light fortnight precedes the dark fortnight. Normally, however, this Vikrami system is not used in northern India. This suggests that the two relevant padas of [text *f*] (one specifying the first half of Magh and the other the eleventh day) are not entirely compatible with each other. All these dates are interesting for another reason as well.

In the modern Kabir Panth, the eleventh day of the bright half of Magh is celebrated as the death anniversary of Kabir.[12] An important

---

12. This is true in at least the Kabir Chaura and allied branches of the Panth. I am not certain that the Dharmadasis accept this same date.

fair (*melā*) and feast (*bhaṇḍārā*) is held every year on this date at Magahar, the reputed site of his death. According to F. E. Keay [1931: 103], the main annual fair and feast at Damakhera, the main center of one of the two principal subdivisions of the Dharmadasis, was held annually on Basant Panchami (fifth day of the light half of Magh). If this was true in about 1930 when Keay did his field work, it is no longer so.[13] Nowadays the Damakhera feast is held on the full moon day of Magh. No explanation, apart from tradition, is given for the choice of this date, but curiously enough it is also the date celebrated as the birthday of Ravi-das by his followers. Whatever the exact significance of these dates may be, it is at least clear that the dates of Basant Panchami and Magh Ekadashi (the fifth and eleventh days of the bright half of Magh) both had some connection with Kabir as far back as the time of the early *Kabir Parachai* manuscripts.

The *Apsarā* and Hari

This is not one of the more popular Kabir legends, but it is included in many legend collections. Most manuscripts of the *Kabir Parachai* do not name the *apsarā* (celestial nymph). They do, however, compare her to the famous apsarā Rambha. A few manuscripts seem to call her Rambha. On the other hand, she is called "Manorama" in Gangasharan Shastri's [1976: 202-12] modern retelling of the legend. In the Dharmadasi versions of the legend by Paramananda-das [1956: 121-22] and Brahmalinamuni [1960: 442-51], the goddess Lakshmi herself, the wife of Hari-Vishnu, plays the same role.

Ananta-das says that one year after (the unexpected feast), Hari sent an *apsarā* to test Kabir's chastity. In spite of her great beauty and her repeated requests, Kabir refuses to become her lover:

> I will not take your hand, mother. My lord Ram would be angry with me. To me your eyes and words seem like poison. My life is bound to Hari alone. Whoever gratifies your hopes is certain to make his

13. Keay [1931: 109] does seem to make an error when he claims that the thirteenth day (?of the light half) of the month of Bhadon (August-September) marks the birthday of Kabir. This date is rather considered to be the date when Kabir installed the first head of the Kabir Panth (either Dharmadas or his son Churamani according to different sadhus). Naturally only the Dharmadasi monasteries hold feasts on this date. All branches of the Kabir Panth now accept the full moon day of the month of Jyeshtha (or Jeth) (May-June) as Kabir's birthday.

> home in hell. Any man who falls in love with you will fall into the river of worldly existence and never reach the other shore. . . . Mother, give up hope of convincing me. Isn't there anyone for you in heaven? [11.11-11.13, 11.16]

The *apsarā* finally concedes defeat and returns to heaven. She tells Hari what had happened. He is so pleased with Kabir that he appears to him in his divine form, complete with conch, discus, club, lotus, Kaustubh jewel, and the mark of Bhrigu's foot. He rides on Garuda and displays four arms. Kabir is overwhelmed by this vision and falls at Vishnu's feet.

Hari then offers to grant Kabir anything he desires: lordship over all the earth, residence in the world of the gods, four magic powers (over physical elements),[14] a new body, as well as the eight *siddhi*s (supernatural yogic powers) and nine *nidhi*s (treasures). Kabir replies that he is incapable of requesting anything: "I have little wisdom. I don't know what to request. How can I recognize the ocean of pleasures?" After this, "Hari put his four hands on Kabir's head. He made him unaging, immortal, and indestructible."

Although Hari appears on earth in human disguises in several of the legends of the *Kabir Parachai*, this manifestation of the god in an anthropomorphic (*saguṇ*) divine form is obviously somewhat curious in the context of a legend about a *sant* such as Kabir who proclaimed a God *without* attributes (*nirguṇ*). One must, however, keep in mind that Ananta-das may simply be retelling a popular legend. Furthermore, Ananta-das himself was not necessarily a proponent of so rigorously a *nirguṇ* conception of God as Kabir was. Interestingly enough, the two main recensions of the manuscripts of Ananta-das's *Kabir Parachai* manifest a sharp difference of opinion precisely about the relation between the *saguṇ* and *nirguṇ* conceptions of God.

In the Niranjani Panthi recension we have used for our text and translation, it is explicitly stated that the two conceptions are both valid [12. *dohā*]: "*Nirguṇ* and *saguṇ* are one. In all bodies It remains inherent. Like the waves of ocean, It assumes a form and then rejoins Its source." On the other hand, the Dadu Panthi recension (based on the 1693 V. S. and related manuscripts) clearly gives precedence to the *nirguṇ* conception. In place of "*Nirguṇ* and *saguṇ* are one," the 1693 V. S. [text *f*] manuscript reads: "*Nirguṇ* is unstained by qualities."

---

14. This list of four magic powers [vs. 12.9] is particularly interesting since the terms used are not those commonly found in Hatha Yoga texts for similar powers. See the text and translation below.

This manuscript immediately precedes this statement with the following two padas not found in our tradition: "*Nirguṇ* Brahman is Niranjan and Nath. He, having joined with Kabir, is indeed his companion." Similarly, this Dadu panthi recension manuscript omits most of the description of the manifest form of the four-armed Vishnu. Since, however, the basic point of the legend is to reward Kabir with a darshan of the manifest Vishnu and to further offer him all manner of supernatural powers and even residence in heaven, the legend itself is logically incompatible with a strict *nirguṇ* conception of God. This incompatibility helps to justify our choice of the Niranjani Panthi recension based on the India Office and related manuscripts (below, pp. 81-83).

Other versions of this legend are roughly similar.[15] Nonetheless, Chandradatta's *Samskrita-bhaktamala*, which otherwise seems to mostly follow Priya-das's commentary, contains an interesting variant. Chandradatta writes that after the unexpected feast, a prostitute "endowed with beauty and art" came to Kabir's house and asked to be permitted to live there and to please Kabir with "dances, songs and other pleasures." Kabir tells her that he has no use for pleasures, songs, and dances: "You should consider me to be an eunuch, I am not a man for women." Kabir does, however, agree to let her stay in his house: "In my house there is (? an image of) the glorious Lord Hari. He is passionate and sensual. Do your dancing in front of him. If you desire pleasure, then Hari himself will come in the night to enjoy you." The woman devotes herself to dancing in front of the god until one day she goes into a wood and disappears. Everyone decides that she must have been an *apsarā*. Is Chandradatta using this legend to show Kabir as a worshipper of the *saguṇ* form of Hari or does he wish to show Kabir as leaving the worship of this inferior *saguṇ* form to others? The answer is not clear.

The conversation between Kabir and Vishnu that concludes the legend of the *apsarā* and Hari in most versions of the legend is utilized by Gangasharan Shastri [1976:207-11] to launch a somewhat underhanded attack against the Dharmadasi branch of the Kabir Panth. The attack takes the form of another legend. Kabir first asks Vishnu if Buddha and Mahavir were not proponents of an atheistic philosophy that denies the reality of God, accepting only the reality of the individual souls (*jīv*). Vishnu tells Kabir that after his death some people will misinterpret his words and propound the soul-only doctrine. Two hundred years after Kabir, a good householder named Shudra will, Vishnu says, follow

15. Priya-das [Nabha-das 1969:490-91], Chatur-das [Raghav-das 1965:54], Chandradatta [1926:chap. 84, vv. 20-29], Paramananda-das [1956:120-23], Brahmalinamuni [1960: 442-51], Gangasharan Shastri [1976: 202-207].

Kabir's doctrine. His teacher will be called Balapir Kabir. Shudra's eldest son will oppose this doctrine. In the end, Balapir's teachings will be accepted by Shudra, but Shudra's younger son will abandon his father's path and propagate a false path through compositions that calumniate Vishnu, Brahma and the other gods. These proponents of the soul-only doctrine will break their ties with the head monastery and establish an independent seat at Kudaramal.

Although the characters of this legend are not given their real names, it is clearly a hostile retelling of the story of Kabir's disciple Dharma-das (here Shudra) and his two sons Narayan-das and Churamani. The latter, under the name Muktamani Nam Sahab, founded the famous Kudaramal monastery. Gangasharan Shastri may be identifying Balapir Kabir with Pramod Guru, called "Balapir," but this Balapir was the great-great disciple of Churamani and not his father's guru. To make matters still more confusing, the soul-only doctrine that Gangasharan Shastri takes such pains to calumniate refers to the *pārakh* doctrine associated with the *Kabir Bijak* commentator Puran-das (A.D. 1805-37). This doctrine (and an associated Jain-like puritanism) is in fact accepted by many sadhus even in the Kabir Chaura branch of the Kabir Panth. It is, however, dominant only in the Burhanpur branch and its offshoots, a branch that has long been independent of the Dharmadasis.

Kabir's Death at Magahar

This may be the best known of all the Kabir legends. Several songs attributed to Kabir himself definitely seem to refer to it. Most interesting is a song from the *Kabir Bijak* in which Kabir says:[16]

> You say that he who dies at Magahar
>   will become a donkey.
> Have you lost faith in Ram?
> If Ram dwells in my heart,
> What is Kashi? What is the barren
>   ground of Magahar?
> If Kabir leaves this body in Kashi,
> What debt is owed to Ram?

16. *Kabir Bijak, shabda* 103 [Kabir 1972: 145]. Compare this with *Kabir Granthavali, dhanāshrī* 5 [Kabir 1969: 382-83], and his song found in the Sikh *Guru Granth Sahib, dhanāsarī* 3 [Kabir 1966: 143].

Ananta-das begins his version of the legend with a similar statement:

> Kabir performed a miracle on the occasion of this death. He decided on the plan of dying at Magahar.
>
> Kabir said: "Everyone says that dying in Kashi leads to salvation and that anyone who dies in Magahar will become an ass in his next birth. Kashi destroys everyone's sins, but I will preserve Hari's glory [by finding salvation at Magahar]." [13.2-13.3]

Soon after Kabir's death, his Hindu and Muslim followers form two rival groups. The Hindus want to burn him and the Muslims want to bury him. They finally agree to send for thirty-two loads of flowers with which they cover his body. All the *sant*s assemble and dance, sing, and play drums and conches. Kabir becomes immortal without abandoning his body. All his devotees are astonished when they see that only the flowers remain. Everyone returns home with great lamentation. Kashi is completely desolate. Meanwhile, back in heaven, Shiv and Brahma go to greet Kabir. Indra offers him his divine throne. Vishnu tells Kabir: "Heaven is yours. Live here forever."

Other versions of this legend make only a few changes in it.[17] Nonetheless, several Kabir Panthi texts add two important characters to the story: the Hindu king Virasimha Baghel and the Muslim nawab Bijali Khan. They lead Kabir's Hindu and Muslim followers respectively during the dispute over the disposal of Kabir's corpse. As already noted, Ananta-das mentions Virasimha Baghel in connection with the legend of the *paṇḍā* of Jagannath (above, pp. 29-32), and the historical synchronism with this king is important for determining the probable dates of Kabir (above, pp. 17-18).

One important feature of Ananta-das's version of the Magahar legend not found in most later versions is the implied distinction he makes between Kabir's Muslim and Hindu followers, on the one hand, and the *sant*s on the other. It is possible that the term *sant* may here simply refer to the non-orthodox Hindu sadhus associated with Kabir, but it seems rather to have a broader implication and may refer to all the persons who followed Kabir alone and refused to identify themselves as either Hindus or Muslims. In any case, the *sant*s seem not to take any part in the quarrel of the Hindus and Muslims over Kabir's corpse. Even in Ananta-das's version of the legend, however, Kabir's Hindu

---

17. See Priya-das [Nabha-das 1969: 491], Muhsin Fani [1843: vol. 2, p. 191], Chatur-das [Raghav-das 1965: 55], Chandradatta [1926: chap. 84, vv. 29-44], Paramananda-das [1956: 140-43], Brahmalinamuni [1960: 593-614]. The legend is not found in Mahipati's *Bhakta-vijay*.

identity is at the end categorically reaffirmed when he is welcomed into heaven by Vishnu and the other Hindu gods.

Magahar, the site of Kabir's death, is now identified with a town of that name in Basti District near the city of Gorakhpur. As has been noted (above, p. 17), the tradition linking this town with Kabir's death is quite an old one. There does, however, exist some evidence that connects Kabir's death with other places.[18] According to one theory, Magahar is not the town near Gorakhpur, but a place just on the other bank of the Ganges across from Varanasi. Alternatively, it may be taken as a corruption of the word for the ancient Magadha region (northern Bihar). Abu'l Fazl (A.D. 1598) mentions tombs or samadhis of Kabir at both Puri in Orissa and Ratanpur in Avadh [Vaudeville 1974:33-34]. The samadhi at Puri still exists (above, p. 16), but the tomb at Ratanpur can no longer be identified. Of these several places, the claim of the town of Magahar near Gorakhpur to be the true site of Kabir's death is clearly much the strongest.

The Magahar legend is the last of the legends found in Ananta-das's *Kabir Parachai.* Priya-das's commentary on Nabha-das's *Bhaktamal* contains the same legends (including Kabir's initiation by Ramananda), no more and no less, in exactly the same order. The many verbal similarities between the texts of Priya-das and Ananta-das have been catalogued in detail by Lalata Prasad Dube [1968:206-22], not only for the *Kabir Parachai* but for Ananta-das's *parachaī*s of several other *sant*s as well. There seems to be little doubt that Ananta-das's *parachaī*s were the principal source used by Priya-das for his versions of the legends of Kabir and these other *sant*s. Similarly, the versions of the Kabir legends in Chandradatta's *Samskrita-bhaktamala* and in Chatur-das's commentary on Raghav-das's *Bhaktamal* seem to be largely dependent on either Priya-das or Ananta-das or on both.

18. On this subject, see Vaudeville [1974:33-34], K. N. Dvivedi [1965:68-70], P. Chaturvedi [1964:141-43], G. H. Westcott [1953:15-17].

CHAPTER 3

OTHER LEGENDS

The *Kabir Parachai* cycle includes only a portion of the Kabir legends found in modern hagiographical collections such as those of Paramananda-das, Brahmalinamuni and Gangasharan Shastri. The principal versions of the more popular of these additional legends are discussed in the present chapter. Still more legends exist both in oral and written traditions, but they are less well-known and less influential.

Most of the additional legends found in sources later than the *Kabir Parachai* are associated either directly or indirectly with the Kabir Panth. Several of these legends have to do with the founding of one or other of the subsects or branches of the Kabir Panth and in fact serve as "foundation charters" for these branches. Some are clearly borrowed by Kabir Panthi authors from other traditions. The cycle of legends connected with Ibrahim bin Addham, for instance, has been imported wholesale from Sufi sources. Similarly, the legend of Saman and Seu originally had nothing to do with Kabir. Other legends are somewhat more difficult to categorize. One of the most popular legends, and one with a wide range of quite different versions, is that of Kabir's birth.

Kabir's Birth

Most versions of the legend of Kabir's birth reflect the desire of Kabir's followers to somehow deny, or at least mitigate, the opprobrium attached to his Muslim and low-caste family heritage. The most extreme versions—such as that of Brahmalinamuni's *Sadguru-shrikavira-charitam* [1960]—not only deny this heritage but also declare Kabir to be a full incarnation of an anthropomorphic Vishnu. Other versions are content simply to assert that Kabir was only the *adopted* son of his Muslim parents, without specifying exactly who his real parents were. Several texts of the Dharmadasi branch of the Kabir Panth, including Paramananda-das's *Kabir Manshur*, invent a whole cycle of legends about Kabir's previous births in the style of the Puranas or Jatakas.

The oldest extant version of Kabir's birth legend seems to be that found in a verse of Raghav-das's *Bhaktamal* (? A.D. 1720), a text associated with the Dadu Panth. This verse clearly refers to Kabir's having been found by a Julaha of Kashi, but it makes no mention of the Lahar Lake where the event took place according to later Kabir Panthi versions. Raghav-das's verse may be translated as follows:

> There appeared in the eastern region the man (*jan*) Kabir, a devotee of the Absolute without attributes (*nirguṇ bhagat*). One day a Muslim weaver went outside of Kashi on his way somewhere. Under a tree someone had left a child who was calling out. The weaver took it home with him and entrusted it to his wife. All their clansmen were called, and a big celebration was held. When Kabir had grown up, he worshipped Ram and had no attachment to anything else [1965: 177 (vs. 349)].

Another early version of Kabir's birth legend appears in Mahipati's *Bhaktavijay* [1982: vol. 1, pp. 8, 57-58, 78-80], a text that belongs to Varakari tradition. Mahipati claims that Vishnu told various sages living in heaven to become avatars on earth. Uddhav was told to become Nam-dev, and Shuk was told to become Kabir. Vishnu changed them into infants and put them in shells. Kabir's shell fell into the Ganges, and Nam-dev's shell fell into the Bhimarathi. Kabir repeated "Ram, Ram," and Nam-dev repeated "Vitthal, Vitthal." A Muslim weaver named Kamal found Kabir's shell and brought the child home to his wife. Motherly love filled her breasts with milk, and she raised Kabir as her own child. Although this version of Kabir's birth legend is otherwise unknown, Kabir is earlier identified as an avatar of Shuk-dev in Ananta-das's *Rai-das Parachai* [1982: 42].

More typical of Kabir Panthi versions of the legend is that of Paramananda-das's *Kabir Manshur* [1956: 100-108]. This text asserts that Kabir is the fourteenth manifestation on earth of Kabir Sahab, alias Jnaniji, in the Kali Yuga. In heaven, the Satpurush told Jnaniji to rescue men, especially Dharma-das, from the bonds of Kal, the god of death. Dharma-das, he said, had taken to image worship, which was nothing other than the worship of this same Kal. In V. S. 1456 (A.D. 1398-99), the light of the Satpurush came to earth on the Lahar Lake in Kashi. The light astonished a disciple of Ramananda named "Ashtananda" who was present on the shore. Ashtananda ran to tell his guru. Meanwhile, the light was transformed into a small human child. At this moment, Niru, a Muslim weaver of the Julaha caste, was returning to Kashi with his bride Nima. According to Paramananda-das, Niru and Nima had originally belonged to a Hindu Brahman caste that had sometime previously lost its religious status (*dharma-bhrashṭa*). Niru went down to the water to drink and saw the child floating among the lotuses. She picked up the child and brought it to Niru. She wanted to keep it, but Niru insisted that she leave it where she had found it, for fear of what people might say. Then the child itself spoke to Nima, telling her to bring it home with them and offering salvation in return. Niru finally agreed.

When they arrived at Niru's house, a Brahman came to give the child a name. The child called out: "Listen, pandit! My name is Kabir. Don't bother giving me a different name." Niru then called a *kāzī* and asked him to give the child a name. The *kāzī* looked for a name at random in the Koran, but to whatever page he opened the book, he found only the name Kabir. This name was considered inappropriate since it was a name of God. The *kāzī* insisted that Niru kill the child. Niru tried to kill it with a knife, but the knife passed through its neck. The child explained to Niru that its body was merely a vision, not real flesh and blood. There being no other solution, the name Kabir was finally accepted.

Brahmalinamuni's version [1960:65-94], written in Sanskrit with the author's own Hindi commentary, is similar to that of Paramananda-das, but Brahmalinamuni characteristically changes several details in order to give the legend a more anti-Muslim and pro-Brahman bias. In his version Kabir's foster parents were not born in a caste that had fallen from Brahman to Julaha status; they were the Brahmans Gaurishankar and Sarasvatidevi, worshippers of Shiv as Lord Vishvanath of Kashi. Their devotions annoyed some Muslims (*yavanalog*) who then forced Gaurishankar and Sarasvatidevi to drink water from their hands. This caused a loss of caste (*jāti-bhrashṭa*). The Muslims (*mlechchha*) then renamed them Niru and Nima. Gaurishankar found that no one would give him proper employment, and he had to resort to weaving for his living. He and his wife contemplated suicide, but a divine voice told them to remain firm since their misery soon would end. They continued to worship Shiv in the privacy of their home.

According to Brahmalinamuni, when Gaurishankar and Sarasvatidevi arrived at Lahar Lake they were already middle-aged. The wife saw the child and wanted to bring it home, but her husband told her to leave it. The infant Kabir then told them both the history of their former births and promised that he would save them from the bonds of worldly existence. They took Kabir home, put him on a throne, and began to worship him. Each day a gold coin was found on the throne, thus ending Gaurishankar's economic worries. Kabir, not being of flesh and blood, ate nothing. This greatly upset his foster parents. He told them to bring a seven day old calf. When it was brought, it immediately began to give milk without even being milked. Kabir consented to drink this milk simply to please them.

When Gaurishankar decided that it was time to give the child a name, he arranged for the proper Vedic ceremony and called in an astrologer. Gaurishankar told the astrologer that the child had been found on the full moon day of the month of Jyeshtha (May-June). The astrologer consulted his almanac and discovered that: "This child must be an avatar of God." The child then announced that its name was "Kavir." The astrologer was amazed and went home happy. In Brahmalinamuni's version, no Muslim *kāzī* comes to name the child. Since he wants to derive the word from the Sanskrit *kavi* ("poet, seer"), rather than from the more obvious Persian-Arabic name "Kabir," Brahmalinamuni prefers the name "Kavir" to "Kabir."

Brahmalinamuni then describes how more and more poeple came to see the child. They wondered whether it was a manifestation of Shiv, Vishnu, or the eternal Paramatman. Kabir finally enlightened his foster parents about his exact identity: "I am that Brahman without qualities (*nirguṇ*) that dwells in the world of Truth, the home of the immortals. . . . My true form is unknowable." Kabir then described his various previous avatars: Satsukrit, Munindra, and Karunamay. Finally he delivered a philosophical discourse that in fact presents Brahmalinamuni's own interpretation of Advaita Vedanta. Brahmalinamuni does not go so far as to identify the avatars of Kabir with the avatars of Vishnu. In this matter, he preserves something of the traditional view of his Dharmadasi branch of the Kabir Panth according to which Shiv, Vishnu, and Brahma are secondary, inferior gods created by the demiurge Kal-Niranjan. Nonetheless, Brahmalinamuni also has Kabir deliver a strong defense of the classical Brahmanic model of society and religion. At one point in his discourse, Kabir says [1960: 83]: "He and he alone will obtain salvation who acts above all to preserve the proper conduct of the *varṇa*s and *āshrama*s as taught in the Vedas and who obtains devotion and knowledge through purity of mind." Brahmalinamuni has obviously moved a long, long way from the socio-religious ideology of Kabir's songs and verses.

Gangasharan Shastri, the present-day head of the Kabir Chaura branch of the Kabir Panth, also tends to Sanskritize and Hinduize Kabir, but his *Kabir Jivanacharitra* also preserves some of the anti-Brahmanic spirit of the earlier versions of the legends. His description of the appearance of Kabir at Lahartara (Lahar Lake) also eliminates at least some of the supernatural excesses of the Dharmadasi accounts of this event. According to Gangasharan Shastri, Kabir does not descend from heaven as a ball of light; he is simply found playing in the lake. When Niru, here also called "Nur Ali," refuses to take the child home, it is not Kabir himself but rather a heavenly voice that tells the couple to take the child home. Niru then asks the child's real identity. The voice answers:

> This child is a yogic being of infinite births, not born from the womb. . . . By his yogic illusion he abandons many bodies and takes new ones. . . . Many times he has come to the aid of the world. . . . He is a portion of me. I have myself sent him by my own desire for the sake of the welfare of men [Gangasharan Shastri 1976:8].

From this it is clear that Gangasharan Shastri also claims that Kabir is some sort of a divine avatar, but he does so in a manner that is much more modest and equivocal and without the trappings of the Purana-like mythology favored by the followers of the Dharmadasi branch of the Kabir Panth.[1]

Other versions of the legend of Kabir's birth are current in oral tradition. One of the better known of these versions is, I think, first mentioned by G. H. Westcott:

> The first legend relates that his mother was a Brahman widow who went with her father on a pilgrimage to the shrine of a famous ascetic. To reward the devotion of the pilgrims the ascetic prayed that the woman might become the mother of a son. The prayer of so holy a man could not fail to find fulfillment and in due course the Brahman widow became the mother of Kabir. The mother, to escape dishonour, exposed the infant, who was discovered and adopted as her own by the wife of a weaver.
>
> According to another version of this story Ramananda, who was the ascetic referred to, said that he could not recall his blessing but would arrange that the birth should not be after the usual manner, but that the infant should issue from the palm of its mother's hand.[2]

---

1. For a more detailed discussion of the variations in the concept of Kabir as an avatar, see Uma Thukral [1989].

2. Westcott notes that this version depends on a fanciful etymology for "Kabir" (or rather "*kar-vīr*"): the hero (*vīr*) from the hand (*kar*).

> His promise was realized and the infant was placed on a lotus flower in the midst of the Lahar Tank. It was there discovered by Nima, the wife of Niru, and by her taken to her husband's house [1953:3-4].

Westcott claims to have gotten most of his versions of the legends from a text called "*Kabir Kasauti*" published in Bombay in A.D. 1885. The text must have been different from the more recently published version of Laihana Simha's *Kabir Kasauti* [1962]. This latter text contains a version of Kabir's birth legend similar to that of Paramananda-das's *Kabir Manshur*.[3]

The Visit of Jahan-gasta

The legend about the visit of Jahan-gasta seems to be an old one. Kshitimohan Sen [1974:96] claims that it is found in the early *Nirbhayajnan*. It is directed against the empty ritualism and obsession with the rules of dietetic purity of orthoprax Muslims. Although this message is perfectly compatible with Kabir's ideology, it is possible that the story may have a Sufi origin.

According to Gangasharan Shastri, Jahani-gasta was a Muslim *sant* of Arabia.[4] In a dream he was told to visit Kabir. Kabir learned of his coming and tied up a pig in front of the ashram. When Jahani-gasta saw the pig, he decided to return to Arabia without meeting Kabir, but Kabir called out to him to stay. Jahani-gasta asked Kabir why he had tied up such an impure thing at his door. Kabir replied that he had taken the impure thing from inside and put it outside, while Jahani-gasta had kept it inside. Jahani-gasta asked Kabir to explain further. Kabir said: "I have removed the pig in the form of lust, anger, greed, error, passion, hatred, and egoism from inside and tied it up outside, while you, in opposite fashion, have kept the pig . . . within yourself."

Kabir Saves the Temple of Jagannath at Puri

This legend, like that of Kabir pouring water on the burning feet of the *paṇḍā* of Jagannath, connects Kabir with the temple of Jagannath in Puri (above, pp. 29-32). Like the *paṇḍā* legend, it displays Kabir's

---

3. Laihana Simha 1962:5-8. See also above, pp. 44-45.

4. Gangasharan Shastri 1976: 194-96. See also Paramananda-das [1956: 157-58].

magical powers while associating him with this famous temple and with Vaishnavism in general. The oldest known versions of the legend seem to be those of the *Anurag Sagar* and of Paramananda-das's *Kabir Manshur*.[5]

According to the latter text, Kabir rescued the temple of Jagannath during the time of the second of his fourteen manifestations in this Kali Yuga. Krishna, after his own death, wanted to establish himself as Jagannath in Puri. In a dream he told king Indradaman to construct a temple. The king tried to do so several times, but each time the ocean swept the temple away. Kabir appeared and told the king to try again. Kabir built a platform on the shore, stuck his staff in the ground in front of it, and sat facing the ocean. When the ocean attempted to attack the temple, it could not get past Kabir's staff. The ocean then took the form of a Brahman and went to Kabir to ask permission to destroy the temple. Kabir told him that he would not be permitted to do so. In exchange Kabir allowed the ocean to destroy the Vishnu temple at Dvaraka in Gujarat. The ocean accepted the bargain and destroyed the Dvaraka temple. Gangasharan Shastri's version of the legend [1976: 145-52] is similar although he does not accept the Dharmadasi theory of the multiple incarnations of Kabir.

Kabir's Wife and the Libidinous Merchant

In terms of its ideological message, this is one of the most interesting of Kabir legends. It combines protests against economic and sexual exploitation of poor low-caste people by local merchants with an insistence that even the poor owe charity and hospitality to religious ascetics.

Although such a message is quite compatible with the general ideological tenor of many Kabir legends, the story is found only in two non-Kabir Panthi sources: the Muslim *Dabistan-i-Mazahib* attributed to Muhsin Fani and the Varakari author Mahipati's *Bhaktavijay*.[6] The reason why Kabir Panthi authors do not mention this legend is quite simple. As has been noted (above, pp. 18-19), the sadhus of the Kabir Panth refuse to accept that Kabir could ever have been married. Other religious

5. *Anurag Sagar*, in Yugalananda 1953: vol. 2; Paramananda-das 1956: 157-58. See also the English translation of the former text [*Anurag Sagar* 1984] and the version of Brahmalinamuni [1960: 740-52].

6. Muhsin Fani 1843: vol. 2, pp. 189-91; Mahipati 1982: vol. 1, pp. 178-85, 398-400. The latter source in fact gives two slightly different versions of the same story.

groups have had no such difficulty in accepting the early tradition of Kabir's marriage. Sikh tradition, for instance, accepts that Kabir, like Guru Nanak, was married. This particular legend, however, is not found in Sikh sources.[7]

According to the *Dabistan-i-Mazahib*, a number of dervishes came to Kabir's house. Since there was no food to offer them, Kabir asked his wife to try to get some groceries on credit. She told him that there was a shopkeeper who had been eyeing her, and he might extend the needed credit. Kabir told her to go ask him. The grocer agreed to give her the food if she would return to visit him at night. She agreed to do so. Once home, she expressed a desire to break her promise to visit the shopkeeper, but Kabir insisted that she keep her word. That night rain began to fall heavily, and Kabir carried his wife through the mud to the grocer's shop. When she arrived, the shopkeeper noted that she had no mud on her feet. He asked her how this could be, and she told him how her husband had carried her. The shopkeeper was filled with shame and fell at Kabir's feet to ask forgiveness. Afterwards the shopkeeper gave away everything in his shop to the poor and became a sadhu.

The Resurrections of Kamal and Kamali

The legends about how Kabir resurrected Kamal and Kamali are found only in Kabir Panthi texts. The reason is quite simple. One of the main aims of these legends is to deny that Kabir was the natural father of Kamal and Kamali. The legends also serve to demonstrate

7. Unfortunately, no written collection of Sikh legends seems to include any legends about Kabir's married life. A few legends about Kabir's wives were collected by M. A. Macauliffe from the Sikh scholars who helped him with his A.D. 1909 translation of the *Guru Granth Sahib* [M. A. Macauliffe 1963: vol. 6, p. 122-316].

Macauliffe [Ibid., p. 123] mentions the following works as sources of the legends he relates: "The work *Kabir Kasauti* of the late Lahina Singh of Panjor in the Patiala State, the *Kabir Manshur* of Sadhu Paramanand (Hindi), the *Kavi Charitar* (Gujarati), the *Bharat Khanda cha Aravachin Kosh* and the *Bhakta Vijay* of Mahipati (Marathi)."

The absence of well-known old Sikh legends about Kabir—apart from the meeting between him and Nanak described in some of the *janam-sākhī*s (below, pp. 17-18)—was confirmed for me by W. H. McLeod (personal communication). Mohan Singh [1934: 5, 30] refers to a Punjabi manuscript [no. 528, Punjab University Library] composed in 1693 (? A.D.) at Anandapur that contains verse *parachāī*s of "Kabir, Dhanna, Trilochan, Namdev, Jaidev, Ravidas, Balmi, Sukdev, Baddhak, Dhru, and Prahlad." Mohan Singh is "of the opinion that Ananta-das's *Parichaya* formed the basis of the Punjabi *Parchis*" in this manuscript. Whether or not this Punjabi manuscript can still be located is an open question.

Kabir's superhuman powers. As has been noted (above, pp. 18-19), Kamal was clearly an historical person. He is mentioned by name in a couple of verses attributed to Kabir.[8] A number of Kamal's own verses survive in oral tradition. In these verses Kamal refers to himself as "Kabir's son" (*Kabir kā bālaka*).[9] Sikh tradition and the Varakari tradition of Mahipati accept that Kamal was Kabir's natural son.[10] Kamali is a more shadowy figure although she is mentioned in both Kabir Panthi and non-Kabir Panthi sources.

According to the *Kabir Manshur* version of Kamal's resurrection [Paramananda-das 1956: 118-19], Kabir accompanied sultan Sikandar and sheikh Taki back to Delhi after he had survived the ordeals they had imposed on him. At Prayag, Taki and Sikandar saw a corpse floating in the Ganges. Taki challenged Kabir to revive it. Kabir said: "Listen, corpse! Get up through a miracle of God (*kudarat kamāl se*)." The corpse revived and was promptly dubbed Kamal ("miracle"). Other versions of this legend are similar.[11]

Sometime later, sheikh Taki's daughter died [Paramananda-das 1956: 159-60]. Eight days after her death, Taki told Kabir that he would have faith in Kabir if he could revive her corpse. Kabir went to her grave and called out: "Get up, daughter of sheikh Taki!" On the third try, she returned to life and rose from the grave. Taki was overjoyed, but his revived daughter told him: "I am not yours. I was brought back to life by the call of Kabir Sahab. For this reason I will live at his feet. I will not go to your house." She was renamed "Kamali" and became known as Kabir's daughter. She is said to have attained the light of knowledge through Kabir's favor. Other versions of this legend are similar.[12]

---

8. In a famous verse of Kabir in the *Guru Granth Sahib* [Kabir 1966] (*saloku* 115), he complains about Kamal's behavior. Vaudeville [1974: 42] translates this verse as follows: "Kabir's lineage was lost [*lit.* drowned] when his son Kamal was born: He forgets to invoke Hari and brings wealth into the house. . . ."

9. See especially, K. K. Bhatta [1975: 12, 29-30, 36-47].

10. Mahipati [1982: vol. 1, pp. 94-99] describes the birth of Kamal from Kabir's wife, Kamal's visit at age seven to Dvaraka in Gujarat, and his being rebuked by Kabir for having accepted a diamond from a merchant as payment for having done *kīrtans* to Hari. Mahipati also converts the story of Samman and Seu into one of Kabir and Kamal (below, pp. 52-53). Kamal is also called Kabir's son in Raghav-das's "*Bhaktamal*" [1965: 81 (vs. 183)].

11. See Brahmalinamuni [1960: 156-64]; Gangasharan Shastri [1976: 103-107].

12. See Brahmalinamuni [1960: 180-94] and Gangasharan Shastri [1976: 107-111].

In Brahmalinamuni's *Sadguru-shrikavira-charitam*, Kamali delivers a long speech, most of which is an attack against meat eating. Brahmalinamuni's text also includes legends of the past lives of Kamal and Kamali. Given Brahmalinamuni's pro-Brahman and anti-Muslim ideological predilections, it is not surprising that he claims that Kamal and Kamali were Brahmans in a previous life. These Brahmans did penance and were rewarded with the promise that in their next life they would be enlightened by Kabir. Since Brahmalinamuni also accepts that Kamal and Kamali were originally the son and daughter of sheikh Taki, however, the ideological message is somewhat equivocal. As a result of their practicing religious penance, the two Brahmans are reborn as Muslims and then are enlightened by Kabir, who Brahmalinamuni considers to have been the adopted son of an outcaste Brahman (although also an avatar of God). Even Brahmalinamuni's often reactionary ideological viewpoint has some egalitarian aspects.

Samman and Seu (Kabir and Kamal) Steal for Food

This legend has several versions. The older ones include a *parachaī* attributed to Ananta-das and a verse in Raghav-das's *Bhaktamal.* Neither of these two early versions makes any mention of Kabir.[13] All Kabir Panthi texts call the protagonists "Samman and Seu" (and variants). The Varakari author Mahipati, however, changes their identity. Samman and Seu become Kabir and Kamal. In Brahmalinamuni's version, it is Kabir, Dharma-das, and Kamal who visit Sammanan. Kabir uses the visit to humble Kamal's pride. In Gangasharan Shastri's version, it is only "Kabir and some *sant*s" who visit Samanan. Shastri's version is considerably bowdlerized and omits the beheading of Shiv (Seu) altogether.

According to Paramananda-das's *Kabir Manshur* [1956: 155-56], one day Kabir, sheikh Farid and Kamal arrived at the house of the lay devotee Samman. Samman had neither money nor food in the house. He asked his wife Neki and their son Seu what they could do. Seu suggested that he and his father go out and steal some food. Father and son went out at night and made a hole in the wall of a merchant's house.

13. For Ananta-das's *Saman Seu Parachai*, see the India Office library manuscript A 12/1 [*Vaisnava Poems*, pp. 73b-76b]. For other versions of this legend, see Raghav-das [1965: 259 (vs. 753)]; Mahipati [1982: vol. 1, pp. 99-108]; Paramananda-das [1956: 155-56]; Brahmalinamuni [1960: 465-80]; Gangasharan Shastri [1976: 82-85]. Different texts give different variants of the protagonists' names (Saman, Samman, Sammanan, Samanan, Seu, Shiv).

Seu entered and collected just enough food to feed their three guests. As he was escaping out through the hole, the merchant caught hold of his feet. Seu told his father: "I have been caught. Now our honor will turn to dust. You must quickly cut off my head so that I will not be recognized." Samman took a sword and cut off his son's head and ran home with the head and the food. He put the head in a niche of the house and told his wife to prepare the food for their three guests. Samman set three places for them to eat, but Kabir insisted that all six of them eat together in one line. Kabir called out to Seu to come. The head answered: "Honorable guru, how can I come? My severed head is sitting here and my trunk is lying somewhere else." Kabir replied: "They cut off the heads of thieves, adulterers, bandits, and bad characters; they don't cut off the heads of devotees. Come quickly here to me!" Seu's trunk came running, joined up with its head, and Seu revived. Seu ran to Kabir and fell at his feet. All the six sat down and ate together. Samman begged Kabir, Farid, and Kamal to stay one day more, but Kabir urged his companions to move on lest Samman do something even more terrible for their benefit.

Mahipati's *Bhaktavijay* [1982: vol. 1, pp. 98-108] tells more or less the same story with Kabir and his son Kamal as the protagonists in place of Samman and Seu. Mahipati's versions also ends slightly differently. After Kamal had been beheaded by Kabir, the merchant whose house they had robbed reported what had happened to the king. The king ordered that the headless corpse be impaled. After taking their meal in Kabir's house, the visiting *sant*s, accompanied by Kabir, walked to the edge of the town. On the way they saw Kamal's impaled trunk. The trunk joined its hands and bowed to them. The *sant*s asked Kabir how this could be. Who was the thief? Kabir told them what had happened. They then told Kabir's wife to bring Kamal's head. They took the trunk down from the stake and put the head back on it. Kamal returned to life and again bowed to the *sant*s. The impaling of the headless trunk must be an old element of the story, for it is already found in Raghav-das's *Bhaktamal* [1965: 259 (vs. 753)].

This legend—like that of Kabir's wife and the libidinous merchant—is obviously intended to describe Samman's and Seu's limitless devotion and generosity to the *sant*s. This, of course, is a favorite theme in Indian legends that arise from priestly and monastic circles. As in the legend of Kabir's wife, the Samman-Seu legend also embodies a strong element of social protest. In this case, the protest is directed against the poor being forced to steal in order to eat and then being treated as criminals for having done so.

There are clearly interesting psychoanalytical implications to this legend as well. Similar Oedipal beheadings, the symbolic equivalents of castrations, are in fact a frequent theme in Indian myths and legends, particularly those associated with the god Shiva. Well-known examples include those of Shiva beheading his son Ganesha, his father-in-law Daksha, and his rival Brahma (grandfather of the gods). The name Seu is in fact a corruption of Shiva, and it seems quite likely that the legend of Samman and Seu originally arose in a Shaivite context. Another Shaivite legend that invites comparison is that of the South Indian Nayamnar saint named "Siruttonda" who offers the flesh of his only son to feed a Bhairava ascetic.[14]

Kabir and Gorakhanath

One of the favorite targets of the caustic satire of Kabir's own verses and songs are the Shaktas. Apparently included among them are the followers of Gorakhanath, the famous early proponent of Hatha Yoga. Until recent times, the Naths or Kanaphata Yogis have been an important rival of the Kabir Panth for the support of low-caste people. In the various areas where the Kabir Panth now has its greatest influence —eastern Uttar Pradesh, Bihar, Madhya Pradesh, and Gujarat—the Naths no longer exercise much influence. Given their former strength, however, it is not surprising that many Kabir Panth texts contain a legend about Kabir's victorious encounter with Gorakhanath. A Kabir Panthi text of uncertain date, the *Gorakh Goshthi* [1930], purports to record the debate between Gorakh and Kabir, but it does not mention the legendary events surrounding the debate. The earliest extant versions of the legend seem to be those of Paramananda-das's *Kabir Manshur* and the *Kabir-charitra-bodh.*[15]

All versions of the legend reduce the encounter between Gorakhanath and Kabir to a miracle contest. Paramananda-das's version [1956: 111] states that one day Gorakh arrived and called out to Kabir: "Come, Kabir, you and I will have a talk about knowledge." Gorakh then planted his iron trident in the ground and climbed up and sat on one of its prongs, inviting Kabir to come up and sit on another. Kabir took out a ball of thread and, holding one end, threw it up into the air. He then climbed up and took his own seat on the other end of the thread, inviting Gorakh to come up and join him.

14. See Sekkizhaar [1985: 353-64].

15. Paramananda-das 1956: 111, 166-67; Yugalananda 1953: vol. 11. See also Brahmalinamuni [1960: 327-49], and Gangasharan Shastri [1976: 50-54].

In Gangasharan Shastri's version [1976: 50-54], Gorakhanath arrived at Ramananda's ashram, rather than at Kabir's place, and challenged Kabir's guru to a debate. Ramananda deputized Kabir to confront Gorakhanath. The story then proceeds as in Paramananda-das's version.

Paramananda-das [1956: 166-67] later adds two other episodes to the legend that are not found in most other versions. In one Gorakh challenged Kabir to find him in a pond. Gorakh changed into a frog and dived in, but Kabir quickly grabbed him. Kabir then challenged Gorakh to find *him* and dived in, converting himself into water itself. Gorakh naturally failed to find him. Some time later, Gorakh sent two poisonous snakes to bite Kabir. When the snakes did not return, Gorakh went to Kabir's hut and asked him to come out. Kabir told Gorakh to enter instead, since he was busy serving his two newly arrived guests. Kabir then gave instruction to Gorakh and Gorakh accepted Kabir as his teacher.

Gangasharan Shastri [1976: 50-54] claims that after Gorakh had accepted Kabir as his teacher, Kabir gave him the new name of Ramaraksha-das. Gangasharan Shastri is aware of the historical impossibility of a meeting between Kabir and the original Gorakhanath, who lived at least two or three hundred years earlier. He suggests that the Gorakh who met Kabir was a later yogi who used the same name.

Kabir's Disciples

The earliest named disciple of Kabir (apart from king Virasimha Baghel) seems to be Padmanabh, unless the *Nirbhayajnan* date of A.D. 1576 is in fact correct (above, p. 9), in which case Dharma-das would be the earliest. Padmanabh is the only person identified as a disciple of Kabir in Nabha-das's *Bhaktamal* (*c.* A.D. 1600).[16] Curiously, he is also the only known disciple of Kabir not credited with the founding of an important branch of the Kabir Panth, although some sadhus of Gujarat do claim spiritual descent from him.[17] Apart from Nabha-das's

16. Nabha-das 1969: 533 (vs. 146). See also the similar verse in Raghav-das's *Bhaktamal* [1965: 78-80 (vs. 181)].

17. The sadhus of one of the three panths called the "Ram Kabir Panth" are said to make this claim. Their genealogy descends from Padmanabh's reputed disciple Nilakantha. This particular Ram Kabir Panth is now divided into two main branches. One has its center at Dudharej near Vadhavan, and the other has one center at a village called "Shapar" and a second in "Jamakhambhaliya." All these sites are in Gujarat. On this rather confusing topic, see Brahmalinamuni [1960: 427-41, 251-55], P. Chaturvedi [1964: 291-96], K. K. Bhatta [1975: 96-152], K. N. Dvivedi [1965: 189-90].

mention of Padmanabh, the earliest mentioned disciples are Tatva and Jiva, who appear as disciples of Kabir in Priya-das's commentary (A.D. 1712) on a verse of Nabha-das's *Bhaktamal* [1969: 536-40 (vs. 69)] that praises Tatva and Jiva, but does not make them Kabir's disciples. Raghav-das's *Bhaktamal* [1965: 80 (vs. 182)] also contains a verse dedicated to Tatva and Jiva that fails to mention any relationship between them and Kabir although the commentator Chatur-das does mention this connection. The next oldest list of Kabir disciples (unless it is an interpolation) is found in a verse of Raghav-das's *Bhaktamal* [1965: 178 (vs. 353)], written in about A.D. 1720. This verse lists nine disciples: Kamal, Kamali, Padmanabh, Ram-kripal, Nir, Khir, Jnani, Dharma-das, and Har-das. We have already discussed Kamal and Kamali (above, pp. 50-52). Of the rest, only Padmanabh, Dharma-das, and perhaps Jnaniji are clearly identifiable.[18]

Modern Kabir Panthi tradition claims that Kabir had four principal disciples: Shruti-gopal, Jagu-das, Bhagavan-das (Bhago-das) Gosvami, and Dharma-das. This tradition also accepts Tatva and Jiva, Kamal and Kamali, and Padmanabh as important disciples of Kabir. Knowledge of scholarly arguments by modern academics (principally K. N. Dvivedi) against the possibility of Dharma-das being a direct disciple of Kabir have led some scholar sadhus (principally Gangasharan Shastri) of other branches of the Kabir Panth to question whether or not Dharma-das can be included among Kabir's immediate disciples.

Kabir and Padmanabh

The main legend about Padmanabh is first recounted in Priya-das's commentary on Nabha-das's *Bhaktamal* [Nabha-das 1969: 534-36]. Paramananda-das's *Kabir Manshur* ignores the story, but it is found in Brahmalinamuni's *Sadguru-shrikavira-charitam* [1960: 418-27] and in Gangasharan Shastri's *Kabir Jivanacharitra* [1976: 122-24]. According to Priya-das, there was once a merchant of Kashi whose body was being destroyed by leprosy and worms. Left with no way to maintain himself, he went to the Ganges with the intention of drowning himself. A big crowd gathered to watch. Padmanabh came by and asked what was happening. He asked that the merchant be untied and told him to bathe in the Ganges and then recite the name of Ram three times with devotion in

18. Jnaniji is said to be the founder of another of the three Ram Kabir Panths, this one better called the "Uda-dharma or the Uda Panth." See above note 17 and K. K. Bhatta [1975: 66-95].

his heart. The merchant did so and his leprosy immediately vanished. Padmanabh later went to visit his guru, Kabir, and was rebuked for having so little faith in the name of Ram. "Just a hint of the Name," said Kabir, "would have accomplished your aim." Most versions of this legend are similar, although Brahmalinamuni prefers the name "Satya" to the name "Ram."

Tatva and Jiva

The main legend about Tatva and Jiva is first told by Priya-das, while other versions are found in Mahipati's *Bhaktavijay*, Chatur-das's commentary (*c.* A.D. 1800) on Raghav-das's *Bhaktamal*, the long version of Paramananda-das's *Kabir Manshur*, Brahmalinamuni's *Sadguru-shrikavira-charitam*, and Gangasharan Shastri's *Kabir Jivanacharitra.*[19]

The original home of Tatva and Jiva has a significant bearing on the meaning of the legend. Nabha-das and Raghav-das say simply that Tatva and Jiva belonged to a "southern region." Mahipati places their home somewhere in the far South between Pandharapur and Rameshvar. Modern Kabir Panthi tradition locates their home in Gujarat. There is a site near Bharuch (Broach) in Gujarat whose huge banyan tree is said to be the one that was originally planted by Tatva and Jiva. The branch of the Kabir Panth that today claims descent from them has its main monastic center not in Gujarat but at Phatuha near Patna in Bihar.

Priya-das says that Tatva and Jiva were two Brahman brothers who dedicated themselves to serving the sadhus. Nonetheless, they were unable to find a guru they could accept. They placed a dry stick in the ground outside their docr and watered this stick with the water they used to wash the feet of each sadhu who visited them. They vowed to accept as their guru the sadhu whose "foot nectar" would make the stick sprout green leaves. One day Kabir arrived at their door. When Tatva and Jiva watered the stick with the water used to wash Kabir's feet, it immediately sprouted green leaves. The brothers asked Kabir to initiate them with the Name. Afterwards, Kabir told them to visit him in Kashi whenever they needed help.

Tatva's and Jiva's caste fellows were outraged that the brothers had taken a low-caste person as their guru. No one would eat in the same "line" with the two brothers or allow their children to marry the two

19. Nabha-das 1969: 537-40; Mahipati 1982: vol. 1, pp. 387-89; Raghav-das 1965: 80-81; Paramananda-das 1984: 585-88; Brahmalinamuni 1960: 216-55; Gangasharan Shastri 1976: 122-24.

brothers' children. Tatva and Jiva then went to Kashi and asked Kabir what they should do. Kabir advised them to intermarry their own children. They accepted Kabir's advice and returned home to begin the preparations for the wedding. When their caste fellows learned what Tatva and Jiva planned to do, they were even more outraged. In the end, their caste fellows capitulated and agreed to provide Tatva's and Jiva's children with marriage partners. Tatva and Jiva returned to Kabir to get his permission for this change of plans. Kabir told them to accept the offer, but to impose the condition that their caste fellows accept the religious path of bhakti. After debating the issue, the caste fellows agreed.

This legend seems in part to revolve around a somewhat misperceived difference between South Indian and North Indian marriage practices. In the South, the marriage system is built around the marriage of cross-cousins, the children of a brother and sister. What Kabir in fact proposes is a marriage between parallel cousins, the children of two brothers. This is definitely prohibited even in the South. What seems most likely to have happened is that the northern authors of the Kabir Panthi and Varakari versions of the legend did not fully understand the southern marriage system and incorporated this misunderstanding in a story whose principal ideological messages are only tangentially concerned with marriage customs.

One major ideological aim of the Kabir Panthi and Varakari versions of the legend is to condemn and ridicule the rigid insistence by Brahman castes on the rules of ritual pollution. Another ideological feature of the legend is the ambivalence it shows toward the Brahmans. The text implicitly intends to praise Kabir by showing how *even* Brahmans became his disciples at the same time that it claims equal (or greater) religious worth for Kabir as a representative of low-caste persons.

Kabir and Dharma-das

Dharma-das is said to have been a wealthy merchant of the Kasaundha Baniya caste who lived in the town of Bandhogadh in Baghelkhand. The followers of the Dharmadasi branch of the Kabir Panth believe that Kabir directly entrusted the creation of the Kabir Panth to him and his son Churamani only. The Dharmadasi branch has apparently always been centered in the Chhattisgadh region of south-eastern Madhya Pradesh. Today the Dharmadasis are divided into two main rival factions with centers at Damakheda in Raipur District and at Kharsiya in Raigarh District respectively. Dharmadasi texts that relate the legend of Dharam-das's life include Paramananda-das's *Kabir*

Manshur, the *Janmavali Dharam Das ki*, Brahmalinamuni's *Sadguru-shrikavira-charitam*, and a recent semi-scholarly study published with the patronage of the former head of the Damakheda faction, Grindha-muni Nam Sahab.[20]

Brahmalinamuni's version of the Dharma-das legend is one of the most commmplete. He writes that Dharma-das was originally a worshipper of *saguṇ* Vishnu. His guru in Bandhogadh was one *shrī* Rup-das. Dharma-das was extremely devout and practiced all the rules of charity toward the poor and guests. One day Dharma-das arrived at Mathura on a tour of sacred bathing places. After bathing in the Yamuna, he set about preparing his food. When he looked in the fire, he saw that an army of ants was desperately trying to escape from a burning log. He was filled with compassion and vowed not to eat the food. He put it on a plate and went out to find a suitable donee. Just then Kabir arrived in Mathura. Dharma-das offered the food to Kabir. Kabir told him: "Listen, merchant Dharma-das! When you were making this food, millions of ants were killed. Do you want to burden me with all this sin?" As Kabir spoke, all the rice grains on the plate turned into ants and began to crawl back to the ground.

Dharma-das then asked Kabir who he was. Kabir said: "In this Kali Yuga my name is Kabir. . . . I gave you a boon in a previous life. For this reason I have come here to enlighten you." Kabir then asked Dharma-das to identify his guru and the religious path hc followed. Dharma-das did so. Brahmalinamuni then puts in Kabir's mouth his own preference for classical Advaita Vedanta. Kabir explained that the external practices that Dharma-das followed did not lead to the "Parabrahman taught in *shruti, smrit*, and other shastras. . . . The direct means to salvation is knowledge of truth (*tattva-jñāna*) alone." Dharma-das then asked Kabir to give him instruction, but Kabir told him to ask his own guru first. Kabir then left, telling Dharma-das to look for him among the *sants*. Dharma-das then returned to Bandhogadh.

At this point in the story, Brahmalinamuni launches an attack against those who argue—in part on the basis of a verse by a woman *sant* named Ratnabai—that Kabir appeared to Dharma-das at Mathura *after* Kabir's death at Magahar. Brahmalinamuni also recounts the story of Ratnabai's initiation by Kabir at Mathura *after* the departure of Dharma-das.

The historical question of when Dharma-das was initiated by Kabir has aroused considerable scholarly and sectarian controversy. K. N.

20. Paramananda-das 1984: 588-90; *Janmavali Dharam Das ki* (manuscript in possession of mahant Grindhamuni Nam Sahab of which I have a film copy); Brahmalinamuni 1960: 266-320; Jagannath Sahab Gurugosvami and Narottam Sharma "Narendra" 1984.

Dvivedi [1965: 169-76] has argued that Dharma-das was initiated by a vision of Kabir over one hundred years after Kabir's death. Gangasharan Shastri [1976: 269-76], the current chief mahant of the Kabir Chaura branch of the Kabir Panth, has seized on Dvivedi's arguments to attempt to discredit the legitimacy of the Dharmadasi branch. The recent semi-scholarly study of Dharma-das's life patronized by mahant Grindhamuni Nam Sahab reasserts the contemporaneity of Kabir and Dharma-das by giving the latter a birth date of V. S. 1452 (A.D. 1395) and a death date of V. S. 1569 (A.D. 1512) [J. S. Gurugosvami and N. Sharma "Narendra" 1984: 9, 30]. K. N. Dvivedi's arguments for a much later date are partly based on several verses such as that of Ratnabai that refer to Dharma-das as having met an incorporeal Kabir, and on various official letters and charters (*panjā*) belonging to earlier mahants of this branch. The latter documents are no longer available to scholars, but Dvivedi's arguments are reasonably convincing in any case.

Brahmalinamuni takes up the story again after Dharma-das's return to Bandhogadh. Dharma-das then went to *shrī* Rup-das's ashram and asked him what was the best means to salvation described in the shastras. Rup-das observed that some great man must have induced Dharma-das to ask this question. He advised Dharma-das to ask the great man this question. Having received his guru's permission, Dharma-das became increasingly anxious to meet Kabir again. He told his wife, Amini Devi, that they should arrange a feast for the *sant*s. Invitations were sent out in all directions. Kabir arrived, but in disguise. After the feast Kabir made himself known to Dharma-das. King Ramasimha of Bandhogadh heard that Kabir had arrived at Dharma-das's house and went to greet him. Kabir stayed there for many days. Finally he gave his complete teaching to Dharam-das and to Amini Devi. Since their son Narayan-das had chosen not to become a follower of Kabir, Kabir promised that they would have another son who would be a portion of the *paramātman* and would become an *āchārya* of the Kabir Panth. Dharma-das was told to give Amini Devi a pan leaf with the name of the *paramātman* written on it. He did so. From this act eventually a son was born called "Churamani," who later became the mahant Muktamani Nam Sahab. According to most Dharmadasi sources, Churamani was the first *āchārya* of the Kabir Panth. After giving religious instruction to Dharma-das and Amini Devi, Kabir vanished.

Dharma-das prayed that to meet Kabir once again. From time to time Kabir returned to him. On one visit Kabir told Dharma-das to give the leadership (*āchārya-pad*) of the Kabir Panth to Churamani. Dharma-das did so and then went with Kabir to Jagannath Puri in Orissa. There Dharma-das died (above, p. 16). Churamani, who was at Kudaramal (Bilaspur District, M.P.), came to perform his father's last rites and then returned to Kudaramal where, according to the Dharmadasis, he established the first seat (*gaddī*) of the Kabir Panth. The Dharmadasis claim that all the other branches of the Kabir Panth are offshoots of the Kudaramal *gaddī*. Dharma-das's elder son Narayan-das is said to have stayed at Bandhogadh. He claimed the *gaddī* of the Kabir Panth for himself, but few accepted his claim. Brahmalinamuni writes that a few monasteries of his followers still exists, but I have been unable to verify this claim. The Kudaramal monastery still survives, but the chief *gaddī* of the Dharmadasi branch later moved several times before dividing into the current rival centers at Damakheda and Kharsiya.

Bhagavan-das (Bhago-das) Gosvami

Bhagavan-das is considered to be the founder of the Bhagatahi branch of the Kabir Panth. Its chief monastery is located at Dhanauti in Siwan District of northwestern Bihar. The legend of Bhagavan-das Gosvami is quite prosaic. Short versions are narrated by Brahmalinamuni [1960: 409-13] and Gangasharan Shastri [1976: 164-69]. A somewhat more detailed version is found in *shrī* Guru Prasad Gosvami's *Kabir Pantha ki Bhagatahi Shakha* [1981: 55-60], a text written by a mahant of his branch.

According to Guru Prasad Gosvami, Bhagavan Gosvami was born at Sulemabad, presumably the Nimbarka center of this name near Ajmer in Rajasthan. From an early age, he demonstrated a desire to become a *sadhu*. He began to stay in a temple in his village. Then he left in search of a worthy guru. He arrived at a temple in Galita village in Jaipur District. Its mahant was Sukilla-das. Bhagavan Gosvami became his disciple but was still not satisfied. Bhagavan Gosvami left Sukilla-das's tutelage and arrived at Pithaurabad near Kalinjar (apparently the site by this name in Bundelkhand). He took up residence in an empty temple and each day offered worship to the temple's image of Ram-Krishna. One day Kabir arrived. Kabir convinced Bhagavan Gosvami that image worship is useless since God is within one's own self. Bhagavan Gosvami asked to become Kabir's disciple. Together they went to Bihar, eventually arriving at Dhanauti. There Kabir imparted teachings through songs and verses that were written down by Bhagavan Gosvami. This collection later became the *Kabir Bijak*, the text is now accepted as authoritative by the Kabir Panth. Kabir returned to Kashi and Bhagavan Gosvami stayed in Dhanauti. From his monastery there, he spread the teachings of Kabir throughout the surrounding region. Bhagavan Gosvami died at Dhanauti, aged 70, in A.D. 1576. *Shrī* Guru Prasad

Gosvami notes that some people have claimed that Bhagavan Gosvami, also called "Bhago-das or Bhagu-das," was a brother of Jagu-das, another important disciple of Kabir. It is also said by some that Bhagavan Gosvami was first a disciple of a follower of Hari-vyas of the Nimbarka sect and that he belonged to the Ahir caste.

Jagu-das (Jago-das)

Jagu-das, also called "Jago-das and Jagu Sahab," is considered to to be the founder of the branch of the Kabir Panth that today has rival centers at Bidupur in Vaishali District, Bihar, and at Shivapur, a suburb of Varanasi. The legend of Jagu-das's life, like that of Bhagavan Gosvami, is rather prosaic. Brief versions are found in the texts of Brahmalinamuni [1960: 414-18] and Gangasharan Shastri [1976: 145]. The Bidupur and Shivapur monasteries have published more partisan versions of the legend in books written by Munishvar Ray "Munish" [1977: 39-44] and *shrī* Shankar Das [1955: 54-58] respectively.

According to Munishvar Ray "Munish," Jagu Sahab was born in the village of Tulasiya near Cuttack (Katak), Orissa, in the year A.D. 1413. His father Jagaradatta was a ritual priest (*devalak*) of the Jagannath temple at Puri. His mother's name was Haso Mata or Hamsabai. When Kabir came to Puri to save the Jagannath temple from being destroyed by the ocean (above, pp. 48-49), Jagu Sahab's parents were influenced by him. Some years later, Jagu Sahab's mother took her initiation as an ascetic from Kabir and delivered her unenlightened son to him. By being exposed constantly to the teachings of Kabir, the son eventually "awoke" from his ignorance. Kabir gave Jagu-das his initiation as a sadhu in A.D. 1429. Munishvar Ray's version of the legend claims that Jagu-das was the first of Kabir's disciples to be initiated. Jagu-das spent the rest of his life spreading the teachings of Kabir. His monastic seat was at Cuttack, but several spiritual generations later the seat was moved to Bidupur in Bihar.

Brahmalinamuni's version of the legend differs enough to be worth briefly summarizing. He accepts that Jagu Sahab's father Jagaradatta was a ritual priest (*purjārī*) of Jagannath and a Brahman and resident of Cuttack. Jagu Sahab's mother's name was Kamaleshvari Devi. His parents were both disciples of Kabir. They were old but had no son. By the blessing of the Kabir, Kamaleshvari Devi gave birth to a son in V. S. 1538 (A.D. 1481). The child was born with thirty-two teeth. He cried out constantly: "Sadguru Kavir, Sadguru Kavir!" His parents prayed to Kabir for an explanation. In a "sky voice," Kabir told them that this was not really their son, rather he was a great ascetic come to bring them salvation. After this the child stopped crying. His parents then gave him the name Jagu-datta. Kamaleshvari Devi taught her son the wisdom of Kabir. In V. S. 1545 (A.D. 1488), his parents took Jagu to Kashi. They found Kabir in Vanakatha forest near Kashi and Kabir initiated Jagu-datta there. This Vanakatha forest is said to be the site of the present-day Shivapur suburb of Varanasi where one of the two chief monasteries of this branch of the Kabir Panth is located.

Sarvananda Alias Sarvajit Alias Shruti-gopal

This legend tells how a southern Brahman pandit named "Sarvananda" became a disciple of Kabir. According to the *sadhus* of the Kabir Chaura branch of the Kabir Panth, when Kabir initiated Sarvananda, he gave him the new name of "Shruti-gopal" (also called "Surat-gopal"). This Shruti-gopal became Kabir's principal disciple and the founder of the Kabir Panth. The earliest extant version of the legend of Shruti-gopal appears to be that found in Paramananda-das's *Kabir Manshur* [1956: 161-63], a text of the rival Dharmadasi branch. This version makes no mention of Sarvananda taking the name Shruti-gopal, of the location of his home, or of his founding the Kabir Panth. Brahmalinamuni's [1960: 384-409] more recent Dharmadasi version is similar. Apart from their concern to insist that Dharma-das and his son Churamani, and not Shruti-gopal, were the founders of the Kabir Panth, however, these Dharmadasi versions of the legend do not differ much from the recent version of Gangasharan Shastri [1976: 132-39] of the Kabir Chaura branch. A brief but interesting text of uncertain date was published by the Kabir Chaura monastery in A.D. 1930 as the *Pam. Sarvajit ki Goshthi* [1930]. It claims to record a conversation between Kabir and Sarvananda that took place before Sarvananda's conversion.

According to Paramananda-das's *Kabir Manshur*, the Brahman Sarvananda was a very learned pandit. He travelled throughout India debating rival scholars. When no opponents remained, he said to his mother: "Listen, mother! Now you should call me Sarvajit ("Conqueror of all"), since there is no pandit anywhere who can rival me." His mother replied: "Listen, son! Have you ever gone to Kashi to debate with Kabir Sahab?" Sarvananda admitted that he had not. His mother said: "Until you have defeated Kabir, you can never be called Sarvajit." Sarvananda decided to challenge Kabir to a debate. He packed all his sacred books on a bullock and set off for Kashi. He found Kabir there, and the great debate began. Kabir made every effort to make Sarvananda understand the truth, but Sarvananda accepted nothing. Kabir concluded to himself that Sarvananda was hopelessly afflicted with the disease of useless talk and would never be cured in this way. Kabir said to him: "Listen, Sarvananda! Tell me what you want." Sarvananda replied: "You should write that you accept my victory." Kabir said: "I do not know how to write. You write it yourself." Sarvananda then wrote: "Kabir Sahab lost and Sarvananda won." He showed the paper to those assembled there and set off for home with this certificate of victory.

When he arrived, he greeted his mother and told her about his great victory over Kabir. She insisted on seeing the certificate of victory. Sarvananda gave it to her, and she read: "Sarvananda lost and Kabir Sahab won." Sarvananda was dumbfounded and returned to Kashi to get a new certificate from Kabir. Kabir let him write a new certificate. Sarvananda returned home with it, but when his mother looked at the new certificate she again read: "Sarvananda lost and Kabir Sahab won." Sarvananda returned to Kabir a third time, but the ultimate result was the same. Sarvananda finally concluded: "Without a doubt, Kabir Sahab is the omnipotent Lord Himself." Sarvananda then became Kabir's disciple.

Gangasharan Shastri adds only a few details in his version. He asserts [1976: 133-34] that Sarvananda was born in a town called "Suramya-puram" near Ootacamund (Utakamanda) in Tamilnadu in the year V. S. 1495 (A.D. 1438). Sarvananda's father's name is said to have been Bhava-bhanjanam and his mother's name Kalyani Devi. When his mother asked him if he had gone to Kashi to debate Kabir, Sarvananda gave an interesting answer: "I have gone several times to Kashi and defeated the hypocritical Brahmans there, but no one ever told me that Kabir was a great pandit. I heard that he was a *mahātmā* (holy man). For that reason I never met him. My business was only with those who tote books." Gangasharan Shastri increases the number of bullock loads of books to sixteen and has Kabir simply decline to debate with Sarvananda. In this version, it takes only one transformed certificate of victory to convince Sarvananda of Kabir's greatness and for Sarvananda to return to become Kabir's disciple, renamed "Shruti-gopal," "the chief *ācārya* of the Kabir Panth whose disciple lineage today continues in the Kabir Chaura monastery of Kashi."

The text and commentary of the *Pam. Sarvajit ki Goshthi* [1930: 2-5] add one interesting episode to the legend. As the Sarvananda was nearing Kashi to visit Kabir, he became very thirsty. He arrived at a well where some women were drawing water. Without thinking, he pleaded for water. One of the women was none other than Kamali, Kabir's "daughter" disciple (above, pp. 50-52). She gave him water. When he had drunk, he asked her who she was. The other women told him that she was Kabir's disciple Kamali. Sarvananda complained to Kamali that she had caused him, an orthoprax Dravidian Brahman, to "lose caste" by giving him the water. She replied: "Listen, pandit! Why didn't you ask me before drinking the water instead of now complaining that you have lost caste?"

Through the mouth of Kamali, the author of this text then launches into a lengthy attack against the idea that physical bodies can be either pure or impure. Caste practices like setting aside separate cooking and eating places, Kamali argues, have no logical justification whatsoever. This episode also appears in Brahmalinamuni's text [1960:387-89], but he characteristically modifies its ideological message. Instead of asking Kamali for water, Sarvananda simply asks her the location of Kabir's ashram. She replies with a symbolic verse that criticizes Sarvananda's reliance on book learning, rather than his belief in caste pollution. She tells him: "Kabir's house is on a mountain peak, where the path is so slippery that even an ant cannot get a foothold, much less a pandit's bullock loaded (with books)."

Kabir's Travels

The legends of Kabir's travels in and beyond India are for the most part colorless lists of places visited, occasionally mentioning how Kabir met and defeated a local pandit or sadhu. Four of these legends, however, merit some discussion: his visits to Totadari and to Balkh and his encounters with Ram-das and with Nanak. All these legends appear in the long version of Paramananda-das's *Kabir Manshur*, in Brahmalinamuni's *Sadguru-shrikavira-charitam*, and in Gangasharan Shastri's *Kabir Jivanacharitra*.

Totadari is a famous sacred bathing place on the way to Rameshvar in the extreme South of India. Totadari is said to have been the chief seat of Ramanuja and his followers. Paramananda-das's *Kabir Manshur* [1956:156-57] claims that one day Kabir and some other disciples of Ramananda arrived at Totadari leading a buffalo that carried their blankets and cooking materials. Ramanuja's spiritual descendants at Totadari were all Brahmans and were very careful to observe the rules of caste purity in bathing, cooking, and eating. If even the shadow of an Untouchable fell on their cooking places, they would not eat. They accepted that Kabir should eat with them but wanted him to sit in a separate line (*paṅgat*). Since to insist on this would be impolite, they devised a pretext to exclude him: "Whoever can recite the verses of the

Veda should sit and eat in our line; whoever cannot recite the Veda should sit apart." Since low-caste persons have no right to recite the Veda, this should have solved their problem. All the Brahmans recited a few verses from the Veda. Finally it came Kabir's turn. He put a hand on the head of the buffalo and said: "Listen, buffalo! Why are you standing there not saying anything? Hurry up and recite well some of the Veda." The buffalo began to recite. Everyone was astonished and begged Kabir to forgive them.

Gangasharan Shastri's version of this legend [1976: 140-42] is quite similar. Brahmalinamuni, however, adds another episode [1960: 256-66]. On one occasion Ramananda was invited to Totadri. He and his disciples were asked to sit apart because some of them were Shudras. Kabir appeared and created an illusion. He was seen sitting between each and every orthoprax Brahman. The Brahmans then begged Kabir and Ramananda to forgive them. Brahmalinamuni, in keeping with his rather conservative social ideology, uses these episodes not to attack caste restrictions in general, but only to attack such restrictions when they are directed against "sadhus and *sants*." In Brahmalinamuni's view, such persons are above the rules of *varṇāshrama-dharma*. In all other cases, the rules should be enforced. Brahmalinamuni himself was, of course, a Kabir Panthi sadhu.

Kabir's efforts to convert the sultan named "shah Ibrahim Addham of Balkh" (now in Afghanistan) to a religious life are first told in the *Sulatan Bodh*, one of the many texts collected by *svāmī* Yugalananda in his *Kabir Sagar* [1953: vol. 6, pp. 33-127]. *Svāmī* Yugalananda claims to have based his edition of the *Sulatan Bodh* on several manuscripts, some of which were over one hundred years old. Rather than one legend, this text presents a whole cycle of legends that are clearly only nominally connected with Kabir. Kabir is simply identified with an unnamed *jindā* fakir who repeatedly appears to effect Ibrahim's religious conversion. The real historical subject of this legend cycle is a famous early Sufi of Balkh, Ibrahim bin Adham (*c.* A.D. 730-778). Sufi versions of this legend cycle are found in texts written in both Persian and Urdu. One of the former, Faridu'd-Din 'Attar's *Tazkiratu'l-Auliya'* ("Memorial of the Saints"), has been translated into English.[21]

A detailed historical analysis of the complex origins and development of the Ibrahim bin Adham legends cannot be attempted here. Even a full summary of the many episodes in the Kabir Panthi *Sulatan Bodh*

21. See A. J. Arberry [1979: 62-79] and Bankey Behari [1975: 37-52]. The Persian text was edited by R. A. Nicholson [1905]. On the Sufi Ibrahim bin Adham, see also S. A. A. Rizvi [1978: 33-34], Russell Jones [1971: vol. 3, pp. 985-96], R. A. Nicholson [1912: 215-20].

would require too lengthy an exposition. A summary of the frame story, all that in fact connects the legend to Kabir, will have to suffice. For this, I will rely mostly on Brahmalinamuni's version.[22]

Ibrahim, sultan of the city of Balkh, spent the first half of his life performing his worldly duties and enjoying worldly pleasures. In his later life his mind turned to religion. He decided that he would like to have a direct vision of God. His courtiers suggested that he invite sadhus and fakirs from all over and seek their advice. The sadhus and fakirs arrived, but none of them could satisfy Ibrahim's request. Ibrahim became angry with them and threw them all in jail where they were forced to turn huge millstones. One day Kabir appeared in Balkh. Kabir told Ibrahim to release the sadhus and fakirs, but Ibrahim demanded that Kabir show him God first. Kabir insisted that the sadhus and fakirs be released first. Ibrahim asked: "How can I believe you?" Kabir replied: "If you don't believe me, ask this buffalo." Kabir placed his hand on the buffalo, and the buffalo told Ibrahim that Kabir had spoken the truth.

Kabir then magically appeared in the jail and comforted the sadhus and fakirs. To ease their physical distress, he made the millstones turn of their own accord. Ibrahim saw this miracle and released the sadhus and fakirs. Kabir then vanished. Ibrahim for a while turned toward religion, but eventually he fell back into the web of worldly entanglements. Kabir reappeared in various disguises to reawaken Ibrahim's religious inclinations. Each time the sultan turned toward religion, only to again become absorbed in worldly affairs. Finally Ibrahim, decided to become an ascetic and abandoned his palace in the middle of the night. This caused great sorrow among his courtiers and queens. After more adventures, Ibrahim again met Kabir and recevied a vision of God.

Kabir's meeting with Ram-das is a simpler legend. According to Paramananda-das's *Kabir Manshur*,[23] Ram-das was a wealthy Brahman landholder who lived on the bank of the Narmada river. One day as he went to the river to bathe, he met Kabir. He asked Kabir to give him a vision of God. Kabir told him that at noon the next day God would visit his house. Ram-das went home and made elaborate arrangements to welcome God. The house was cleaned and purified, and delicious delicacies were prepared. A throne was set up and decorated. When all was ready, a muddy buffalo wandered up and sat down in the middle of the floor. Ram-das was furious and picked up a stick and beat the

22. Brahmalinamuni 1960: 534-84. See also Paramananda-das [1984: 573-82], and Gangasharan Shastri [1976: 113-117].

23. Paramananda-das 1956: 156-57; Brahmalinamuni 1960: 496-508; Gangasharan Shastri 1976: 125-29.

buffalo with it. After the buffalo had fled, Ram-das cleaned up the mess and sat down again to wait for God. He waited all day, but God never appeared. The next day Ram-das again met Kabir at the river and complained: "Ascetic, I didn't get a vision of God as you said I would." Kabir laughed and replied: "Listen, Ram-das! I told you no lie. Vishnu certainly did arrive at your house, and you gave him a real proper welcome. You beat him with a stick and chased him away." Ram-das realized what had happened and was ashamed. Paramananda-das concludes with this judgment about Ram-das: "He was a devotee, but he lacked the characteristic of the devotees who see their Beloved as present in every object. For this reason he was cheated of his vision of God."

Kabir's meeting with Guru Nanak (A.D. 1469-1538) is mentioned in Sikh as well as Kabir Panthi sources, athough each sect's legend about what happened at this meeting do not coincide. The meeting is historically quite possible, but no historical evidence exists apart from the legends themselves. W. H. McLeod, a scrupulously skeptical scholar of Sikh tradition, tends to doubt that the meeting ever took place, and does not find any direct evidence of the influence of Kabir on Nanak.[24] Large numbers of Kabir's songs and verses were, of course, later (A.D. 1604) incorporated into the *Guru Granth Sahib* of the Sikhs. Kabir Panthi tradition accepts Guru Nanak as an important *sant* whose doctrines are akin to, and influenced by, Kabir. Nonetheless, the Kabir Panth has not attempted to appropriate Guru Nanak in the same way that the Sikhs have appropriated Kabir.

Paramananda-das's *Kabir Manshur* [1956: 163-65] tells two separate legends that connect Kabir with Guru Nanak. In one, the eighty-four Nath Siddhas, Kabir Sahab and Guru Nanak met together in some unspecified location. A merchant follower of Nanak arrived there. Thinking it would be improper to greet the guru without having something to offer, the merchant reached into his pocket, found a sesame seed, and duly presented it to Guru Nanak. Guru Nanak then asked Kabir how they could divide the sesame seed among so many ascetics. Kabir told him to crush it in some water and then distribute it. Guru Nanak observed that there was no water anywhere nearby. Kabir then magically made water flow in a nearby dry riverbed. Everyone drank the sesame seed crushed in the water and was satisfied. The eighty-four Nath Siddhas then offered to give Kabir anything he asked for. Kabir asked for a "full five paisas' worth of poverty." The Siddhas did not

---

24. W. H. McLeod summarizes the Sikh legends and comments on them in his *Guru Nanak and the Sikh Religion* [1976: 56, 85-86] and in an article on "Guru Nanak and Kabir" [1966: 87-92]. See also his translation of *The B40 Janam-Sakhi* [1980].

possess this and went to the Creator, Brahma, to request it. Because of his pride as Creator, Brahma could not supply it either. The Siddhas then went to Shiv. Because of his pride as Destroyer, Shiv did not have it either. They then went to Vishnu, but he claimed to have only *three* paisas' worth of poverty. Vishnu told them that it was only Kabir himself who had a full five paisas' worth. The eighty-four Siddhas returned to Kabir and fell at his feet.

The second legend is set in the Punjab. Kabir came to visit Guru Nanak. Guru Nanak offered to perform any service that Kabir would like. Kabir asked him to fill his begging bowl with milk from a five day old calf. Guru Nanak found a calf, but it ran away when he tried to milk it. Kabir told Guru Nanak to go and ask the calf to give the milk in Kabir's own name. Guru Nanak placed the begging bowl under the calf and made his request. The milk flowed from the calf's udder of its own accord and filled the bowl. Kabir told Guru Nanak: "Listen, Nanak! You have done much devotion, but there is still something lacking in its performance. You will set in motion a sect and many individuals will follow your command."

Brahmalinamuni [1960: 509-35] does not repeat these legends, but he does relate a long conversation between Kabir and Guru Nanak as well as elements of the legends of Guru Nanak known from Sikh sources. He claims that Guru Nanak had a meeting with Kabir in V. S. 1554 (A.D. 1497) when the former bathed in a river. Kabir told Nanak to abandon worldly existence and imparted religious teachings to him for three days. These teachings largely consist of Brahmalinamuni's version of Advaita Vedanta. After this, Guru Nanak became a sadhu. His followers, says Brahmalinamuni, later "spread the Hindu religion in the Punjab." Brahmalinamuni also claims that Kabir accompanied Nanak on his famous journey to Mecca. When they both slept with their feet pointed toward Mecca, people moved their feet in a different direction to correct the insult, but Mecca itself then moved, remaining in the direction of their feet.

These two episodes are based on legends borrowed from Sikh tradition. The story of Guru Nanak's religious awakening (without any help from Kabir) after bathing in a river is told in several Sikh *janam-sāhkīs* as is his voyage (without Kabir) to Mecca and the moving of Mecca with his feet.[25] The Sikh versions obviously express a competitive spirit, even animosity, towards Islam. In Brahmalinamuni's Kabir Panthi versions, this competitive spirit is directed against Nanak and the Sikhs as well as against Islam.

---

25. See W. H. McLeod [1976: 35, 37, 49, 54, 60-61, 73, 75].

CHAPTER 4

THE TEXT OF THE *KABIR PARACHAI*

There are basically two different recensions of the text of Anantadas's *Kabir Parachai.* Nether recension can claim to be significantly better or older than the other. Nonetheless, I have preferred to work more closely with the one I have called the "Niranjani Panthi" recension for reasons that will be explained below. Chapter five below is a translation of this recension, and chapter six is a corrected edition of its Hindi text. Appendix A below presents a transcription of the 1693 V. S. (A.D. 1636) manuscript from the Rajasthan Prachyavaidya Pratishthan (number 11583). This manuscript is apparently the oldest one extant and also gives readings that are generally representative of the second recension of the text, the one that I have called the "Dadu Panthi" recension (see below, pp. 74-83).

Almost all the manuscripts of the *Kabir Parachai* are written in the mixed *sadhukkaḍī* dialect of Hindi favored by the *sant* poets of northern India up until recent times. This dialect varies from poet to poet, but in the manuscripts of the *Kabir Parachai* it is more western than eastern and mixes together grammatical forms and vocabulary taken from a number of different regional dialects: Braj, Avadhi, Khadi-boli, Punjabi, Hariyanvai, Rajasthani, and Bhojpuri. The *Kabir Parachai* also uses a fair sprinkling of Perso-Arabic vocabulary. The differences between the two recensions of the text and between the different individual manuscripts seem to be minimal in this regard.

The *sadhukkaḍī* dialect of the *Kabir Parachai* allows quite varied grammatical forms, a somewhat loose meter, and a wide range of

which suggests that both of the two surviving recensions of the *Kabir Parachai* are especially associated with sects other than the Ramanandis: one with the little studied Niranjani Panth or Sampraday and the other with the Dadu Panth.[2]

One important piece of evidence that connects what I have called the "Dadu Panthi" recension of the *Kabir Parachai* with the Dadu Panth is the presence in the text of this recension of two verses that the *Kabir Granthavali* attributes to Kabir himself.[3] The *Kabir Granthavali* is the collection of Kabir's compositions that has been preserved and transmitted by the sadhus of the Dadu Panth. The two verses in question do not appear in the Niranjani Panthi recension of the *Kabir Parachai.*

On the other hand, there are five *pada*s (equivalent to one and one quarter verses in all) found in *both* the Dadu Panthi and Niranjani recensions of Ananta-das's *Kabir Parachai* [verse 13.16 and 13.17a] that correspond in sense, though not in exact wording, to a verse found both in the *Kabir Granthavali* [*sākhī* 38.5] and in the Sikh *Adi Granth* [*saloku 81*] [Kabir 1966]. The basic trope of this verse—that even oceans of ink and tons of pens do not suffice to write all of God's praises—is found at least as early as a quite similar Sanskrit verse found in the early medieval hymn to Shiva, the *Mahimnastava.*[4]

One single *pada* (quarter verse) attributed to Kabir in both recensions of the *Kabir Parachai* [8.3b] is also found in the *Kabir Bijak* [*ramainī* 49.3a]: "Who is it who ordered (the sacrifice of) goats and chickens?" This passage is too short to be of much significance.

The most convincing evidence that associates the two recensions with the Niranjani and Dadu Panths respectively comes from the larger manuscripts in which the texts of the *Kabir Parachai* are found. In most cases each manuscript contains a number of different texts besides the *Kabir Parachai.* Although these different texts often come from more than one sectarian tradition, often one tradition clearly predominates. In such cases, it is safe to assume that the whole manuscript was originally

2. Practically the only serious scholarly discussion of the Niranjani Panth seems to be the few pages dedicated to it in P. Chaturvedi's *Uttari Bharat ki Santa Parampara* [1964: 337-356]. Also useful are P. Chaturvedi's preface and Mangal-das Svami's introduction to a published collection of the poems and verses of several Niranjani Panth authors [Mangal-das Svami 1962].

3. A verse of the Dadu Panthi recension placed after verse 4.5 of the corrected edition of the *Kabir Parachai* is the same as *Kabir Granthavali, sākhī* 38.1. Similarly another verse placed after 12.4 of the *Kabir Parachai* is the same as *Kabir Granthavali, sākhī* 5.1 [Kabir 1969]. Uma Thukral first noted these two equivalences.

4. See W. N. Brown [1983], verse 1 appendix. Vedanta Deshika has written another verse using a quite similar image [K. K. A. Venkatachari 1988].

copied by one or more sadhus belonging to that sectarian tradition. In a few cases, the sectarian affiliation of the copyist sadhu is expressly mentioned in the colophon of the manuscript. Other colophons sometimes mention the site where the copy was made, and this site is sometimes identifiable as a center of a specific sect. Whenever the sectarian affiliation of the manuscript can be identified, the Dadu Panthi manuscripts exclusively contain the Dadu Panthi recension of the *Kabir Parachai*, and Niranjani Panthi manuscripts equally exclusively contain the Niranjani Panthi recension.

For example, Nagari Pracharini Sabha manuscript number 877 contains a text of the Niranjani Panthi recension of the *Kabir Parachai.* It also contains the *parachaī*s (not by Ananta-das) of Hari-das and Seva-das, both important gurus of the Niranjani Panth,[5] as well as many verses and songs of Seva-das. This manuscript collection clearly belongs to Niranjani Panthi tradition. Likewise, the colophon of the India Office manuscript (A 12) states that it was copied in 1843 V. S. (A.D. 1786) by Baishnav Niranjani Sobharam Svami at a place called Pokara (modern Pushkar near Ajmer). The copyist's name clearly identifies him as a member of the Niranjani Panth and the text of the *Kabir Parachai* belongs to the Niranjani Panthi recension.

Not surprisingly, the largest number of extant manuscripts of Ananta-das's various *parachaī*s are now located in Rajasthan, most notably in the libraries of the Rajasthan Prachyavidya Pratishthan [RPP] in both Jodhpur and Jaipur, of the Rajasthani Shodh Samsthan [RSS] in Jodhpur, of the Jaipur Palace museum, and of the Shri Dadu Mahavidyalay in Jaipur.[6] In the manuscript collections of these libraries, the following larger manuscripts clearly belong to Dadu Panthi tradition: Rajasthani Shodh Samsthan manuscripts 8432, 7642, and 2934 and Rajasthan Prachyavidya Pratishthan (Jaipur) manuscripts 1 and 3. All these manuscripts contain texts of the Dadu Panthi recension of the *Kabir Parachai.*[7]

5. On these two *parachaī*s, see T. N. Dikshit [1957: 62-69, 157-163]. On the spiritual genealogy of Hari-das and Seva-das, see P. Chaturvedi [1964: 356].

6. Almost all the manuscripts of the Rajasthan Prachyavidya Pratishthan and of the Jaipur Palace libraries are described in published catalogues. The most important are those of O. Menariya [1974 and 1978] and that of G. N. Bahura and L. G. Dikshit [1961]. The Jaipur Palace library collection catalogue, prepared by G. N. Bahura, has also been published, but only a part of the Rajasthani Shodh Samsthan catalogue has appeared in print.

7. I was unable to see the manuscripts of the Shri Dadu Mahavidyalay. Most of these must belong to the Dadu Panthi recension. Since Callewaert has used several of these manuscripts, details about them should be available in his edition of the *Kabir Parachai.*

On the other hand, in addition to India Office manuscript A 12 and Nagari Pracharini Sabha manuscript 877, the following manuscripts clearly belong to Niranjani Panthi tradition: Rajasthan Prachyavidya Pratishthan (Jodhpur) manuscripts 11092 and 12422, and Rajasthani Shodh Samsthan manuscript 8633. All these manuscripts contain texts of the Niranjani Panthi recension of the *Kabir Parachai*.[8]

Manuscript Dates and Textual Differences

Other salient aspects of the comparison between the Niranjani Panthi and Dadu Panthi recensions of the *Kabir Parachai* include: (1) the age of the manuscripts, (2) the inclusion (or exclusion) of section one, (3) details of textual logic, and (4) their respective preferences for *saguṇ* and *nirguṇ* metaphysics.

The oldest extant manuscript of the *Kabir Parachai* appears to be manuscript 11583 in the collection of the Rajasthan Prachyavidya Pratishthan in Jodhpur. The colophon of the manuscript has been read as giving the date 1693 V. S. (A.D. 1636). The text belongs to the tradition of the Dadu Panthi recension. Callewaert has used other seventeenth century manuscripts of this recension in his critical edition. The oldest manuscript of the Niranjani Panthi recension of the text seems to be the Jaipur Palace museum library manuscript 1843. Its colophon gives the date 1722 V. S. (A.D. 1665). Another early manuscript of the Niranjani Panthi recension is manuscript 8561 of 1754 V. S. (A.D. 1697) from the Rajasthan Prachyavidya Pratishthan (see below, p. 87). In addition, the story of Kabir's initiation by Ramananda, a story found only in the Niranjani Panthi recension of the *Kabir Parachai*, is also found in Priya-das's commentary of A.D. 1712 on Nabha-das's *Bhaktamal* [1969: 480-82]. This commentary is almost certainly based on Ananta-das's *Kabir Parachai.*

One of the biggest differences between the two recensions of the *Kabir Parachai* is that the Niranjani Panthi recension includes section one, and the Dadu Panthi recension excludes it. This section relates

---

8. It is also worth noting that a few of the manuscripts in which the *Kabir Parachai* is found seem to be associated with yet another Rajasthani sectarian tradition, that of the Ram-snehi Panth. Most important in this regard is Hindi Sahitya Sammelan manuscript 1900 (see below, pp. 85-86). Two other manuscripts that seem to be associated with this sect are Rajasthan Prachyavidya Pratishthan (Jodhpur) manuscript 12420 and Rajasthani Shodh Samsthan manuscript 95 (below, pp. 87, 90). All these texts give somewhat anomalous readings but are generally somewhat closer to the Niranjani Panthi recension than to the Dadu Panthi recension.

the legend of Kabir's initiation by Ramananda. Some scholars have suggested that this section may be a latter addition to the *Kabir Parachai*, written to provide a possibly fictional geneological link between Kabir and Ramananda. In fact, there are no real grounds for such a conclusion. The first section relates the story of Kabir's initiation by Ramananda, but the Dadu Panthi recension also begins with the statement that Kabir was Ramananda's pupil. Thus, whatever the historical status of section one, the geneological connection between Kabir and Ramananda is accepted in both recensions.

Both Ramanandi tradition and his own *Pipa Parachai* genealogy affirm that Ananta-das belonged to the Ramanandi Sampraday. As suggested above (pp. 25-26), Ananta-das's emphasis on the genealogical connection of Ramananda with Kabir and various other *sant*s may have been intended to foster a more liberal, egalitarian ideology within his own, generally more conservative sectarian tradition. In addition, as a Ramanandi, Ananta-das would be expected to emphasize a more *saguṇ* conception of the Absolute than Kabir himself. Such a *saguṇ* conception is in fact more evident in the Niranjani Panthi recension of the *Kabir Parachai* than in the Dadu Panthi recension (see below, pp. 81-83).

The juncture of the first two sections of the *Kabir Parachai* is somewhat anomalous in both recensions of the text. The Niranjani Panthi recension ends the first section with two *dohā*s in place of the usual single final *dohā*. The text of the Dadu Panthi recension begins with a *dohā* (the second of the final two *dohā*s of section one of the Niranjani Panthi recension) in place of the usual beginning *chaupāī*. The inclusion of two *dohā*s taken from the *Kabir Granthavali* (see above, p. 76) in the middle part of two sections of the Dadu Panthi recension is also somewhat anomalous.

A few specific passages seem to be better logically organized in the Niranjani Panthi recension of the *Kabir Parachai* than in the Dadu Panthi recension. These passages are noted in the footnotes to the translation found in chapter five below. One example is particularly interesting. Verses 3.11-3.13 tell how: (1) Hari, in the form of Kabir, buys various foodstuffs; (2) Hari then has four workmen carry the food to [Kabir's] house; (3) the Brahmans see the foodstuffs and are pleased; and (4) each Brahmaṇ is given two-and-half *ser*s of the foodstuffs. The Dadu Panthi recension changes this order of events. Hari first buys the foodstuffs; the Brahmans see the foodstuffs; each Brahman is given two-and-one-half *sers*; and the workmen carry the food to [the Brahmans'] houses. In this reading, the workmen must be assumed to take the goods to the *Brahmans'* houses, but one would think that each Brahman would have been capable of carrying away his two-and-one-half kilos without the help of the workmen.[9]

Another interesting difference of readings between the two recensions occurs at verse 11.3. Here a list of perfumes seems to be greatly simplified in the Dadu Panthi recension, suggesting that the editors of this recension may not have understood the difficult original verse and substituted an easier one.[10]

One reader of an earlier draft of this book accepted that the Niranjani Panthi recension does have a more logical arrangement of some episodes, but argued that this fact suggests that this recension is less rather than more authentic than the Dadu Panthi recension. Invoking the general principal that the more difficult reading (*lectio difficilior*) should be accepted as earlier, this reader commented that it is more likely that "the original text had the episodes in a somewhat illogical order, whereupon a later redactor rearranged and rationalized them."

Unfortunately, things are not quite so simple. In the case of the *Kabir Parachai* manuscripts, it is more generally true that the later the manuscript, the more likely it is that its readings are corrupt, both in terms of language and logic. It is also true, however, that later copyist-editors occasionally do attempt to "improve" the versions of the text that they have inherited. The undated, but probably late, Hindi Sahitya Sammelan manuscript [no. 1900] of the *Kabir Parachai* is the clearest example of such an attempt that I have encountered. Even in this case, however, the copyist-editor really did little more than Sanskritize the spellings of some words, simplify a few difficult or corrupt readings, and complete a few "hanging" half verses.

To my mind, the arguments of the reader who favors the Dadu Panthi recension are inadequate. The most blatant example of a confused arrangement of an episode—that of the Brahmans receiving two and one half *ser*s of foodstuffs—represents simply too obvious a confusion to have been introduced by the original author of the *Kabir Parachai.* On the other hand, the greatly simplified list of perfumes found in the Dadu Panthi recension of verse 11.3 is a particularly clear case in which the Niranjani Panthi recension has the presumably older *lectio difficilior.*

9. Other examples of passages where the Niranjani Panthi recension seems to be somewhat more consistent include those at verses 9.6, 12.2, and especially the problem of the relation of *saguṇ* and *nirguṇ* conceptions of the Absolute. It is also possible to find a few verses in which the Dadu Panthi recension seems to be somewhat more consistent than the Niranjani Panthi recension.

10. Another interesting passage in which the Niranjani Panthi recension has a good, but more difficult reading, is found in verse 11.1.

All these textual considerations indicate three major justifications for our preference for the Niranjani Panthi recension: (1) the claims of this recension to historical priority are no less convincing than those of the Dadu Panthi recension; (2) the Niranjani Panthi recension is superior in the sense that it is generally more consistent in terms of narrative logic and theology; and (3) the presence of the disputed first section in the Niranjani Panthi recension gives it a greater "genealogical" importance in the sense that the presence of this section strongly suggests that this recension was the source for Priya-das's commentary on Nabha-das's verse on Kabir and, through this commentary, the source of most post-Priya-das versions of the legends.

In this context, a rough comparison can be made with the creation and flood stories found in the Old Testament. Scholars have considerable knowledge of the Sumerian and Babylonian antecedents of these stories [see Pritchard 1969]. They also are aware of the existence of at least two contradictory earlier Jewish versions of the story of the creation, both included in Genesis itself (despite the efforts of the priestly redactors to unify the text). Whatever the significance of these earlier versions of the creation and flood stories, no one can dispute the central historical importance of the Old Testament versions of these stories. The *Kabir Parachai* has obviously not attained the same status as a fixed canonical point of reference within Kabir Panthi tradition that Genesis has attained in Judeo-Christian tradition. Nonetheless, the *Kabir Parachai*, especially its Niranjani Panthi recension, obviously does represent a key "moment" in the evolutionary development of the Kabir legends.

Saguṇ and Nirguṇ

The most theologically interesting difference between the two recensions of the *Kabir Parachai* is their contrasting attitude toward the relation between the *nirguṇ* and *saguṇ* conceptions of the Absolute. As has been noted (above, pp. 38-39), the Dadu Panthi recension of the text opts for a more strictly *nirguṇ* conception while the Niranjani Panthi recension expressly identifies the two conceptions, claiming that *nirguṇ* and *saguṇ* are one.

To explain this contrast, at least five different influences must be taken into account. These include the theological positions of Kabir himself, of the Dadu Panth, of the Niranjani Panth, of Ananta-das and the Ramanandi Sampraday, and the internal logic of the legends themselves. Kabir himself is generally acknowledged to have been an unswerving advocate of a *nirguṇ* conception of the Absolute. Both the

Dadu Panth and the Niranjani Panth also belong to *nirguṇī* tradition. At some point, however, perhaps as early as the seventeenth century, some sadhus of the Niranjani Panth tended to seek a compromise between *nirguṇ* and *saguṇ* conceptions of the Absolute [Chaturvedi 1964: 337-356].

On the other hand, the Ramanandi tradition to which Ananta-das presumably belongs definitely advocates a *saguṇ* conception of the Absolute. Since Ananta-das is known only as the author of several "biographies" of *nirguṇī* saints such as Kabir, Rai-das, Pipa, Dhana, etc., however, it must be assumed that he had a special sympathy for *nirguṇī* tradition. In terms of the logic of the situation, it seems likely that Ananta-das held the view that the *saguṇ* and *nirguṇ* manifestations of the Absolute are in some sense ultimately one, the view explicitly enunciated in the Niranjani Panthi recension of the *Kabir Parachai.*

The published text of Ananta-das's *Rai-das Parachai* describes a debate and miracle contest between Kabir, Rai-das, and Sen in which Kabir steadfastly holds a *nirguṇ* conception, and Rai-das and Sen argue that *nirguṇ* and *saguṇ* are one [Ananta-das 1982: 45-46]. Although Kabir bests his companions in this episode, at the end Ananta-das seems to interject a verse that supports their view that *nirguṇ* and *saguṇ* are one. A preliminary look at various manuscripts of this text seems to indicate that this verse is not found in Dadu Panthi manuscripts, a fact that leaves Ananta-das's own position somewhat uncertain. Once Callewaert publishes his critical edition of this and Ananta-das's other *parachaī*s, it should be somewhat easier to make an accurate assessment of Ananta-das's position.

A final factor affecting the view of the *Kabir Parachai* with respect to the *nirguṇ* and *saguṇ* conceptions of the Absolute is the internal logic of the legends themselves. Some of these legends in fact require the acceptance of a *saguṇ* conception of Hari-Vishnu. How else can this god be portrayed as taking the form of a merchant to deliver foodstuffs to Kabir's house, as taking the form of Kabir himself to give away food to the Brahmans, as taking the form of many Kabirs to entertain the guest at the unexpected feast, and—most significantly—as taking a divine four-armed form to give Kabir a darshan as a reward for refusing the *apsarā*'s efforts to seduce him. The Dadu Panthi recension drops most, but not all, of the description of the four-armed divine Vishnu, but this omission in fact contradicts the basic *saguṇī* character of the story. The final scene of Kabir's bodily ascent into heaven also presupposes the acceptance of a *saguṇ* conception of the gods and their heaven. It is possible that a philosophically *nirguṇī* Ananta-das felt himself free to be a *saguṇī* storyteller, but on the face of it it seems unlikely.[11]

The Manuscripts

During the preparation of the corrected edition and the translation of Ananta-das's *Kabir Parachai*, we consulted about twenty different manuscripts of the text. I was able to make photocopies of nine different manuscripts. I also was permitted to make a detailed comparison of the Nagari Pracharini Sabha manuscript number 877 with a copy of the India Office manuscript. I also consulted R. K. Varma's printed text, a draft of Callewaert's critical text, and a transcribed concordance prepared by Callewaert which includes five manuscripts I was unable to consult directly.

For the corrected text which follows, I have made line by line comparisons of eight texts: India Office library manuscript A 12 [text *a*], Nagari Pracharini Sabha [NPS] manuscript 877 [text *b*], Rajasthani Shodh Samsthan [RSS] manuscript 7133 [text *c*], Hindi Sahitya Sammelan [HSS] manuscript 1900 [text *d*], R. K. Varma's [1983] published text [text *e*], Rajasthan Prachyavidya Pratishthan [RPP] manuscript 11583 of 1693 V. S. [text *f*], the draft of Callewaert's critical edition [text *g*], and Rajasthan Prachyavidya Prathishthan [RPP] manuscript 8561 [text *h*]. Six of these texts [*a, b, c, d, e, h*] are of the Niranjani Panthi recension and two texts [*f, g*] are of the Dadu Panthi recension. These latter two texts are mostly used for the purposes of comparison, and only major variant readings of these two texts are recorded in the notes to the corrected edition. Nonetheless, a transcription of the *Kabir Parachai* found in the 1693 V. S. manuscript [RPP 11583] is also included in this book, and translations of the major variant readings found in it and in Callewaert's critical edition are included in the notes to the translation of the text. The corrected text uses the India Office manuscript [A 12] as its "default choice," only departing from its readings when other readings are clearly preferable.

11. It must be admitted, however, that the story of the debate between Rai-das, Sen, and Kabir in Ananta-das's *Rai-das Parachai* seems to be a case where Ananta-das tells an explicitly *nirguṇī* legend. Another version of this legend is found in Sen's own *Kabir Rai-das Samvad*, a text I hope to edit and translate in the near future. Even in these two texts, however, one or more gods make their appearance in anthropomorphic form during the course of the debate.

The details of the eight texts used for this corrected edition and other texts consulted are given below.

1. India Office library (London) manuscript A 12, entitled *Vaisnava Poems* [text *a*]. This manuscript is dated 1843 [V. S.] (A.D. 1786). The text is of the Niranjani Panthi recension. It was copied at Pokara by Baishnav Niranjani Sobharam Svami, a sadhu of the Niranjani Panth. The catalogue claims that most of the compositions collected in the manuscript are by Sikh authors, but this statement seems to be an error. The manuscript includes Ananta-das's *parachaīs* of Nam-dev (21a-23b), Kabir (23b-35a), Rai-das (35a-47a), Dhanaji (47a-55b), Ranka and Banka (55b-64b), Angadaji (64b-71b), Trilochana (71b-73b), Saman and Seu (73b-76b), and Pipa (76b-123a). The letters of the manuscript are quite legible but not highly uniform. The text has relatively few scribal errors; a few are corrected in the margins by the copyist himself. Paper photocopies of a microfilm of the manuscript are sold by the India Office library. Unfortunately, the manuscript was bound sometime after being copied, and the center of each double page is not legible in the microfilm and its photocopies. This means that one to three *akshars* on each line cannot be read unless the manuscript itself is consulted. The failure to use a green filter on the camera has also left the letters written in red virtually invisible.

2. Nagari Pracharini Sabha (Varanasi) manuscript, new number 877 [text *b*]. This manuscript seems to be the same as that formerly numbered 1433/873.[12] This manuscript is included in, and catalogued as part of, a collection of the compositions (*bānī*) of Seva-das, an important leader of the Niranjani Panth. The copy date, as given at the end of the whole manuscript, is 1846 V. S. (A.D. 1789). The copyist was Mukun-das, a disciple of Darasan-das, a disciple of Amar-das. The text of the *Kabir Parachai* in the manuscript is of the Niranjani Panthi

12. What seems to be the same manuscript 877 is numbered as 1437/873 by T. N. Dikshit [1957: 42] and as 873 by L. P. Dube [1968: 29]. The NPS library does not seem to have a concordance of the new and former catalogue numbers of its manuscripts. T. N. Dikshit lists another *Kabir Parachai* (2350/1400) as being found in the NPS library. Perhaps it is the same as the manuscript with the new catalogue number nagari/2/1383 which was the only other *Kabir Parachai* manuscript I was able to locate in the NPS library collection. L. P. Dube [1968: 29-31] claims that the NPS manuscript (old number) 873 (= new number 877) was copied in 1855 and 1856 V. S. Dube's dates for this manuscript, however, are later by ten years than the 1846 V. S. (A.D. 1789) date I read in the colophon. One of us is evidently mistaken. I was unable to find the *Pipa Parachai* manuscript copied in 1740 V. S. (A.D. 1683) containing Ananta-das's complete genealogy that Dube claims is also found in this library. As noted above (p. 10), manuscript 877 contains a *Pipa Parachai* in which the relevant verse omits two names from Ananta-das's genealogy.

recension. The *Kabir Parachai* gives virtually the same readings as the India Office manuscript [text *a*]. This is not surprising considering that both manuscripts were copied within a few years of each other, and both are clearly associated with the Niranjani Panth.

In addition to Seva-das's *bānī* and the *Kabir Parachai*, the manuscript includes the *parachaī*s of Pipa [p. 637], Dayalaji Hari-das [p. 643], Seva-das [p. 661], Trilochan [p. 675], Dhana [p. 676], Nam-dev [p. 677], Kabir [pp. 678-85], Rai-das [p. 686], Ranka and Banka [p. 690], and Seu and Saman [pp. 693-94]. All these *parachaī*s are attributed to Ananta-das except for those of Hari-das and Seva-das, both leading figures in the Niranjani Panth. The *Nam-dev Parachai* includes the verse that gives its composition date as 1645 [V. S.] (A.D. 1588). The *Pipa Parachai* in this manuscript includes a defective version of the verse giving the genealogy of Ananta-das starting from Ramananda. The verse omits the names of Krishna-[das] and Vinodi [see L. Dube 1968: 29-31]. I was not allowed to photograph or copy this *Kabir Parachai*, but was allowed to make a line by line comparison between it and a copy of the India Office manuscript and note down any variant readings.

3. Rajasthani Shodh Samsthan (Jodhpur) manuscript 7133 [text *c*]. This text was copied in 1867 V. S. (A.D. 1810). The letters of the manuscript are well-made and legible. The readings generally follow closely those of Niranjani Panthi recension as found in the India Office A 12 and Nagari Pracharini Sabha 877 manuscripts. The only other *parachaī* contained in the manuscript is the *Angad Parachai.* The director of the Rajasthani Shodh Samsthan, Dr. Narayan Simha Bhati, kindly arranged for me to get permission to photography this and two other manuscripts in the institute's library.

4. Hindi Sahitya Sammelan (Allahabad) manuscript 1900 [text *d*]. This text is not dated. The nagari letters are exceedingly well-made and modern in style. The spelling of words often shows a tendency toward Sanskritized *tatsama* forms. This text includes section one and generally follows the Niranjani Panthi recension of the text, but in several minor passages it shows a closer agreement with the Dadu Panthi recension. Some of the more difficult passages seem to have been "corrected" in order to yield easier (but not necessarily better) sense.

The same manuscript also contains the *parachaī*s of Pipa and Angad. It begins with a collection of verses by Santa-das and features many *pad*s and other compositions of Ram-charan. It also includes the popular *Dhru-charitra* and *Prahlad-charitra* by Jan Gopal, the *Hari-chanda-sata* by Dhyan-das, and the *Moh-marad-raja ki katha* by Jan Jagannath, pupil of Turasi-das. The manuscript clearly belongs to the Shahapura branch of the Ram-snehi Panth, another important sect of Rajasthan. This would explain its somewhat anomalous readings that combine elements of both the Niranjani Panthi and Dadu Panthi recensions of the *Kabir Parachai.* The officials of the Hindi Sahitya Sammelan kindly made a paper photocopy of this text for me.

5. The text published as an appendix to R. K. Varma's *Kabir: Ek Anushilan* [text *e*] [R. K. Varma 1983:95-107]. This *Kabir Parachai* includes section one and follows the Niranjani Panthi recension quite closely. The published text includes quite a few bad readings that may well be mistakes either by transcription or by the printer. The spelling of many words (particularly the use of *kh* for the *sh* that appears in most manuscripts) may well be a Sanskritized correction made by the transcriber of the text (presumably Varma himself). The published text ends at verse 13.9. This suggests that the last page of the manuscript was probably lost. According to what R. K. Varma told me in an interview [Allahabad, 9 September 1986], the published text is based on a single undated manuscript that he had loaned to a student who had never returned it (perhaps T. N. Dikshit).

6. The Rajasthan Prachyavidya Pratishthan (Jodhpur) manuscript 11583 [text *f*]. The colophon of this manuscript gives the date 1693 V. S. (A.D. 1636) in faded and difficult to read numbers. I have examined the colophon carefully and tend to agree with the original cataloguer that this is the date given there. If so, this seems to be the oldest extant manuscript containing the *Kabir Parachai*, and one evidently copied within about 50 years of its original composition. The text of the *Kabir Parachai* generally follows the readings of the Dadu Panthi recension.

This manuscript contains a number of other compositions by several different authors including *pad*s by Jan Haridas (presumably the Haridas associated with the Niranjani Panth) and by Bajid (Dadu Panth); the *Prahlad-charitra* and *Jad-Bharat-charitra* by Jan Gopal (Dadu Panth); compositions attributed to Nath Panth authors such as Prithvi-nath and Gorakh-nath; *pad*s by famous earlier *sant*s such as Kabir, Rai-das, and Sur-das; compositions by the less well-known authors Murari Mishra, Ganga-kavi, and Khem-das; and also Anantadas's own *parachaī*s of Pipa and Nam-dev. The heterogenous character of the collection makes it difficult to identify the sectarian association of the manuscript as a whole.

A paper photocopy of the manuscript was very kindly made and sent to me in 1986 by the director of the institute, Dr. Padmadhar Pathak, who also allowed me to photograph several other manuscripts in the institute's collection. I could not examine the manuscript personally until my return visit to Jodhpur in 1990. The 1693 V. S. manuscript is showing signs of wear and tear. The letters are rather crudely formed, but for the most part it is legible. There are a number of relatively minor differences between the readings of the text of the *Kabir Parachai* in this manuscript and those of the other manuscripts Callewaert has used for his edition of the Dadu Panthi recension.

7. A draft version of W. Callewaert's critical edition of the Dadu Panthi recension [text *g*]. For the details of the procedures and manuscripts used in preparing this text, the reader is referred to Callewaert's forthcoming publication. Since I worked with a draft version of his edition, some of my notes may prove to refer to readings that were subsequently modified. I would like to thank him for letting me use the draft version of his critical text and also a concordance of eight transcribed manuscripts of the *Kabir Parachai.* The concordance includes my texts *a* [India Office A 12], *d* [HSS 1900], and *f* [RPP 11583] as well as five other manuscripts.

8. The Rajasthan Prachyavidya Pratishthan (Jodhpur) manuscript 8561 [text *h*]. This manuscript was copied in 1754 V. S. [A.D. 1697], making it one of the older manuscripts of the text. It is incomplete, most of it having been either lost or destroyed. What survives includes the verses from 8.14 to the end of the text [13. *dohā*]. The letters are somewhat crudely made but are generally legible except where the manuscript is partially destroyed. The text generally follows the Niranjani Panthi recension. It is apparently the second oldest extant manuscript of this recension of the text (after Jaipur Palace museum library manuscript 1843 dated in 1722 V. S. [A.D. 1665]). The director of the Rajasthan Prachyavidya Pratishthan, Dr. Padmadhar Pathak, kindly allowed me to photograph the manuscript.

9. Rajasthan Shodh Samsthan (Jodhpur) manuscript number 95. This manuscript was copied in 1871 V. S. (A.D. 1814). The letters of the manuscript are well made and legible. The same manuscript also includes the *parachaī*s of Nam-dev, Rai-das, Dhanna, and Saman and Seu. This manuscript includes section one and generally follows the Niranjani Panthi recension. Particularly in section one, however, the text contains a number of quite different, sometimes corrupt, readings. Some of these readings are given in the notes to the translation. The manuscript contains other compositions chiefly by poets belonging to the Khedapa branch of the Ram-snehi Panth, a fact that may explain the somewhat anomalous readings found in the text of the *Kabir Parachai.* I have closely examined the readings of this and the following manuscripts only for difficult passages or where their readings are particularly interesting. Dr. N. S. Bhati kindly arranged for me to photograph the document.

10. Rajasthan Prachyavidya Pratishthan (Jodhpur) manuscript 37981. This manuscript is not dated but appears to belong to the

eighteenth century. The letters are neither well nor crudely made. The manuscript also contains *parachaī*s of Nam-dev, Trilochan, Rai-das, and Pipa. The *Kabir Parachai* text includes section one and generally follows the Niranjani Panthi recension. The director of the institute, Dr. Padmadhar Pathak, kindly allowed me to photograph the manuscript.

11. Rajasthan Prachyavidya Pratishthan (Jodhpur) manuscript 25269. This manuscript is not dated but probably belongs to about the late eighteenth century. The letters are well made. The first section is omitted and the text generally seems to follow the Dadu Panthi recension of the text. The director of the institute, Dr. Padmadhar Pathak, kindly allowed me to photograph the manuscript.

12. Rajasthan Prachyavidya Pratishthan (Jodhpur) manuscript 35150. This manuscript is not dated but belongs to the eighteenth or nineteenth centuries. The letters are well made but only black ink was used (not black and red). Section one is omitted and the readings generally follow the Dadu Panthi recension of the text. The director of the institute, Dr. Padmadhar Pathak, kindly allowed me to photograph the manuscript.

13-17. These five manuscripts are transcribed in Callewaert's draft concordance. I do not have detailed information on their dates or provenance. This will presumably be available in Callewaert's critical edition when it is published. Callewaert's numbers for these manuscripts are as follows: [02], [21], [03], [04], [06]. All except [04] are of the Dadu Panthi recension of the text.

18. Nagari Pracharini Sabha (Varanasi) manuscript nagari/2/1383. This manuscript is not dated and seems to belong to the eighteenth or nineteenth centuries. It does not include section one and probably follows the Dadu Panthi recension of the text. This is the only one of the four manuscripts found in Eastern India whose text I was able to examine that seem to follow this recension. The same manuscript contains the text of the *Kabir Granthavali* (i.e., the Dadu Panthi collection of Kabir's verses). This and the following manuscripts I was able to examine but either was not allowed to photograph or felt that they were not worth photographing.

19. Rajasthani Shodh Samsthan (Jodhpur) manuscript 154. This includes a *Kabir Parachai* [3] as well as *parachaī*s of Nam-dev [1], Ranka and Banka [2], Rai-das [4], Pipa [5], Dhanna [6], Saman and Seu [7], and Trilochan [8]. It seems to belong to the twentieth century. The *Kabir Parachai* includes section one and seems to follow the Niranjani Panthi recension of the text.

20. Rajasthai Shodh Samsthan (Jodhpur) manuscript 207. This includes a *Kabir Parachai* [19] and a *Nam-dev Parachai* [18]. It is undated but seems to belong to the 19th century. It omits section one and seems

to follow the Dadu Panthi recension of the text.

21. Rajasthani Shodh Samsthan (Jodhpur) manuscript 2935. This includes a *Kabir Parachai* and the *parachaīs* of Rai-das [6], Nam-dev [7], Trilochan [8], Dhanna [9], and Saman and Seu [10]. The manuscript is dated 1851 [V. S.] (A.D. 1794). The *Kabir Parachai* omits section one and seems to follow the Dadu Panthi recension of the text.

22. Rajasthani Shodh Samsthan (Jodhpur) manuscript 4471. This includes a *Kabir Parachai* [28] as well as *parachaīs* of Rai-das [29], Pipa [30], Trilochan [31], Dhana [32], Seu and Saman [33], Angad [34], and Nam-dev [35]. It is undated but seems to belong to the nineteenth century. It includes section one and seems to follow the Niranjani Panthi recension of the text.

23 Rajasthani Shodh Samsthan (Jodhpur) 7642. This contains a *Kabir Parachai* as well as *parachaīs* of Rai-das [6], Nam-dev [7], and Pipa [8]. The manuscript is of uncertain date. The *Kabir Parachai* omits section one and seems to follow the Dadu Panthi recension of the text.

24. Maharaja Mansingh Pustak Prakash (Jodhpur) manuscript 1200. This manuscript is not dated but belongs to the nineteenth or twentieth centuries. It includes section one and seems to follow the Niranjani Panthi recension of the text. Its readings appear to be quite corrupt.

This concludes the list of seventeen manuscripts, one published text [number 5 above], one draft critical text [number 7 above], and five transcribed texts [numbers 13-17 above] that I was able to consult before preparing the corrected text and translation given below.

In my subsequent visit to Rajasthan in 1990, I was able to examine many other manuscripts of the *Kabir Parachai* but did not find any containing important new readings of the text. Nonetheless, two of the manuscripts are quite worth describing in more detail.

The Jaipur Palace museum manuscript 1843 is of great historical importance since it is by far the oldest manuscript containing the Niranjani Panthi recension of the *Kabir Parachai.* The colophon of the manuscript clearly states that it was copied in 1722 [V. S.] (A.D. 1665). The manuscript is in surprising, almost suspiciously good condition. It also contains Ananta-das's *Nam-dev Parachai* and *Rai-das Parachai.* It does not contain other texts that might help to determine the sectarian affiliation of its copyist. I would have liked to have included its text of the *Kabir Parachai* among those used to prepare my corrected edition of the Niranjani Panthi recension. I have checked its readings of the text carefully against those of the manuscripts I did use, however, and have not found any significant variant readings. In the circumstances, its incorporation into the edition does not seem to be necessary.

Another interesting manuscript that I examined in 1990 is Rajasthani Shodh Samsthan manuscript 8633, apparently belonging to the eighteenth century. Its *Kabir Parachai* is of the Niranjani Panth recension and the larger manuscript gives pride of place to compositions by the Niranjani Panthi poets Seva-das, Hari-das, and Turasi-das. It also includes compositions by Nath Panthi and Dadu Panthi authors as well as several of Ananta-das's *parachaī*s. Not all these compositions are listed in the catalogue.

Other manuscripts of the *Kabir Parachai* examined in 1990 include the following: Rajasthan Prachyavidya Pratishthan (Jodhpur) manuscripts 11092, 12422, 12420, 12585, 13960, 14423, 14376, 14392, 14741, 14716, 15990, and 17174 (15756 was considered too delicate to examine); Jaipur Palace museum library manuscript 3321; Rajasthani Shodh Samsthan manuscripts 154, 207, 7152, 7191, and 4471; Rajasthan Prachyavidya Pratishthan (Jaipur) manuscripts 1 and 3; and a manuscript in the possession of a Ramanandi sadhu scholar named Parameshvar-das who lives in Jaipur. I was unable to see the several manuscripts containing the *Kabir Parachai* said to be located in the Shri Dadu Mahavidyalay in Jaipur.

A Note on the Translation

The translation of Ananta-das's *Kabir Parachai* which follows in chapter five, is based on the corrected edition of the Niranjani Panthi recension found in chapter six. Translations of the more important variant readings given in other manuscripts—including the 1693 V. S. manuscript of the Dadu Panthi recension and Callewaert's draft critical edition of this recension—are given in the footnotes.

The translation attempts to be as readable as possible without sacrificing accuracy. Since Ananta-das's text has more the character of narrative verse than poetry, Jagdish Kumar, Uma Thukral, and I have preferred to render the text in prose rather than in verse. We have preserved the verse numbers, however, for the convenience of those scholars who may want to compare the Hindi and English texts.

In order to make Ananta-das's often somewhat elliptical syntax more understandable, we have often added to the translation words and phrases not found in the original Hindi text. For instance, phrases that identify the speakers of direct quotations ("Kabir said," etc.) are only rarely found in Ananta-das's text, and we have added them to the translation with as neutral a wording as possible. When the additions to the translation involve somewhat speculative interpretations of Ananta-das's intentions, we have put the additions in brackets.

We have also attempted to keep as few Hindi words in the translation as possible. Thus, the translation refers to "forehead marks" rather than "*tilak*s," and to "worshippers of the Goddess" rather than "Shaktas." Interested scholars can, of course, easily check the Hindi text to find the original reading. Inevitably, a few words have been left in Hindi for want of any reasonable alternative. For example, the term *sant* cannot really be translated as "saint" or as "good person." Similarly, the terms "*nirguṇ*" and "*saguṇ*" are key concepts that are too specific to be respectively rendered simply as "without attributes" and "with attributes." Proper names and Indian words commonly found in English (*e.g.*, bhakti, darshan, guru, sannyasi, shastra, etc.) are not usually translated nor italicized.

in the translation involve somewhat speculative interpretations of Guru Arjan's intentions, we have put the additions in brackets.

We have also attempted to keep as few Hindi words in the translation as possible. Thus the translation refers to "forehead marks" rather than "tilaks" and to "worshipping of the Goddess" rather than "Shakti-puja". Interested scholars can, of course, easily check the Hindi text to find the original reading. Inevitably, a few words have been left in Hindi for want of any reasonable alternative. For example, the term sant cannot really be translated as "saint" or as "good person". Similarly, the terms nirgun and sargun are key concepts that are too specific to be adequately rendered simply as "without attributes" and "with attributes". Proper names and Indian words commonly found in English (e.g. bhakti, dharma, guru, sannyasi, mantra, etc.) are not italicized.

CHAPTER 5

A TRANSLATION OF THE *KABIR PARACHAI*

Section One

1. There was a Julaha[1] living in Kashi who followed the customs of the devotees of Hari.[2] Earlier he spent many days among the worshippers of the Goddess. Afterwards he lived by praising the virtues of Hari.

2. God spoke to him and said: "Unless you become a Vaishnav I will not give you my darshan. Only if you put on the Vaishnav prayer beads and forehead mark will you obtain my darshan.

3. Kabir said: "I belong to a Muslim caste. How can I obtain these prayer beads?"

The inner voice said to him: "Take an initiation[3] from Ramananda."

4. Kabir said: "Ramananda will not even consent to look at me. How can I get his initiation?"

The voice said: "Go at night and stay on the path where he comes out with his followers."[4]

---

1. Julaha is the name of a caste of Muslim weavers.

2. Text d: ". . . custom of remembering Hari."
Ananta-das uses the names Hari, Gobinda, Keshav, Kharari, Murari, Narayan, Raghunath, Raghuvir, Ram, and Sarangapani to refer to the god Vishnu.

3. Text d: "teaching."

4. The last two padas are not found in text d.

5. At night Kabir came and stayed in Ramananda's path.[5] Ramananda stepped on him and said "Ram." The devotee's heart filled with enthusiasm. Then Kabir got up and went home.

6. Kabir put on prayer beads and a forehead mark and acted in a way pleasing to the *sants*.[6] Many people came to see. Kabir Das sang the virtues of Ram.[7]

7. His own family members and his father-in-law[8] came together and lamented:[9] "He has gotten confused. Why has he abandoned the customs of his own home, where Mecca and Medina, the Muslim creed, fasting during Ramadan, and prayers to Allah are our way of worship?"[10]

8. But Kabir was obstinate.[11] On his brow he wore a forehead mark, on his neck prayer beads.

His family said: "Kabir, who has led you astray? Where did you get this heresy from?

9. "One's destiny is found going on one's own path. Ask both the Hindus and the Turks."[12]

Everyone was amazed. They went and appealed to Ramananda.

10. They said: "There is a Julaha who has put on the costume of the Vaishnava devotees. He makes *kirashi*[13] and gives it to them.[14] When

---

5. Text RSS 95 here adds that Ramananda was "going to the Ganges to bathe" (*nhāvaṇa Gaṃga cale*).

6. In other words, he acted like a *sant*.

7. The last two padas are not in text d.

8. The mention of Kabir's father-in-law (*samadhī*) is one of several indications that Anantadas believed that Kabir was married (see above, pp. 18-19). Text d has the, perhaps bowdlerized, reading *saṃbandhī* ("relatives").

9. Text RSS 95: "The women of the house and the family cried." Text RPP 37981 also mentions the women.

10. Text RSS 95: "Mecca, Medina, and prayers to Allah, the Muslim creed, fasting during Ramadan and going to [the tombs of] saints."

11. The translation of the first pada is rather tentative.

12. Text RSS 95 here adds the following: "Kabir recited the Name of the compassionate Lord. On his brow he had a forehead mark and on his neck prayer beads. His mother said: 'Kabir is not acting in a way pleasing to me. The people of the town are coming to see him.'"

13. The sense of this *kirashi* is not clear. The reading *kiratana* (RSS 95) and variants, meaning "religious singing and chanting," makes sense but is not found in older manuscripts.

14. Text RSS 95: "He does *kīrtan* and serves the Lord."

asked about this, he says he does it in your name."[15]

11. Ramananda then quickly called for Kabir. A screen was put in front and back of Ramananda (so that he would not come into direct contact with Kabir). Ramananda said to Kabir: "Tell me! When did I give you prayer beads? Why do you say you are acting in my name?"

12. Kabir said: "I went at night and stayed on the path when you came out with your followers. You said 'Ram' when you stepped on me.[16] You said it to me, and I said it to you.

13. "Then I got up and went home. Absorbed in bliss, I found the nectar of love."[17]

Ramananda said: "Anyone can say 'Ram' in this way. This is not the way one becomes a devotee of Hari."[18]

14. Kabir said: "If the guru and Gobinda show favor and one meets the Satguru, then nothing is difficult. Everything is easy and spontaneous. This is what all the *sant*s say.

15. "Show yourself, Master. Give me your darshan. If you don't give it, I will weep and die."

Ramananda recognized Kabir's pure bhakti. He opened the curtain and gave him an initiation.

16. Kabir had great good fortune. He got Ramananda as his guru and shed the illusions of birth and death.

---

15. Text RSS 95 here adds several additional verses that mention how two men were sent to Kabir's. They told him to come quickly. Kabir thought about it and went quickly. Kabir arrived. Ramananda was seated doing service to God. Kabir then entered inside (?by his insight, not his body). Kabir told Ramananda to put the garland on the god by untying the knot. Then Ramananda called him and asked him when he had given him the prayer beads. He told Kabir that everyone was saying that Kabir was claiming Ramananda as his guru. Kabir answered telling how he had waited on the path when Ramananda was going to bathe.

The story of Ramananda's difficulties in putting the garland on the idol of the god and Kabir's miraculous advice is told in several late sources.

16. Also possible: "I touched your feet."

17. Text d: "I found bliss, auspiciousness, and the nectar of Ram."

18. Text RSS 95 here adds the following verse (which substitutes for the next): "'When a guru gives the name of Gobinda, only then one becomes a devotee. Then only is it accepted.' Kabir replied: 'Give me initiation now, Master . . . Oh Guru, give me the Name of Gobinda. Bring me, who am astray, onto the proper path.'"

Doha a

Kabir won Ramananda as his guru and recgnized the wisdom of Brahman. He became filled with bhakti[19] and achieved nirvana.

Doha b

Kabir was Ramananda's disciple and his *sant*. Kabir came to earth to strengthen bhakti. Ananta-das is singing the story.[20]

Section Two

1. Kabir concentrated his mind and practiced bhakti. He abandoned Maya and worldly fame.[1] First he adopted the role of being a servant. In this way he gave much pleasure to the devotees.

2. He wove cloth, sold it, and brought the money home. If there was any profit, he used it all to eat and feed others.[2]

One day Hari made a test. He came to the market and gave Kabir his darshan.

3. He said: "Kabir, I have heard about you. For that reason, I have come to you."

Hari had taken the form of an emaciated devotee. He requested cloth very humbly.

4. When Kabir began to tear a cloth in half, Hari said: "Give me all of it, devotee, for I am naked."[3]

Kabir gave it to him immediately, without any hestitation. Then Kabir did not return home.

---

19. Text d: "Intellect arose in his body."

20. The half chaupai that replaces this doha in text f reads as follows: "Kabir was Ramananda's disciple. He was a *sant* on account of his thought and strengthened bhakti."

Text g gives the following doha: "Ramananda's disciple was Kabir, who recognized the Lord. He came to earth to strengthen bhakti. Ananta-das is singing the story."

Texts f and g begin with these lines.

1. These two padas are not in text f.

2. Text f: "He made an offering [*aragha*] of a drink [*pachhevarī*]. Then he ate and fed others." The sense and reading are somewhat problematic. The word *aragha* looks more like *aradha*.

3. Or: "I am a naked devotee."

5. He stayed hidden here and there. No one in his house knew his whereabouts. For three days the people in his house went hungry. The children cried, standing and complaining.

6. Then Hari took pity on them in this way.[4] While everyone sat at home, Hari brought them a bullock's load of food.[5] He brought and unloaded many foodstuffs. [The people of the house] protested, but he put it on the porch.[6]

7. Hari said: "Keep it in the house, mother of Kabir. Ram, who is your benefactor, has given it."

Kabir's mother said: "Who is this Ram? From where is this benefactor? If Kabir hears of this, he will kill me.[7]

8. "Who are you, sir? Where did you come from? Whose money was it? Who sent this? Kabir never requests anything, even if thousands of coins are put in front of him."[8]

9. Hari said: "Listen, mother, to what we have to say. In Kashi, Vishvanath is the Overlord. A king came to take His darshan. That king offered money to Kabir.

10. "Your son did not take the money. Then the king got up and begged him to accept it. Kabir said: 'I will accept your request, o king, [but you should use the money to] procure some foodstuffs for a great feast.'[9]

---

4. Text f: "Hari took the form of a merchant."

5. Compare the following pada attributed to Mirabai: "[Hari] who brought a bullock's load to the house of Kabir Das" (*Dāsa Kabīra ghara bālada jo lāyā*).

6. Here text f adds a verse whose sense seems to partially repeat verse 2.7 (also found in text f): "Hari said: 'Mother, keep the goods in the house. If they are left outside, someone will take them away.' Kabir's mother said: 'Whose goods are these? Kabir's behavior is very difficult to understand.'"

7. Text f here adds the following verse: "'He does not take charity. He does not request anything from anyone. He works hard and is attached to Ram. He sells what he makes. Whatever work he does goes to fill bellies.'" The first two padas are also found in text g.

8. Text f here has the following: "'Who are you, sir? Where have you come from? Who was it, merchant? Who sent it?' Hari replied: 'I am a servant of the devotees of Hari. I always stay near the *sants*.'"

Callewaert's text g includes the last two padas of the text we have used (2.8cd) and then adds (indented) the verse found in text f and translated in this note. Callewaert indents texts that he considers to be less authentic.

9. Text f here adds the following two padas, apparently spoken by the king: "'I will not take it for you. Let it be given to feed the *sants*. Dear sir, please accept this much.'"

11. "Then the king procured these goods and had them sent to Kabir's house. In a little while [Kabir] is coming also. A crowd of people are coming to take darshan."[10]

12. Then Keshav vanished without saying anything about his own secret [identity]. Four men[11] ran to Kabir. Somehow or other they brought him home.

13. They said to him: "Master, the offering which has arrived for you, either spend it or keep it."

Kabir came and saw it with his own eyes. Only then did he believe what the others said.

14. Kabir said: "Who gave this? Where did it come from?"

Then his mother told him the whole story. In his heart he knew that Sarangapani had shown compassion to him.

15. He thought: "The Lord has done this for me. Why should there be any fear in my heart?[12]

Doha

"I have abandoned my weaving and stay meditating on the feet of Ram.[13] Now Ram has shown compassion, and my troubles have ended."[14]

---

10. Here texts f, g add the following two padas: "When she had heard all this, Kabir's mother accepted it."

11. Text f: "Some servants."

12. Texts c, d: "life" or "breath". The double "negative" (*jini* and *kāhi*) seems to be for emphasis but the *jini* is not found in texts e (*jiva*), f (*jana*) or g (*tūṃ*). Text f: "Now why and who should the devotee fear?" Text g: "Now why should you have fear in your heart?"

Text d here adds the following two padas: "'Without my asking for it, Hari has sent me wealth. I will keep it for Hari.'"

13. Text a: "'I stay absorbed in love of Ram.'" This doha can be taken as being either in the first or third person.

14. The meaning of the second half of the second line of this doha is mostly inferred from the context.

Text f and g (indented) here add the following chaupai: "Then Kabir began to think in this way, that all the foodstuffs should be distributed: 'I will call the devotees from all over. I will offer all His wealth to him.'"

Section Three

1. Kabir invited the devotees and prepared a great feast. He kept nothing for himself, but gave away everything. The Brahmans and the sannyasis became angry and went to ridicule him.

2. One said: "Some king gave Kabir money and then left. Kabir gave everything to the Shudras. He has shown respect to all, king and commoners alike. Why has he considered the Brahmans to be less worthy?

3. "Kabir has shown no respect to any of us. Let's throw him out of town!"

One said: "Catch him by the nose and cut it off! That will solve all our problems!"

4. One said: "We will beat anyone who holds Kabir in high esteem."[1] Expressing their anger like this, all [the Brahmans and sannyasis] in the town came running.

5. The sannyasis grabbed up their *guptī* and *chakra* weapons. All of Kashi poured out to see the show. From every direction they came and surrounded Kabir's hut. Then Kabir came out to face them.

6. Kabir showed them respect and politely asked them to sit: "Why have you done me the honor of coming here?"

The Brahmans just got angry and reprimanded him: "Get out of town! If you don't, we will kill you."[2]

7. Kabir replied: "For what mistake will you kill me? I have [done nothing except] keep the Name of Ram deep in my heart.[3] Have I waylaid you? Have I eyed another man's woman?

8. "Did I destroy someone's house? Kill somebody? Steal money?"

The Brahmans and sannyasis said: "You performed an act of bhakti,[4] but you did not invite us. You brought the Shudras and fed them instead.

9. "Give us food right now. Otherwise we and you will come to blows."[5]

---

1. Texts f, g add two padas here whose sense is not clear.

2. Texts f, g add here two padas: "The sannyasis were really burning, without there being any fire. They said: 'Kill him quickly [lest he] run away!'"

3. Texts f, g substitute in this pada: "'If I have done something wrong, tell me, what was it?'"

4. Text d: ". . . held a feast."

5. The translation of this last pada is somewhat doubtful.

When he saw what mischief they were up to,[6] Kabir wisely said nothing in reply.

10. He merely said: "Right now there is no food in the house. I will go get some. You sit here in the shade." Having said this Kabir, slipped away. [The god] Keshav wasn't sure what to do.

11. Then Hari took the form[7] of Kabir. He brought money taken from a hidden place.[8] He gave the money to a Baniya and took goods of various sorts in exchange:

12. Flour, rice, and powdered sugar in quantity and all sorts of food cooked with ghee. He sent off four workmen who took everything to [Kabir's] house.[9]

13. When the Brahmans saw this, they were delighted. No one realized that Murari had done it [and not Kabir]. Kabir's prestige was greatly increased.[10] Each man received two-and-one-half *sers*[11] of food.

14. One of them said: "This Julaha has found a treasure. Someone should report this matter to the royal court."

But another said: "Very good, very good! He has done well. He has a noble character."

15. Then Kabir pleased them further by giving them rolled pan. All of them were delighted with Kabir. When their desires were satisfied, their anger vanished. Saying "Praise be! Praise be!" they all went home.

Doha

Kabir is a true devotee. He appeared in Kashi. Whoever directs scorn against him will go to hell.

---

6. The words *thīgā thīgī* are equivalent to modern *dhīṃgā dhīṃgī*.

7. Here *karā* is equivalent to modern *kalā*.

8. Text d reads *gāṃṭhi* ("knot") in place of *gaiba* ("hidden; hidden place; invisible world"), which suggests a confusion with *jaiba* or *jeba* ("pocket"). The reading of texts f, g (*māthaiṃ* in place of *āṃni*) gives "He took money of a hidden place on his head."

9. Texts f, g invert this and the following verse. The reading of the Niranjani Panthi recension texts (a etc.) seems better. The logical order of events is that (1) Hari as Kabir buys the food, (2) it is taken to Kabir's house, (3) the Brahmans see it and are pleased, (4) each receives two and one half *sers*. If the reading of texts f, g is accepted, the workmen must take the goods to the *Brahmans'* houses.

10. The reading *jana* ("devotee") of texts f, g is perhaps clearer than *tina kī*.

11. A *ser* is equal to about one kilo.

Section Four

1. Hari went to where Kabir was. In order not to be recognized, Hari became a Brahman. Hari said: "What are you doing sitting here, brother? Why don't you to go Kabir's?

2. "He is giving food to anyone who opens up his bag. He is making offerings of two-and-one-half *ser*s of flour and rice together with ghee and sugar.[1]

3. "The Brahmans and the sannyasis have taken theirs. Look at what he gave to me."

Hearing this Kabir became very happy. He thought: "Keshav has saved my honor."

4. Then Kabir returned to his own house. No one realized the marvel that Hari had performed. Kabir saw all the food in the house. The Brahmans were still taking it away.

5. Everyone was saying, "Praise be, praise be!" Kabir Das kept his face hidden. He thought: "Praise be to the mighty Hari who is doing my work.[2] I am forever Hari's servant.[3]

6. "Hari alone can bestow greatness. Hari Himself has made me His own?"

Then Kabir fell into a trance.[4] Confidence came to him and illusion fled away.

7. With love in his heart, Kabir sang the virtues of Hari. People came from far away to take Kabir's darshan. They gave gold, silver, and fabrics, but Kabir Das took nothing.

8. He took only that [minimum of] cloth and food that the devotees of Hari gave with sincere emotion. He disregarded the persistence of king and subjects alike. For that reason pilgrimages to Kabir's place increased.[5]

---

1. Texts f, g invert the second two padas of this verse with the first two of the next.

2. Text f, g: "'Praise be, praise be to my mighty Lord!'"

3. Here texts f, g, insert a verse the same as *Kabir Granthavali, sākhī* 38.1: "I did nothing. I was incapable of doing anything. My body was unable to do it. Whatever was done was done by Hari. Because of Him, Kabir became great (*kabīra*)."

4. Of the varied readings, *tāli* has as one of its senses "a yogic trance." The sense is an uncommon one, however, and is not given for *taralī*.

5. The translation of this verse is somewhat tentative.

9. Day-by-day the crowd got bigger. As a result, when Kabir tried to meditate, his mind often was distracted. Then an idea came to him: "I will rid myself of all this popularity."

10. Early in the morning, he went to a prostitute's house and took her out with him. Everyone was astonished. Kabir threw his arm around the prostitute's neck. She returned the embrace and went off with him.

11. He filled a pot with holy water. Pretending it was liquor, he drank and drank. He went out into the bazaar acting as if he had forgotten all his wisdom.

12. The townspeople laughed at him, and the hearts of the devotees of Hari were filled with sorrow. The Brahmans and Baniyas taunted him. When the devotees of Hari saw all this, they hid their faces.

13. The Brahmans, and Baniyas said: "Everyone wants to perform bhakti, but how can low-caste persons do it? Kabir performed bhakti for about ten days. Now look! He has taken up with a prostitute.[6]

14. Going along, Kabir arrived at the place where the king of the city was holding court. On other days the king would get up to receive Kabir. Giving up his throne, he would offer the seat to Kabir.

15. That day the king showed Kabir no respect. He had Kabir sit at the back of the assembly. Everyone was astonished. How could such a devotee get so spoiled?

Doha

Everyone in the city was astonished. Everyone was thinking about it. But what [real harm] could all this scorn do? The Creator Himself protects Kabir's head.

Section Five

1. On that occasion Kabir poured out the water [in his pot] and saved the *paṇḍā*[1] of Hari [in the distant temple of Jagannath in Puri] from being burned. The king asked him to explain: "Tell me, Kabir, what have you done?

---

6. Texts a, b invert the order of the two half verses.

1. Roughly: "the Brahman priest."

2. "What charade have you demonstrated? I don't understand its inner meaning."

Kabir said: "Listen, king. No one will believe me if I simply tell what happened?

3. "A *paṇḍā* of Jagannath got burned. A pot broke and fell on his feet. I sprinkled water and saved him from being burned. My eyes saw everything that happened both here and there."[2]

4. Then the king searched everyone's face. He said: "Is Kabir telling the truth or is he misleading us?[3]

One devotee made a comment that was pleasing to the king and people alike:

5. "Whether Kabir is drunk or not drunk[4] when he speaks, how can anything he says be doubted?"

The king immediately wrote a note so that the exact moment of Kabir's action would not be forgotten.

6. He sent two men[5] to Jagannath. The devotee Kabir went home. In ten days the men reached Jagannath and called for the burned *paṇḍā*.

7. They said to him: "*Paṇḍā*, tell us truthfully. How did your feet get burned?"

The *paṇḍā* said: "I got burned while pouring off water from boiling rice. The pot broke and fell on my feet.

8. "Then Kabir ran up with [cool] water. He showed compassion and brought it to soothe my burning feet."

Hearing this, the men expressed a doubt: "Who was this Kabir? What sort of man is he?

9. The *paṇḍā* replied: "He belongs to the Julaha caste of Muslim weavers and lives in Kashi. Everyone knows him as the slave of Hari. He comes here to take the darshan of Jagannath. With great joy he sings the virtues of Hari.[6]

---

2. Text *f*: "'By the grace of Hari, my eyes saw that.'" Text *g*: "'Although I remained here, my eyes saw that.'"

3. For *bāhai* see also verse 7.13d. The modern verb is *bahakānā*.

4. Dictionaries permit "drunk" for *chhāka*. Compare *Kabir Granthavali, pad* 1.20.4.

5. In texts *d, f, g* only, the number of men is not given.

6. Texts *f, g* invert the last two padas and give slightly different readings for them. They may be translated as follows: "'He sings the praises of Hari with love. People come from far away to take his darshan.'"

10. "As soon as I saw that Kabir,[7] he poured out water on my burning feet."

By this time the messengers were quite satisfied. They turned around and set off for home.

11. In ten days they arrived in Kashi. The people of the town ran to ask what had happened. The messengers told the king the secret: "We did not force the *paṇḍā* to say anything.

12. "Of the witness the *paṇḍā* gave us, we have kept nothing from you."

Then the king became so upset that he forgot the presence of the ministers and other people.[8]

13. The king thought: "Kabir is a great man. I didn't understand his inner wisdom. All the wonderful miracle that has occurred is his doing."[9]

The king went and asked the queen what to do. He explained to her what had happened.

14. The queen said: "Don't delay! Run and fall at Kabir's feet."

The king said: "I am very frightened. If Kabir curses me, who will save me?

15. "I must go to meet Kabir right away. Otherwise nothing good will happen. But what present can I bring him? If he sees money, he only gets angry."

Doha

On his shoulder the king put an axe. On his head he put a bundle of straw.[10] Then the king and his whole family went off to meet Kabir. All of Kashi was a spectator.

---

7. Also possible: "'As soon as Kabir saw me.'"

8. For this difficult verse, see the note to the accompanying corrected text. The two padas inserted here in texts *f, g* may be translated as follows: "The king thought: 'I must meet Kabir right now. Otherwise nothing good will happen.'" These padas appear in our text in verse 5.15.

9. This second pada is a difficult one. Texts *f, g* give equally difficult readings that are quite different from those of texts *a-e* and somewhat different even from each other. They may be tentatively translated as follows: "'For this reason I insisted on getting an answer from him.'"

10. In texts *f, g*: "a bundle of wood." The reference is to a customary penance similar to that mentioned in Tulasi-das's *Ram-charit-manas* 6.29.4.

Section Six

1. King Virasinghadev Baghel gave up all his royal dignity for Kabir's sake.[1] Kabir saw the king coming at a distance. He got up and ran to meet him, his heart filled with love.

2. Kabir said: "Throw down the bundle on your head. There is no anger in my heart. For me there is no question of either hatred or love, nor any difference between king and commoner."

3. The king went and prostrated himself before Kabir. Kabir embraced him. The king kept holding onto one of Kabir's feet. The rest of the king's family held onto the other one.

4. They said: "Master, forgive our mistake. Except for you, who can save us? Master, don't turn your back on us. What else can we do but repeat this again and again?"

5. Kabir said: "You have done something good. Your coming here has honored me. Whoever gives greatness to others is himself great. A great person is one who consumes wealth by sharing it with others.

6. "Great is he who recognizes truth from falsehood. What does a fool know of greatness?"

The king's heart filled with happiness. He took Kabir's darshan and returned home.

7. Kabir tried to erase his own fame, in the same way as a modest well-born woman hides a pregnancy. But how can such acts be hidden when day-by-day they become more evident.[2]

8. If someone praises himself, he gets no pleasure from it. He merely gets frustrated. If a woman caresses her own breast, how can she satisfy her sexual longings?

9. Thus, the whole world has become confused. Only he who meditates on Hari knows the true path.[3] Honor was again offered to Kabir. The whole world ran to take his darshan.

---

1. Literally: "lost his shame." Virasinghadev Baghel is a king known also from the *Virabhanudayakavyam* and other historical sources. He died in about A.D. 1530. See above, pp. 14-15.

2. In text *f*, pada *c* (there *d*) reads: "The sun when it rises cannot be hidden."

3. In text *f*, this pada reads: "When the devotee of Hari worships Hari, he becomes united with Hari."

10. Ram restores everything that has fallen into ruin. Ram saves those who are drowning in the ocean of existence.

The *kāzī*s and the mullahs were troublemakers. The Brahmans and the Baniyas were big sinners.

11. They all were full of hatred. They all waited for the opportunity to kill Kabir. The more they learned about Kabir, the more they got irritated. In this way, many days passed. Every day Kabir debated them and was victorious.

12. But Kabir's mother was malicious. She did not like bhakti. She nagged at Kabir.[4] She and her daughter-in-law created quarrels every day. Praise be to Kabir who put up with all this.[5]

13. There were enemies outside and inside the house, but Kabir lived in Ram's shadow. The whole of worldly existence is the enemy of the true devotee. From beginning to end, Hari is their protector.[6]

14. One time it happened like this. A conjunction of fate cannot be expunged. Shah Sikandar came to Kashi. The *kāzī*s and mullahs were pleased.

15. Right away the petitioners went off to Sikandar. The Brahmans and Baniyas also got together and went with them.[7] Even Kabir's mother ran to join them. No one understood. Everyone was confused.[8]

16. They were all eager to go and make their petitions, as if Kabir had killed one of their own men.[9] But God protected Kabir. Ananta-das is singing his praises.

---

4. Literally: "grabbed his topknot."

5. In texts *f, g* these four padas are placed after verse 6.15b of this edition. Texts *f, g* invert the order of the two half verses and substitute, for pada *c* of this edition, a somewhat different text which reads: "In the house was Kabir's bad wife." In this same pada, text *e* gives "many" (*bahuta*) instead of "daughter-in-law" (*bahū*). The texts which give *bahu*, with short *u*, may be understood either way. Text *g* then repeats and indents (*i.e.* considers less authentic) padas *c,d* of this edition. In the final pada, the word *dhani* ("praise be") less likely means either "young girl" or "husband," both of which can also yield possible translations.

6. In text *g* these four padas also are indented and placed after verse 6.15b of this edition. They are not found in text *f*.

7. Here text *f, g* add padas equivalent to verses 6.12-13 of this edition.

8. This last pada perhaps refers only to Kabir's mother.

9. Text *d* has "family" in place of "men." Text *d* also here adds two padas not found in other texts. They read as follows: "All of them met together and made their petitions. They said: 'One sinner has shown us disrespect.'"

Doha

They said: "Shah Sikandar, long life to you! Remove our pain. No one has ever before done to us what Kabir has done."

Section Seven

1. Sikandar said: "What has happened, brothers? Has he snatched away a village or a district?"

They replied: "No, he hasn't taken a village or a district. Instead, this Julaha has done an unconventional thing.[1]

2. "He has abandoned the customs of the Muslims and has broken the touchability[2] rules of the Hindus. He has scorned the sacred bathing places and the Vedas. He has scorned the nine planets, the sun and the moon.

3. "He has scorned Shankar and the Mother. He has scorned Sharada and Ganapati. He has scorned the rites of the eleventh day of the fortnight, the offerings to the sacred fire and the ceremonies for the dead.[3] He has scorned the Brahmans, whom the whole world worships.[4]

4. "He has scorned service to one's mother and father, sisters, nieces, and all the gods. He has scorned the hope of all religions, the six systems of metaphysics and the rites of the twelve months.[5]

5. "In this way he has corrupted everyone. He has separated himself from both the Hindus and the Muslims.[6] For this reason, no one respects

---

1. Text *f*: "'Kabir has given us a great deal of trouble.'"

2. The word *chhiti* means "touch" and, by extension, "touchability."

3. Shankar is another name of the god Shiv or Shiva. The Mother is the Goddess, often considered as the wife of Shiv. Sharada is the goddess of learning, often called "Sarasvati." Ganapati, often called "Ganesh," is a god of obstacles and son of Shiv.

4. Text *g* here substitutes two padas similar to the first two of the four added padas that text *f* adds after verse 7.4.

5. For the last two padas, text *f* substitutes two other padas and adds four more. The six padas may be translated as follows:

"'He has scorned the doctrines of the six systems; he has scorned the numberless sacred bathing places. He has scorned the prayer beads, the forehead mark, the sacred thread, . . . [?], the Saligram and the ten avatars. Kabir has said that all this is false. He has fostered [?] neither the Hindus nor the Turks.'"

6. For the second pada, text *f* gives: "'He has put [read *baiṭharyā*] Hindus and Turks in the same place." Text *g* is similar.

us as long as this Julaha remains in Kashi.

6. "For this reason you should put an end to our troubles. You indeed are our father. You indeed are our mother."[7]

When he heard all this, Sikandar got furious. He sent two guards [to go get Kabir].[8]

7. Sikandar said: "Bring him quickly! Don't delay! I will have him killed even if he begs me for his life."

The soldiers[9] went and told the news to Kabir: "Shah Sikandar has called for you, brother."

8. Kabir said: "How is it that Sikandar knows about me? Who told him? How did he find out?"

The soldiers said: "Your mother created a fuss. Together with the *kāzī*s and the Brahmans, she has appealed to Sikandar against you."[10]

9. Kabir went off with them, knowing that if he did not go they would take him by force. He said: "I have just given religious instruction to all the *sant*s. You shouldn't pass judgment on me."

10. Because he was so agitated, the demon Sikandar then sent two more men who also arrived at Kabir's.[11] Kabir was taken and made to stand there where Sikandar had set up camp.[12]

---

7. Text *d*: "'Great [?] Badashah, you are our benefactor.'" Text *f*: "'Great [?] Badashah, you are our authority.'"

8. Text *e*: "He gave two guards the order [to go get Kabir]."

9. It seems probable that these "soldiers" or "messengers" (*payādai*) are the same two "guards" (*chharīdāra*). In texts *f, g*, the word used is *chharīdāra*.

10. Text *f* here adds the following six padas:

"'The petitioners said that Kabir had given them trouble, that he had obliterated all doctrines and taken a single doctrine [possibly "a bad doctrine" (*kumata*)], that he had abandoned the path of the Muslims, that he had not approved of the conduct of either the Hindus or the Turks [Text *g* here substitutes: "and that he had not respected the touchability rules of the Hindus"]. The Badashah gave us the order that as soon as we recognized you, we should bring you to him.'"

11. Text *f* here substitutes the following two padas: "They at once came quickly and told the Badashah the news."

12. Texts *f, g* here add the following two padas: "Shah Sikandar came and sat. Kabir was brought before him."

11. Kabir's dark body put to shame [even the beauty of] the god of love. Kabir wore prayer beads and a forehead mark.[13] He had a pleasing voice[14] and clear eyes. Soothing words flowed from his mouth.[15]

12. Then the *kāzī*[16] instructed him: "Offer obeisance in the royal court, brother."[17]

Kabir replied: "What do I know about offering obeisance? Don't you be crazy, *kāzī*."[18]

13. Sikandar said: "If this is the way it is, we will see you go to hell. You have abandoned the true path and taken a bad path. Why is this, Julaha? Who has mislead you?

14. "One gets salvation by following one's own traditional path. Ask both the Hindus and the Turks."[19]

Kabir then spoke these extraordinary words while the whole assembly looked on in stunned silence:[20]

15. "The Hindus and the Turks are the ones who will fall into hell. The *kāzī*s and the mullahs are clumsy fools.[21] I have found salvation through bhakti.[22] I have sung about the virtues of Ram through the guru's grace."

---

13. In text *f* the second pada reads: "On his head there shown *tulachhī* [= *tulasī*] and a forehead mark."

In text *g* the same pada reads: "On his head there shown the guru and Gobinda."

14. In text *d*: "face."

15. In texts *f*, *g*: "When he spoke, his words were nectar."

16. Texts *f*, *g*: "The *kāzī*s and the mullahs."

17. The word *tasalīma* can also imply "a confession." Text *f* has: "'Offer obeisance and then bow your head.'"

18. In this verse, there is a play on the words *divānā* ("court") and *divānā* ("crazy").

In texts *f*, *g*, the last pada reads: "'You have become a little crazy, *kāzī*.'"

19. For this pada, text *f* gives: "'Ask the opinion of both the Vedas and the Puranas.'" This reading is clearly inferior in this context.

20. More literally this may be translated as "the assembly looked on as if dead," as "the assembly looked [at Kabir] as if he were already dead," or as "[Kabir] looked at the assembly as if it were dead."

21. Text *f*: "'The *kāzī*s and the Brahmans are both mistaken.'" Text *g*: "'These *kāzī*s and Brahmans are big fools.'"

22. Text *f*: "'I have come to the bhakti of love.'"

16. "Kabir was faithful to Ram alone. He had no concern for anyone else, even when king and commoners alike were angry at him.

Doha

Kabir said: "If Ram is my protector, no one can kill me. Badashah, I am not afraid.[23] Whatever God does, that is what will be."

Section Eight

1. The *kāzīs* took out their Holy Book and displayed it. While this was going on, the Brahmans broke in: "Remove his prayer beads and forehead mark. Then stone him to death.[1]

2. The *kāzīs* said: "Listen, every one! If a Muslim becomes an infidel, he must be stopped."[2]

Kabir said: "Why don't you think before you act? *You* are the real infidels. *You* are the ones who are going to die.

3. "What sort of a Holy Book is it that permits a cow to be killed? Who orders the sacrifice of goats and chickens?[3] The god of death will crush the chests of all those I see killing living beings.

4. "Kings and commoners alike will fall into hell. Whoever speaks the Name Ram will have no fear."

As he listened, Sikandar got enraged. It was as if someone were pouring an offering of ghee on a sacrificial fire.

5. It was as if someone were twisting the tail of a cobra; as if someone were poking a sleeping lioness;[4] as if someone were stirring up the bonfires of Holi; as if someone had plucked out a leopard's eye.

---

23. Or: "'I do not fear the Badashah.'"

1. In text *g*: "'Look, he has obliterated your dharma. For this have him killed with seven stones.'" Text *f* is similar but slightly defective.

2. In text *f*: "'Then everyone will learn to remain on the proper [path]. A Muslim may not become an infidel.'" Text *g* is quite similar. It is possible that these two padas are also spoken by the Brahmans, but the following padas suggest that Kabir is aiming his reply at the Muslims and the Hindus, one after the other.

3. This pada is the same as *Kabir Bijak, ramainī*, 49.3a.

4. Text *f* here substitutes the following pada: "as if someone had put the torch to a cannon."

6. Sikandar said: "You are a fool not to fear me. Now let's see a true miracle.[5] Tie Kabir's feet and bind him with chains.[6] Drown him in the water of the Ganges."[7]

7. As soon as the order was given, they grabbed Kabir and dropped him into the Ganges at midstream. The chains came loose[8] as he fell into the water. He began to float and did not drown.

8. Full of rage, the demon Sikandar said: "You were saved in the water, but *now* who will save you?"

Then they tied Kabir up and threw him into a house. All around they lit a fire.

9. When Kabir Das repeated to himself "Hari, Hari," the fire became as cool as water. Hari recognized Kabir's compassion. The Ganas and Gandharvas made a rain of flowers.[9]

10. The house burned and the ashes flew up. The gods and men then witnessed a true miracle.[10] Narayan gave Kabir still greater beauty. The god applied a cleansing paste to Kabir's body and washed him with water.

11. Everywhere the people shouted "Hurrah, hurrah." The *kāzīs* and Brahmans got very angry. They said: "This Julaha knows magic arts. Shah Sikandar, you mustn't accept this."

12. When Sikandar heard this, he became still angrier. He said: "Kabir, *now* who are you going to depend on?" The demon Sikandar called for a frenzied elephant. It arrived attacking its own shadow.

13. The elephant had no fear of its mahout. It was specially selected from among all the elephants. It was kept tied up with golden chains. Its fodder was thrown to it from a good distance with a long ladle.[11]

---

5. Text *f*: "'He will have to show me a miracle.'" This text also here adds: "'He should quickly call for God the Protector.'"

6. Text *f* makes it his hands that are tied, text *g* his neck.

7. Texts *f*, *g*: "Throw him from the bank of the Ganges."

8. Texts *f*, *g*: "broke."

9. Text *d*: "Hari made [i.e. showed] compassion to Kabir." This seems to be an example of the copyist-editor of this manuscript "correcting" the text so that it yields a somewhat more logical sense.

10. Text *f*: "Sarangapani protected Kabir."

11. Here *kūṃchī* is a difficult word. Dictionaires give *kūchī*/*kūṃchī* meaning "a bush" or "various kinds of brushes" or "key," and *kūṃchā* meaning "flotsam" or "a grain parcher's long-handled ladle." Text *e* gives *kūṃbhī* (? = *kuṃbhī*, an elephant).

14. Its tusks and goad[12] were covered with gold. Here and there they were studded with diamonds and pearls. If it had gotten loose in the town, it would have killed people or even demolished the fort.

15. It had killed valiant warriors in battle. Bards recited panegyrics about it.[13] Kal Bhairav established his abode on its head.[14] It was worshipped with oil, red minium, and incense.

16. This killer[15] had won a big name for itself by winning battles. When it went out on the road, people sang songs about it. It was always[16] adorned with eighty-four bells. It seemed to be the very likeness of [Airavata, the elephant of] the world of Indra.

17. It was brought and made to attack Kabir, but it fled backward and refused to advance.[17]

Doha

When this elephant arrived like Kal,[18] everyone fled. Kabir had no fear. He stayed there absorbed in the love of Ram.

Section Nine

1. Keshav took the form of a lion in order to frighten the elephant. That is why the elephant did not come any nearer. Keshav also let the elephant driver see the lion. The driver turned the tusker away and made it stand there.

---

12. Possibly: "[as sharp as] goads."

13. Texts *f, g* here insert padas 8.16ab of this edition.

14. The name Kal Bhairav refers to the Shiv in his fierce form as the god of death and destruction. The meaning of this difficult pada is problematic. Dictionaries give "home" (*ghara*) or "abode" as an old meaning of *hara*. The word is, of course, also a name of Shiv. It is also possible that *mathohara* is a variant of *mahāvata* or *mathavāha* (= mahout).

15. Text *f*: "elephant" (*kujari*, = *kuṃjara*).

16. Texts *f, g*: "all."

17. In text *d* these two padas are preceded by the following: "No one had ever seen such an elephant. It was made . . . (?) Kabir" (the meaning of *dheshā* is unclear). In texts *f, g* the two padas of 8.17 are followed by the following: "Then it remained there in the dust, full of anger. Seated in front of the devotee Kabir was a lion."

18. Texts *f, g*: "got angry." Kal may be the god of death or, here more likely, Kal Bhairav. It comes to much the same thing.

2. Afterwards Shah Sikandar saw the lion seated in front of Kabir. He said: "Elephant driver, take the elephant away. A miracle has just occurred.[1]

3. "Kabir, your Ram is the true God. Just this once, please save my life.[2] The *kāzi*s and the mullahs do not understand the inner truth. The Creator has accepted your word."

4. When he saw Sikandar's humility, Kabir said: "Raghuvir protects all those who take refuge at his feet. Sikandar, if you had become afraid just now,[3] then Hari certainly would have destroyed you."[4]

5. No bad feeling entered Kabir's heart. That is why the demon Sikandar was not punished. A virtuous person will assume that someone's evil intention is in fact a good one.[5]

6. If a person keeps his emotion fixed on Hari, none of his efforts will fail. Anyone who sees what Hari has done, Hari will make that person his own.

7. Then Keshav disappeared. The demon Sikandar humbly grabbed Kabir's feet and said: "Ask me for gold. Ask me for silver. Ask me for priceless fabrics.

8. "Ask me for villages, districts, or horses. Whatever is given to you will not be enough."

Kabir said: "I don't ask for material things. Such things devour[6] everyone, king and commoners alike.

---

1. Text *f*: "'We have seen, Kabir, your Ram.'"

2. Texts *f*, *g* invert the first padas. Text *f* omits the following two padas.

3. Texts *f*, *g*: "Don't be afraid. Raghuvir will protect you. If, Sikandar, you had not become afraid at this instant . . .'"

4. Text *f*: "'Because of your hatred for the *sants*, Hari would have destroyed you.'"
Here texts *f*, *g* add four padas similar to 9.6cdab. They may be translated as follows: "'Any person who has seen what Hari has done, Hari will make that person his own. Whoever's heart, words, and actions belong to Hari [Text *g*: "Whoever keeps faith in Hari"] will not have any of his efforts fail.'" It is probable that this is narration, not the words of Kabir.

5. Text *g* here adds the following four padas: "The *kāzī*s and Brahmans did not know your inner truth. The Creator has accepted your word. Whoever scorns the devotees will fall into the Kumbhi Hell." The first two padas are similar to 9.3cd and fit better there.

6. Texts *f*, *g*: "lead astray."

9. "Whoever asks for things is not a devotee. Whoever keeps his mind firm is God's own devotee."

Joining his hands in respect, Kabir[7] bowed his head. Then the devotee returned home.

10. Wherever there is distress, Hari removes it. The *kāzī*s and Brahmans[8] were shown to be false.[9] Kabir returned to his own house. By the grace of the guru,[10] Kabir's body became immortal.

11. Then people began to come to see Kabir again. The *sant*s and devotees met and asked him what had happened.

Laughing, Kabir said:[11] "Raghuvir protects those who take refuge at his feet.

12. "When the Badashah gave me a test, he caused no fear in my heart.[12] Nobody can kill someone who has the strength of the devotees.[13]

13. "Bhakti to Hari destroys millions of sins.[14] Hari comes running for his devotees. Ram never protects those who stay aloof from the devotees.

14. "Those who scorn the devotees will, on account of their sins, fall into the Kumbhi Hell.[15] The god of death will slit the throats[16] of those who deceive the devotees.

---

7. Possibly it is Sikandar who does this.

8. Texts *d, g*: "mullahs."

9. Text *f* places these two padas after 9.12b. Text *g* indents them here and repeats them at 9.12b.

10. Here, and possibly elsewhere in the text, "guru" seems to imply a divine "satguru" than a human guru.

11. Texts *a, g*: "Kabir said: 'Hari, Hari.'"

12. Texts *f, g* here add the following padas: "Wherever there is distress, Hari relieves it. The *kāzī*s and the Brahmans were shown to be false." See also 9.10ab.

13. Text *f*: "'Wherever the devotee has the strength of the Lord, no one can kill him.'"

14. Texts *d, f, g* have "devotee" (*bhagata*/*bhakta*) for *bhakti*. This may be translated either as "For the devotee, Hari destroys millions of sins" or "The devotee of Hari destroys millions of sins."

15. Texts *d, g* (indented): "Those who scorn the devotees will fall into the Kumbhipak Hell." This is a virtual repeat of 9.7ab.

16. Text *f*: "'They will be living beings who attain an eternal hell.'" Text *g*: "'The god of death will crush their chests.'"

15. "I see Ram in all living beings. Without bhakti[17] to Hari, no work can prosper. I recognized the guru and Gobinda through devotion.[18] That is why Sikandar could do nothing to me."[19]

Doha

Kabir was submerged in the water and burned in the fire, but his body was not destroyed. When he was to be crushed by the elephant, Hari saved him. Kabir had no fear.[20]

Section Ten

1. In this way Kabir was saved. In every situation Hari became his protector. Then the Brahmans came together[1] and discussed their problem: "This Julaha is giving us too much trouble."

2. They made a peculiar conspiracy. They looked to their own interests in a deceitful manner. They shaved the heads of four Brahmans and had them each put on a disguise of prayer beads and a forehead mark.

3. They were given instructions and sent off secretly: "Invite the devotees from everywhere. Give them a letter in Kabir's name in all the villages up to a radius of eighty *kos*.[2]

4. "You should go early on the ninth day[3] in the first half of the month of Magh."

---

17. Text *d* : "the devotees "

18. Texts *f, g*: "'I recognized the guru and Gobinda in the devotees.'"

19. Here text *f* adds the following two padas: "'When both the devotees and the Lord became helpers, even a hot wind could not come near.'"

Here text *g* adds the following two padas: "'Hari gives refuge to those who are grounded in devotion to Ram.'"

20. Texts *d, f, g*: " . . . The fearless Kabir Das."

1. Text *g*: "The frightened Brahmans."

2. Texts *f*: "a hundred" or "hundreds" of *kos*. A *kos* is equal to about two miles or 3.2 kilometers. The reading *aisī* (texts *a, c*) seems to be a mistake for *asī*.

3. Text *f*: "'Arrive at my door on the eleventh day in the first half of the month of Magh . . .'" This text omits the second two padas and hence does not mention Basant Panchami.

If they set off on the ninth of the first (dark) half of Magh (January-February), this was nine days before Basant Panchami (the fifth day of the light half of Magh). These calculations

They gave the false letter to everyone. It said: "Come quickly on Basant Panchami.

5. "Kabir Das has arranged a feast. He is expecting all the *sant*s to come."
The *sant*s accepted the letter, raising it to their foreheads. Not one of them recognized the heretical disguise of the Brahmans.[4]

6. This is how the Brahmans carried out their conspiracy. They returned home happy at heart. Afterwards, all the devotees of Hari set off for Kabir's as if they were the gathering clouds of the rainy season.[5]

7. About twenty pandits[6] were writing down [the names of those who arrived]. About twenty were seated giving instruction. For twenty days people kept on arriving.[7] Ananta-das is singing the praises of this event.[8]

8. Even going to the front, no one could count how many had come. Everyone assembled on the bank of the Ganges. Hearing this, Kabir stayed hidden as all the *sant*s arrived.[9]

---

use the Samvat rather than the Vikrami calendar. In any case, the nine days between the two dates of the ninth of the first fortnight and the fifth of the second fortnight of Magh do not seem to be sufficient. The reading of the text *f* is perhaps better but implies the use of the Vikrami calendar that is normally used in the south and not the north. See above, pp. 35-37.

4. Text *f*: "All the *sants* set off for Kabir's."

5. Texts *a, g* give *pāvaka ruti* ("hot season"). This is possible but less appropriate. The final two padas are not found in text *f*.

6. Texts *f, g*: "Brahmans." The terms *bīsaka* (texts *a, b, c, d*) and *bīsa yeka* (text *g*) both signify "about twenty."

7. This is impossible if the inviting Brahmans were sent off nine days before the feast and the feast lasted five days (10.10).

8. Texts *f, g* here add two padas and a full doha. All this may be translated as follows: "When Ram Himself is on one's side, who can destroy one's work? All the Brahmans engaged in deceit together. Their hearts were obsessed with hatred. Ram is Kabir's helper. Even now the blind fools do not understand this."

9. Text *d*: "He went in front and said nothing." Text *g*: "Coming down in front, he did nothing."

Text *f* omits this verse and the next and substitutes two other verses (135, 136). Text *g* includes versions of the last two padas of the first verse (135) and the first two padas of the second (136) as an indented text, added after 10.9b. The two verses read: "All the devotees came singing his praises: 'Where can we take Kabir's darshan?' Kabir left the door of his house and then went away. Keshav took Kabir's form. He came before each devotee. He praised them and had camping places given to each. He did whatever they told him. Before each devotee . . . [?]."

9. Then Keshav took charge of the situation. He made himself be recognized as[10] innumerable forms of Kabir. At each camp site he respectfully received the people. He gave to each whatever was asked for.

10. In some places they danced and sang.[11] No one realized what Hari had done.[12] For five days Hari performed this miracle. Afterwards he gave gifts of cloth to the *sants*.[13]

11. Showing respect to all, Hari bid them farewell. The King of the Three Worlds was compassionate.[14] Kabir himself joined in the crowd and found happiness. He felt that his life and birth had been made fruitful.

12. Because of Ram, Kabir's difficulties were always resolved. For the third time,[15] the Brahmans ended up vexed.[16]

When one year had passed, Hari[17] sent an *apsarā*.

13. He said: "Go and see whether you can make Kabir your husband. He lives in Banaras, [the city] of Niranjan.[18] Use any trick you like to

---

10. Text *d*: "He made himself [take] . . ." See also the note to verse 8.9.

11. Texts *f, g*: "Some places some danced, some places some sang."

12. Also possible: "No one knows the ways of Hari." Text *f* has "secret" (*bheda*) instead of "that done" or "ways" (*chirata/charita*).

13. Texts *f, g* here add the following two padas (indented in *g*): "The feast preserved and even increased his greatness. Everyone [text *g*: "In this way"] said: 'Praise be, praise be to Kabir.'"

14. These two padas are not found in text *f* and are indented in text *g*.

15. Text *g*: "For the fourth time." The reference seems to be to the feeding of the Brahmans, the saving of the *paṇḍā* of Jagannath, the encounter with Sikandar, and the just described unexpected feast. Presumably the texts that read "For the third time" take the first two of these episodes as one.

16. Here texts *f, g* add two padas and a complete doha, all indented in *g*. These may be translated as follows: "What profit will result from attibuting faults to one whose work is done by Hari himself [text *g*: "whom Hari himself protects"]? The Brahmans were all astonished. The feast was a success. Hari always accompanies Kabir, like a cow accompanies a calf." Here the doha apparently serves to end the episode.

17. Text *f*: "Indra."

18. It seems that Niranjan is here a name of Shiv, since Shiv is the god of Banaras. In early *sant* usage, however, Niranjan generally refers to *nirguṇ* brahman. This latter sense is roughly the one found in a pada of the Dadu Panthi recension of the present text added after verse 12.16. In later Kabir Panthi usage Niranjan becomes a synonym of the demiurge Kal.

get him to embrace you." The Lord gave her these instructions several times.[19]

14. The *apsarā* arrived in Banaras and appeared before Kabir. It was as if the *apsarā* Rambha had come to visit Sukh-dev.[20] No one could equal her beauty, and she spoke with a sweet voice.

15. When she directed her darting gaze, it seemed as if she were a frightened deer wandering about in a forest.[21] When anyone looked at her, she stole his heart. Never mind men's, even Brahma's resistance collapsed.[22]

Doha

Kabir kept control of his five senses. He recognized his own essence.[23] Ananta-das is singing about Kabir, the beloved of Hari.

Section Eleven

1. Praise be to Kabir, who did not satisfy the wishes [of the *apsarā*].[1] He tasted only the nectar of Hari's lotus feet.[2] The *apsarā* made amorous gestures as she spoke, but Kabir's mind never wavered.

Another possible translation of the first pada of this verse is: "He, [the devotee] of Niranjan lives in Banaras.

The first two padas of this verse are not found in text *f*.

Texts *d, g* have the somewhat easier reading: "is my own devotee," in place of "of Niranjan."

19. Texts *f, g* invert these two final padas.

20. Dictionaries identify Sukh-dev with the legendary sage Shuk-dev. For this pada texts *f, g* give: "Rambha arrived from heaven."

21. In texts *f* the second pada reads: "Brahma became overwhelmed with embarrassment."

Text *g*: "It seemed as if Brahma and the other (gods) would be overcome with embarrassment."

22. These two padas are not found in text *f*.

23. Texts *f, g*: "Kabir recognized the *sant* in himself [?]."

1. Also possible: " . . . who did not keep his own mind [on the *apsarā*]."

Texts *f, g*: "who keeps his mind firm" (*man diḍha rāshai*).

This is one of several passages in this chapter in which the Niranjani Panthi recension has the *lectio difficilior* or "more difficult reading" that may well be historically earlier than the simpler reading of the Dadu Panthi recension.

2. Text *g*: "He speaks with his mind fixed on the lotus feet of Hari."

2. Kabir said: "How can you and I have relations? Mother, fire, and water do not mix. If Raghunath sent you, you have come to give me prestige.

3. "My modest name is of a low-caste.[3] You go about where there are kings and princes. There one has tumeric powder, musk mixed with saffron, camphor, the scent *jubād*, extract of aloe wood, and the scents *phūlav*, and so forth.[4]

4. "All pleasures can be enjoyed at the king's palace.[5] How can a stone absorb water?"[6]

The *apsarā* said: "Kabir, you are keeping your gaze too low. Take a good look at my beauty.

5. "No matter how hard they try, no one is able to win me. Yet I have come to you of my own free will. I cannot be won even by making a pilgrimage to Kalanjar in the month of Kartik, to Prayag in Magh or to Nimashar in Phagun.[7]

6. "For my sake some go to the Ganges to celebrate Ganga Dashahara; for my sake some commit religious suicide at Kashi; for my sake some go to the god of Kedar Mountain. Even so, my Lord, I have come to you of my own free will.

7. "For my sake some bathe in countless holy bathing places; some die suffocated in the smoke [of penance fires]; some go practice asceticism in the Himalayas. Even then, this *apsarā* is not pleased with any of them.

---

3. The word *kamīna* can signify "a man of low-caste" or, as an adjective, "low, insignificant." The reading of text *f* is simpler: "'My birth was in a modest caste.'" This can be taken as another case in which the Niranjani Panthi recension has the *lectio difficilior*.

4. The list contains several rather unusual words. Texts *f, g* give a simpler reading: "'Aloe wood [*agara*], camphor, sandalwood, musk: all enjoyments are found in the fortresses of kings [text *g* better interpreted as "all enjoyments are fulfilled at the king's"].'" This is a particularly clear example of the Niranjani Panthi recension having the *lectio difficilior*.

5. Here text *f* (and *g* indented) adds: "'If you came to my house, what would happen? My caste is Julaha; my name is Kabir. You and I have no common substance. Mother, don't argue with me.'"

6. Here text *f* (and *g* indented) adds: "'How can fire and water mix? Mother, in front of you I am as if a child.'"

7. The different readings for the second half of this verse are quite varied and do not all make clear sense. Kalanjar is a famous site in Bundelkhand, Nimashar (Sanskrit Naimisharanya) is a sacred site in Sitapur District of Uttar Pradesh. Prayag is of course Allahabad. Pilgrimages to these three places are recommended in the *Mahabharata*, the Puranas and other texts.

8. "Unless you enjoy me, your birth[8] will have been in vain. Accept only this much of my proposition: don't keep me for many days, but only for a few."

9. Kabir then spoke in order to make her understand: "Listen, I ask you mother. Why have you come from heaven?[9] Why do you desire me?[10]

10. "If you sit close to me, I will die of shame. If I look down [at my feet],[11] my mind will not waver. Pardon me, pardon me! I beg you! If I think about you, it will be my death.[12]

11. "How can I satisfy everyone's request? I would soon be divided up into pieces. I will not take your hand, mother. My lord Ram would get angry.[13]

12. "To me your eyes and words seem like poison. My life is bound to Hari. Whoever gratifies your hopes is certain to make his home in hell.[14]

13. "Any man who falls in love with you will fall into the river of worldly existence and never reach the other shore.

"[It is like the story of] the woman drawing water at the well while leaving her child at home.[15] There the mongoose killed a snake and went [to the door with blood on its face to wait for the child's mother].

---

8. Texts *f, g*: "wisdom."

9. Text *f*: "'Because of what problem in heaven have you come to earth?'" Text *g* is similar.

10. Text *f*: "'Explain that to me.'" Text *g*: "'I am a very modest Julaha.'"

11. Possibly: "'If you look down [in my direction]. . . . '"

12. Text *f* omits this verse and substitutes the following ten padas:
"The bewitching *apsarā* said: 'I have no such motive. I have come to make you my husband.' Kabir replied: My caste is Julaha. You have no reason to associate with me. From sitting close to me you will die of shame. Looking down, you have not wavered, but to me your eyes and words seem like poison, mother. Your mind is too fickle. Your light appears [text *g*: "eyes look"] bearing the form of Kam. Your allure [text *g*: "essence"] is nothing to me.'" Some of this translation is somewhat tentative. Text *g* gives the first two padas of the corrected text followed by eight padas similar to those of text *f*.

13. The second two padas are not found in texts *f, g*. Texts *c, d* have "Kharari" in place of "Ram."

14. This verse is not found in texts *f, g*.

15. This story is found in the *Panchatantra*, book 5. See the edition of N. R. Acharya [1959: 320-21].

14. "Taking the water pot from her head, she threw it [at the mongoose thinking it had bitten the child]. Afterwards she had to bite her tongue in repentance. In a similar way, whoever associates with you will have to repent in the end.[16]

15. "There was once a black snake in a box. A mouse thought there was sweet food in it. Biting through the box, it entered it. The snake swallowed the mouse and went out through the hole.

16. "This is what will happen to whoever associates with you. Mother, give up hope of convincing me. Isn't there anyone for you in heaven?"[17]

Doha

No matter what she tried, she failed.[18] Kabir never wavered. The *apsarā* went home, and the devotee kept his resolve.

Section Twelve

1. The *apsarā* went and spoke to Hari:[1] "I couldn't get any control over Kabir. I wanted to bewitch him completely, but I was unable to plumb his great depth.[2]

2. "If the sun were to rise in the west, if the mountain were to tremble, if fire[3] were to become cold, if the polar star were to move to the south,[4] even then Kabir wouldn't lose his wisdom.

---

16. Texts *f, g*: "'Thus will be the condition of whoever falls in love [text *g*: "associates"] with you.'"

17. Here text *f* adds a chaupai somewhat similar to the following doha: "Even after all her efforts, she failed. Kabir did not look at her an instant. She shot all her arrows of looks and words. Not one came close to Kabir."

18. Text *f*: "The *apsarā* did her all."

1. Text *f* alone: "Indra."

2. In text *f, g* the second two padas read: "'Making a great deal of effort, I failed. Murari alone dwells in Kabir's heart [text *g*: "Kabir's heart, words and deeds are true."].'"

3. The readings *āghā, āghāsa*, and so forth seem to be unusual *tadbhava* forms of *āg* or *agni*. Text *f* gives an easier *agani* and text *g agni*.

4. Texts *f, g*: "west." The context clearly shows that this is a mistake rather than a more difficult reading.

3. "He regards the pleasures of Maya as if they were merely straw. In the practice of yoga, he excels even Gorakh."

Then Keshav accepted Kabir as His own. He came and gave His darshan to Kabir.

4. Hari showed himself to Kabir with His conch, discus, club, and lotus. He was adorned with the Kaustubh jewel and yellow robes. He displayed the mark of Bhrigu's foot on His chest and was sitting on His eagle Garuda. The tiara on His head dazzled anyone who saw it.[5]

5. Earrings hung from his ears. His eyes were large. He had four arms and wore a Vaijayanti garland. From head to foot His dark body was beautiful. His teeth were like buds of white flowers or diamonds.[6]

6. Around His neck was a double string of elephant pearls. This is the way He dwells in His heaven.[7] Seeing Him, Kabir's body was soothed. Kabir stayed there holding His lotus feet.

7. Hari tried to arouse in Kabir desire for wealth.[8] He told him about the pleasures of the three worlds: "Ask! Ask! Whatever you ask for I will give, whatever you desire.[9]

---

5. In places of this verse and the following one-and-one-half verses, texts *f, g* read as follows:

"Inside and outside He has the nature of light. His essence is indestructible, unattainable, incomparable. In every hair there is the light of infinite suns, the brightness of infinite lighting flashes.

"The streams of His splendor fill everything. The devotee of the Lord plays among them [text *g*: "His splendor is infinite; it has no end anywhere. Kabir sees this splendor within and without.] Tell me. Whose glory is it that appears? Whatever exists on the earth arises and fades away. Only Hari displays the glory of Hari. Who else shows a splendor near to his? [In this last pada text *g* gives a different reading whose sense is not clear].

"Kabir says: 'His splendor is infinite, as if a multitude of suns had arisen. The beautiful women who awoke with her husband saw this miracle.' [This last verse is the same as *Kabir Granthavali, sākhī* 5.1. A common interpretation is that the husband is brahman and the wife the atman].

"His greatness cannot be told in words, but in one's heart one obtains great joy."

6. This verse, like the previous one, is not found in texts *f, g*.

7. The first two padas, like the previous two verses, are not found in texts *f, g*.

8. Text *a* has *saṃgati* that may mean either "sexual relations" or "His company [in heaven]." Text *g* has *māyā*.

Text *f* gives a somewhat different reading for the pada: "Ram tried to produce in Kabir desire for love."

9. These two padas are not found in text *f*. Text *g* indents them.

8. "If you tell me to, then I will make you the lord of the earth. I will preserve, unshaken, the royal umbrella over your head. If you tell me to, I will sit you in the world of Indra. I will keep you there forever and never turn you out.

9. "If you tell me to, I will give you all[10] the miraculous powers: the power of surviving in fire, the power of surviving in earth, the power of flying in air, the power of surviving in water.[11] If you tell me to, I will tell you the True Word. Or leave this aside, and I will tell about other things.

10. "[I will give you the power to] throw aside one body and take up another body.[12] I will give you the eight *siddhis* and the nine *nidhis*.[13] I, together with the goddess Kamala, will serve at your feet."

11. Kabir said: "Listen, Giver of Bliss. I will request nothing, King of the Three Worlds. I have little wisdom. I don't know what to request. How can I recognize the ocean of pleasures?[14]

12. "How can an ant lift up a mountain? How can a firefly outshine the moon? When a peacock flies up it cannot go high in the sky. How can the ocean be held in one's cupped hands?

13. "When a child reaches for a snake, his mother stops him from grabbing it.[15] When a child smears himself with excrement, his mother takes care of him.[16]

---

10. Texts *b, c, d*: "four."

11. In somewhat different order and using somewhat different terms, all texts give the same four powers. These four terms, each referring to a power over a different element, do not, to my knowledge, appear in other texts.

Text *f* here inserts two padas similar in sense (but not wording) to padas 12.10ab (which do not appear in text *f*): "'You can make your own body big. You can play in new bodies at every instant.'"

12. These two padas are not found in text *f*. At the beginning of the next pada texts *f, g, h* add: "'If you tell me to.'"

13. The well-known eight *siddhis* are the magical powers of making oneself large, small, and so forth. The nine *nidhis* (treasures) of the god Kuber include Padma, Mahapadma, Shankha, Makara, Kachchhapa, Mukunda, Nanda, Nila, Kharva. For the *siddhis*, see M. Eliade [1969: 85-90, 383-84].

14. Text *f* omits the last two padas, although the third pada does appear after 12.14d.

15. Texts *f, g*: "'When a child puts his hand in the fire, then his mother takes care of it.'"

16. The last two padas are not found in text *d, f*.

14. "[If a child has] a coin, [his mother] gives him sugar and grabs [the coin]. She guides the child's innocent mind.[17] I don't know how to say what is good and what is not good. That's how my simple mind is."[18]

15. Hearing all this, Keshav was delighted. Praise be to Kabir, whose heart never wavered.[19] Then Hari put His four hands on Kabir's head.[20] He made Kabir unaging, immortal, and indestructible.[21]

16. He gave His grace to Kabir and took away all his pains.[22] The Lord of the Three Worlds then proceeded to His heaven.[23]

Doha

Nirguṇ and *saguṇ* are one.[24] In all bodies It remains inherent. Like the waves of the ocean, It assumes a form and then rejoins Its source.

---

17. The translation of the second pada is somewhat tentative.

18. Text *f* omits the third pada. Text *g* inverts the third and fourth padas. Text *f* here adds the following pada: "'What can I ask for? I have very little wisdom.'"

Texts *f, g* then add the following two padas (indented and inverted in *g*): "'You, Dweller in All Bodies, know everything. Except for [the pleasure of serving at your] feet, whatever one might request is foolish.'"

19. Texts *f, g*: "Then Keshav took Kabir as His own. He knew Kabir to be a devotee and gave him everything [text *g*: "Praise be to Kabir! You kept your heart firm"]."

20. In text *f* the third pada reads: "Hari made Kabir's body of the same essence as His own."

21. Text *g* inverts the first and second lines of this verse.

22. Texts *f, g*: "He gave Kabir fearlessness and took away all the pleasures [text *g*: "pains"]."

23. Texts *f, g* substitutes: "In this way Hari gave salvation to the devotee Kabir."

Texts *f, g* then add the following two padas: "*Nirguṇ* Brahman is Niranjan and Nath. He, having joined with Kabir, is indeed [text *g* "not"] his companion."

In the text *d* the two padas of this half verse are preceded by the following two padas (thus making a full verse): "'Kabir, your devotion is true. You have remained apart from delusion and Maya.'"

24. Text *f*: "*Nirguṇ* is unstained by qualities." Text *g*: "*Nirguṇ* brahman is unperceivable."

Section Thirteen

1. In his childhood, Kabir was lost in illusion.[1] He became truly conscious from the age of twenty. Up to the age of one hundred,[2] he practiced bhakti. After that he found salvation.

2. He displayed a miracle on the occasion of his death. He planned to die at Magahar.

Kabir said: "Everyone says that dying in Kashi leads to salvation[3] and that anyone who dies at Magahar will be reborn as an ass.

3. "Kashi destroys everyone's sins, but I will preserve Hari's glory [by finding salvation at Magahar]."

The Hindus and the Turks [who followed Kabir each] formed a band. One band said: "You should burn him." The other band said: "You should bury him."

4. They ordered thirty-two loads of flowers. A bed of flowers was made under and over him.[4] All the *sant*s came together to dance and sing.[5] They clapped,[6] beat drums, and blew conches.[7]

---

1. Text *f*: "Kabir spent twelve years in childhood."

2. This may also mean: "For a hundred [more] years." This would make a total of 120 years before he found salvation. In the Kabir Panth, he is traditionally given a life-span of 120 or more years.

3. Texts *f*, *g*: "Everyone goes to Kashi for salvation."

4. Text *f*: "They spread out the flowers and made a bed for him in them. How did the Hindus and Turks come to quarrel?"

Here texts *f*, *g* add the following two padas: "One said: 'We will bury him.' One said: 'We will burn him.' Each thought according to his own religion."

5. Note that the *sant*s here seem to be separate from both the Hindus and the Turks.

6. The word *tāla* can also refer to a kind of musical instrument.

7. Here texts *f*, *g* add the following two padas: "From both sides they came to see. They found flowers but did not find Kabir."

Text *f* alone then adds two padas that repeat 13.4cd: "All the *sant*s came together and sang. They clapped, beat drums and blew conches."

5. When Kabir became an immortal, he did not abandon his body. Kabir left[8] this world taking his body with him. The devotees were astonished. When they saw that the flowers[9] [were all that remained], they went home.

6. When some of them heard what had happened, they refused to eat any food. Others felt terrible grief.[10] Without Kabir there was darkness in Kashi, as when there is no moon one sees the stars alone.[11]

7. It was as if the groom were missing from the groom's procession, as if a feast were spoiled because there was no ghee.[12] It was as if one's body got dirty because one had no clothes. This is how desolate Kashi was without Kabir.[13]

8. Wherever Kabir went, his fame multiplied. Shiv and Brahma[14] went forth to greet Kabir. Indra, the lord of the gods, got up from his throne and gave it to Kabir.

---

8. The reading *bhayau* ("became") of texts *a, b, c, e* seems inferior in sense.

9. The word *phūla* can also mean "ashes."

10. Text *f*: "The servant *sants* did not eat any food.. Being separated from Kabir, they felt terrible grief."

Text *g* (second pada only): "Others, in their hearts, felt terrible grief."

11. Text *f*: "Without the moon, the stars do not appear so beautiful."

Text *f* and text *g* (indented) here add the following two padas: "Without a lamp a temple does not appear so beautiful. Without Kabir, who is there in Kashi?"

12. Text *f*: "What is food without ghee?" Text *g*: "It was as if one eats food without ghee." Text *h*: "It was as when food is nothing without ghee."

13. The last two padas are not found in texts *f, g*. Texts *f* and *g* (indented) here add the following fourteen padas:

"In the world of Indra there was great excitement. The thirty-three gods came for the miraculous event [Text *g*: "came together to take Kabir's darshan"]. They performed a great deal of worship, saying: 'Where can we find this devotee of Hari?'

"Brahma said: 'I have had great good fortune. I have waited day and night for the darshan of this *sant*. You have your family in the world of Brahma. Your darshan was hard to obtain. Be gracious!'

"Vishnu said: 'Take heaven. Everything there is given to you. All wealth and luxuries, together with the goddess Shri herself are yours. Everything is available before you.'

"The devotees of Hari look only towards Hari [Text *g*: "don't want any distance from Hari"]. They know brahman alone to be true."

14. Text *f* adds "Vishnu."

9. Vishnu said: "My heaven is yours. Live here forever. This is my wish." The Siddhas showed their great love for Kabir. Kuber offered him his treasures.

10. Sanak and the other sages came together and sat with Kabir. Narad's presence increased their pleasure still more.[15] How can I express it? Vishnu, the Conqueror of All Bliss, was present everywhere in bodily form.[16]

11. Hari Himself sang His own praises. By giving fame to the devotees, he increased love everywhere.[17] He joined together with the devotees and wandered about. The Lord spoke through the bodies of the devotees.[18]

12. I am telling all this story of Yours. By singing and listening to it, salvation will become one's servant.[19] If any man or woman sings it, they will spontaneously find bliss.[20]

13. One's diseases will be destroyed. All one's thirsts will be removed.[21] Wisdom and bhakti will arise in one's heart. He who has no knowledge will obtain knowledge. If you sing about Kabir's virtues with enthusiasm, [all this will be yours].[22]

---

15. These two padas are not found in text *f*. Text *g* indents them.

16. The idea seems to be that Vishnu, as the Absolute, took the form of all the other gods to enjoy Kabir's company, although Kabir himself is also finally an aspect of Vishnu. For the translation I have used the reading *biyāpī* from Callewaert's text *g*.

17. These two padas are not found in text *f*. They are indented in text *g*.

18. Text *f*: "And being in the bodies of the devotees, He spoke." Text *g*: "And He spoke in the body of each devotee."

Here texts *f*, *g* add the following two padas: "He sang His own fame to the devotees. Giving fame to the devotee, He increased love everywhere."

19. Texts *c*, *d*: "mine." These two padas are not found in texts *f*, *g*.

20. Text *f*: ". . . they will become pure and obtain the highest abode." Text *g*: ". . . with certainty they will obtain the highest abode."

21. Text *f*: "Error will be destroyed. All karma will be removed." Text *g*: "Disease will be destroyed. All pains will be removed."

22. The last two padas are not found in text *f*. They are indented in text *g*.

14. Kabir is a part of the Creator. He descended to earth[23] to practice bhakti. Kabir meditated on *nirguṇ* brahman. That is how he crossed to the other shore of the ocean of worldly existence.

15. *Saguṇ* bhakti cannot make our doubts flee as long as our minds are not attached to *nirguṇ*. Hari, how can I describe Your virtues. Singing about them, my heart is kept free from passion.[24]

16. If the Himalayas were burnt and made into ink, if eighteen *bhārs*[25] of pens were brought, if an ink pot were made of the seven seas, if the whole earth were made of paper,[26]

17. And if Sharada[27] were to write them all down, one would still not come to the end [of these virtues].[28] What can Ananta-das say to sing them all?[29]

Doha

What has Ananta-das been able to tell?[30] Hari's story has no end.[31] Through the kindness of the Satguru, I have told some of Kabir's story.

---

23. The phrase *pahaumī avatarā* obviously suggests the decidedly *saguṇ* idea of Kabir being an avatar of Hari-Vishnu.

24. The word *bhikta* seems to be equivalent to *virakta*. Texts *d, h*: "Singing them my heart crosses the wheel [of worldly existence]."
Text *f* omits this verse. It is indented in text *g*.

25. A *bhār* is an old unit of weight equal to twenty *paserīs*. One *paserī* equals five *sers*. One *ser* equals about one kilogram. Thus, eighteen *bhārs* equal about 1,800 kilograms.

26. The texts *f, g* invert the last two padas.

27. Sharada is the Hindu goddess of learning, often called Sarasvati.

28. Text *f*: "Even then one would not come to the end of the virtues of Hari" (No mention of Sharada).
Text *g*: "Even then one would not come to the end of writing the virtues of Hari."
The basic trope of this and previous verse can be traced back at least as far as a similar verse in the *Mahimnastava* (Brown 1983: verse 1 appendix) of about the twelfth century. The trope also appears in a verse attributed to Kabir himself in *Kabir Granthavali, sākhī* 38.5 (Kabir 1969) and *Adi Granth, saloku* 81 (Kabir 1966).

29. Texts *f, g*: "Ananta-das is singing to that glory."

30. Texts *d, f, g*: "Ananta-das has told the story."

31. Texts *f, g*: " . . . but the virtues are infinite, limitless."

CHAPTER 6

AN EDITION OF ANANTA-DAS'S *KABIR PARACHAI* (NIRANJANI PANTHI RECENSION)

Section One[1]

कासी बसै जुलाहा ऐक ।
　　हरि भगतन[2] की पकडी टेक ॥
बहुत[3] दिन साकत[4] मैं गईया ।
　　अब हरि का गुण ले निरबहीया ॥ 1

1. This section is not found in texts *f, g,* nor in other manuscripts of the Dadu Panthi recension.

2. Text *d* alone: सुमरण.

3. Text *a*: बहौतक. Text *b*: बहूत. Texts *c, d, e*: बहुत.

4. Text *a*: साषत. Texts *b, c, d, e*: साकत.

बिधनां बांणी बोलै यूं ।
बैष्नौं बिनां न दरसण द्यूं ॥
जे तूं माला तिलक बणांवै ।
तोर हमारा दरसण[5] पावै ॥ 2

मुसलमांन हमारी जाती ।
माला पांऊं कैसी भांती ॥
भीतौ[6] बांणी बोल्या ऐह ।
रांमांनंद पैं दछ्या[7] लेह ॥ 3

रांमांनंद न देषै मोही ।
कैसैं दछ्या पांऊं सोई ॥
राति बसौ गैला मैं जाई ।
सेवग सहत वै निकसैं आई[8] ॥ 4

---

5. Text *d*: तौ तूं दरसन हमरा. Texts *b, c, e* give close variants of the reading of text as given above.

6. Texts *a, b, c*: भीतौ. Text *d*: बहुयौं. Text *e*: मीतौ.

7. In the microfilm copy of text *a*, only the द is visible. The word appears again in the following verse. Text *b* (?): दच्छा. Text *c*: दषा. Text *d*: सिछ्या. Text *e*: दच्छया.

8. These two padas are not found in text *d*.

राति बस्यौ गैला मैं जाई ।
रांम कह्या अरु भेट्या पाई ॥
जन कै हिरदै बढ्या[9] उछावा ।
कबीर अपनैं घरि उठि आवा ॥ 5

माला लीन्ही[10] तिलक बणाया ।
कबीर करै[11] संतन का भाया ॥
लोकजात्रा दरसण आवै[12] ।
दास कबीर राम गुण गावै[13] ॥ 6

कुटंब सजन समधी[14] मिल रोवैं ।
बिकल भयौ काहे घर षोवै ॥
मका मदीना हमारा[15] साजा ।
कलमां रोजा और निवाजा ॥ 7

---

9. Texts *a, b, e*: बढ्या. Text *c*: बढ्यौ. Text *d*: ब्रह्म.

10. Text *a*: लीन्ही. Texts *b, c, e*: लीनी. Text *d*: पहरी.

11. Text *d* alone omits करै.

12. Text *a*: दरसण पावै. Text *b*: दरसन पावै. Text *c*: दरस जन आवै. Text *e*: दरसन आवै.

13. Text *d* omits the last two padas.

14. Text *d* alone संबंधी.

15. Text *d* alone हीरौ.

तब कबीर कै लागी झाला[16] ।
माथै तिलक गुदी परि माला ॥
रे कबीर तूं किन भरमाया ।
यह पांषंड कहां तैं ल्याया ॥ 8

अपनी राह चल्यां गति होई ।
हींदू तुरक बूझि लै दोई ॥
अचंभा भया सकल संसारा ।
रांमांनंद लग ई[17] पुकारा ॥ 9

मुसलमांन जुलाहा ऐक ।
हरि भगतन[18] का पहरया भेष ॥
किरषि[19] करै[20] उन हूं[21] कूं देई ।
बूझ्यां नांव तुम्हारा लेई ॥ 10

---

16. Texts *a, c, e*: डाला. Text *b*: डीला. Text *d*: झाला.

17. Text *a*: ई. Texts *b, c, e*: गई. Text *d*: लई.

18. Text *a*: भगातन. Text *b* (?), *c*: भगतन. Text *d*: भगतनि. Text *e*: भगतिन

19. Text *a* seems to read either किरुx or किसx with the last syllable not visible on the microfilm copy. Texts *b, e*: किरषि. Text *c*: किर्षि. Text *d*: किर (Is the प of the following पकडै actually a mistake for ष?). Other manuscripts give किरष, कीरत, किरति, and किरतन.

20. Texts *a, b, c*: करै. Text *d*: पकडै. Text *e* omits this word.

21. Texts *a, d, e*: हूं. Text *b*: हू. Text *c*: ही.

तब रांमांनंद तुरत बुलाया[22] ।
    आगैं पीछैं परदा द्याया ॥
रे[23] कहि माला कब दीनी तोही ।
    अब तूं[24] नांव हमारा लेई[25] ॥ 11

हम राति बैसे गैला मैं जाई ।
    सेवग सहत तुम निकसे आई ॥
रांम कह्यां अरु भेट्या पाऊ ।
    हमैं कह्या अरु तुमहैं कहाऊ ॥ 12

तब हूं अपनैं घरि उठि आया ।
    आंनंद मगन[26] प्रेम[27] रस पाया ॥
रे यूं तौ रांम कहै सब कोई ।
    ऐसी भांति[28] न हरिजन होइ ॥ 13

---

22. Most of this pada is illegible in the microfilm copy of text *a*.
23. The word रे is not found in text *e* alone.
24. Texts *a, b, c*: तूं. Text *d*: सै. Text *e*: तू.
25. Texts *a, b*: लेई. Texts *c, e*: लेही. Text *d*: होई.
26. Texts *a, c, e*: मगन. Texts *b, d*: मंगल.
27. Texts *a, b, c, e*: प्रेम. Text *d*: रांम.
28. Texts *a, b* (?): भांति. Texts *c, d, e*: बात.

गुर गोबिंद कृपा जौ होई ।
    सतगुर मिलै न मुसकल कोई ॥
सब आसांन सहज मैं होई ।
    ऐसैं साध कहैं सब कोई[29] ॥ 14

परगट दरसन द्यौ[30] गुसांई ।
    नही देहौ तौ मरिहूं कलपाई ॥
नृमल[31] भगति कबीर की चीन्हीं[32] ।
    परदा षोल्या दिछा[33] दीन्हीं ॥ 15

भाग बडे रांमांनंद गुर पाया ।
    जांमन मरन का भरम गमाया[34] ॥ 16

---

29. Text *d* alone omits this pada.

30. Text *a*: द्यौ. Text *b*: देहू. Texts *c, d*: देहु. Text *e*: द्यौह.

31. Text *a*: नृलमल. Texts *b, e*: नृमल. Text *c*: निरमल. Text *d*: न्रमल.

32. Text *d* alone कींन्हीं. The other texts have variants of चीन्हीं.

33. Text *a*: दिछा. Texts *b, d*: दछ्या. Text *c*: दक्षा. Text *e*: दच्छया.

34. Texts *a, c, d*: गमाया. Text *b*: मिटाया. Text *e*: गंवाया.

रांमांनंद गुर पाईया,
चीन्ह्यां ब्रह्म गियांन ।
उपजी भगति कबीर कै,[35]
पाया पद नृबांन ॥ doha *a*

रांमांनंद कौ सिष है,[36]
कबीर ता कौ संत ।
भगति दिढांवण औतर्यौ,
गावै दास अनंत ॥ doha *b*

---

35. Text *d*: बुधि सरीरां उपजै. The other texts (with minor variants) give the reading as above.

36. In texts *f, g* (and others) variants of this doha begin the text, that is, the opening of the composition. In text *f*, this verse is reduced to the first two padas of the opening chaupai:

रांमांनंद कौ सिष कबीर ।
मति कौ संत भगति दिढ धीर ।

Text *g* of Callewaert, basing itself on his manuscripts 03 and 04, gives the following doha:

रांमांनंद कौ सिष कबीर, जिंनिं चींन्हौ भगवंत ।
भक्ति दिढांवन औतरचौ, गावै दास अनंत ॥

Section Two

करी कबीर[1] भगति चित[2] लाई ।
छाड़ी माया लोक बडाई[3] ॥
पहली तौ दासातन कीन्हौं ।
बहौत सुष भगतन कूं दीन्हौं ॥ 1

कपरा बुनैं बेचि ले आवै ।
बढतौ होइ स षाइ षुलावै[4] ॥
ऐक दिनां हरि अंतर[5] लींन्हौं ।
दरसन आइ चौहटै दीन्हौं[6] ॥ 2

सुन्यौ कबीर[7] तुम्हारौ नांऊं ।
ता तैं आयौ तुम्हारै ठांऊं ॥
भगत कौ रूप कीयौ तन षीनौ ।
बसतर मांगै अति आधीनौ[8] ॥ 3

---

1. Text *a* has a half erased भग between करी and कबीर. Text *d*: कबीर करी. Texts *b, c, e, g* are as given above.

2. Text *b* alone: मन.

3. Text *f* omits these first two padas.

4. Text *f* gives a somewhat different reading of this pada.

5. Texts *a, b, d, g*: अतर. Texts *c, e*: अंतरि. Text *f*: परचौ.

6. Texts *f, g* give slightly different readings of the last two padas.

7. Text *d* alone: करतूत.

8. Text *f* gives somewhat different readings in padas 1, 2, 4.

आधी फारि दैंन जब[9] लागौ ।
सगरी देह[10] भगत हूं नागौ ॥
दीयौ तुरत[11] गहर[12] नहीं लायौ ।
तबै कबीर न मिंदिर आयौ ॥ 4

हाटैं बाटैं रह्यौ लुकाई ।
घर कै काहू सुधि न पाई[13] ॥
दिनां तीन के मानस भूषे ।
बालक रोवैं षरे बिदूषे ॥ 5

तब हरि कीन्हीं ऐसी दया[14] ।
घरि बैठा बालद ले गया ॥
बहौत सौंज ले आंन उतारी[15] ।
बरजत ले बाषर मैं डारी[16] ॥ 6

---

9. Text *d* alone: तब.

10. Text *a*: दे. Texts *b, c, d, e, f*: देह. Text *g*: देहु.

11. After तुरत texts *b, c, e* add: ही. Text *d* adds: हीं.

12. Texts *a, b, c, e, g*: गहर. Texts *d, f*: बार.

13. Text *c* alone: आई.

14. Text *f* has a quite different reading of this pada.

15. Text *g* has a somewhat different reading of this pada.

16. Texts *f* and *g* (indented) here add an extra verse.

घर मैं धरौ कबीर की माता ।
दैहै रांम तुम्हारौ दाता ॥
कैसौ[17] रांम कहां कौ दाता ।
सुनैं कबीर करै अपघाता[18] ॥ 7

को है बीर[19] कहां तैं आयौ ।
का कौ धन किन देइ[20] पठायौ ॥
कबीरा कब हू लेइ न मांगै ।
लाष टका जौ धरीयै आगै[21] ॥ 8

सुनि री माता बात हमारी ।
कासी बिश्वनाथ[22] अधिकारी ॥
ता कै दरसन राजा आयौ ।
तिन[23] कबीर कूं दरब चढायौ[24] ॥ 9

---

17. Texts *a, c, d, e*: कैसौ. Texts *b, f, g*: को है.

18. Text *f* here adds an extra verse. The first two padas of this extra verse are also in text *g*.

19. Texts *a, b, c*: बीर. Text *d*: कवीर. Text *e*: कबीर.

20. Text *a*: देइ. Texts *b, c, d, e*: देन.

21. Text *f* omits this verse. Text *g* omits the first two padas. In text *g*, the third pada is somewhat different. Texts *f* and *g* then add an extra verse, the first two padas of which are somewhat similar to 2.8ab. This verse is indented in text *g*.

22. Texts *a, c*: बिश्वनाथ. Text *b*: बिष्नु नाथ. Text *d*: बिस्वनांथ. Text *e*: विश्वनाथ. Text *f*: नाथ बिस्व. Text *g*: बिस्वनाथ.

23. Texts *a, b, c, e*: तिन. Text *d*: जिन. Text *f*: तहि. Text *g*: तिनिं.

24. Text *a* alone: चटायौ.

दरब न लेई बेटा तेरौ ।
तब राजा[25] उठि कीयौ निहौरौ ॥
मांनी राजा बीनती तेरी ।
सौंज मंगाइ महौछै केरी[26] ॥ 10

तब राजा या सौंज मंगाई ।
सो कबीर घर देइ[27] पठाई ॥
घडी ऐक मैं वै भी[28] आवैं ।
लोकजात्रा दरसन पावैं[29] ॥ 11

तब[30] केसौ अदृष्टि ह्वै रहिऊ ।
भेद आपनौ कछु न कहिऊ ॥
जना च्यारि कबीर[31] कूं ध्याया ।
नीठि नीठि करि[32] घर ले आया ॥ 12

---

25. Text *c* alone here adds जा.

26. Text *f* omits this verse and substitutes two different padas.

27. Texts *a, g*: देइ. Texts *b, c, e, f*: देन. Text *d*: दैन.

28. Texts *a, b*: मैं वै भी. Text *c*: नैं वै भी. Text *d*: पीछैं वै भी. Text *3*: मैं दैषी. Text *f*: लैं सोई. Text *g*: लूं वो ही.

29. Text *c*: आवै.
The reading of the last pada is slightly different in texts *f, g*. These two add an extra two padas here.

30. Text *b* alone: जब.

31. Text *d* alone: कठिर.

32. Text *a*: करे. Texts *b, d, e, f, g*: करि. Text *c* omits this word.

स्वांमी तुम कूं भेट जु आई ।
कै षरचौ कै धरौ उठाई ॥
देषी आइ आपनैं नैंनां ।
तब पतिआयौ पर कै बैंनां ॥ 13

कौनैं दई कहां तैं आई ।
तब माता सब कथा सुनाई ॥
मन ही मन कबीर यूं जांनी[33] ।
कृपा करी है सारंगप्रांनी ॥ 14

ठाकुर मेरौ ऐसी[34] करिहै ।
अब जिनि[35] जीयरा[36] काहि डरिहै[37] ॥ 15

---

33. The reading of this pada in text *f* is somewhat different.

34. Text *e* alone: जैसी.

35. Texts *a, b*: जिनि. Texts *c, d*: जिन. Text *e*: जिव.

36. Texts *a, b* (?): जीयरा. Texts *c, d*: जीवडा. Text *e*: जीइरा.

37. Texts *f, g* have somewhat different reading of this last pada. Text *d* adds the following two padas here:

विन मांग्यां ही रिधि दई पठाई ।
हरि कै लेषै देहु उठाई ॥

तांनौं बांनौं छादि कैं,[38]
रह्यौ चरन चित[39] लाइ ।
अब तौ रांम[40] दया करी,
झषि पचि मरै[41] बलाइ[42] ॥ doha

Section Three

भगत बुलाइ महौछौ कीन्हौ ।
कछू[1] न राष्यौ सगरौ दीन्हौ ॥
कोप्या[2] बांभन अरु सन्यासी ।
करन चल्या कबीर की हासी[3] ॥ 1

38. Texts *a, b, e*: कैं. Text *c*: कै. Texts *d, f, g*: करि.

39. Text *a*: रांम ल्यौ. Text *f*: रांम चित. Texts *b, c, d, e, g* have the reading given above (with minor variants).

40. Text *f* alone gives गोब्यंद in place of सौ रांम (and minor variants).

41. Text *c* alone: करै.

42. Texts *f* and *g* (indented) here add an extra chaupai.

1. Texts *a, b*: कछु. Texts *c, d, e, f, g*: कछू.

2. The syllable प्या is not written correctly in text *a*.

3. Text *a*: दासी. Texts *d, e*: हांसी. Texts *b, c, f, g*: हासी.

राजा कोई दे गयौ दर्बू[4] ।
दे घाल्या सुद्रन[5] कूं सरबू ॥
राजा परजा सब ही मांनें ।
बांभन कहा घाटि करि जांने[6] ॥ 2

कछू न राषी बात हमारी ।
नग्र मांझ ते देहु निकारी ॥
ऐक कहैं नाक धरि काटौ ।
तातैं मिटै[7] हमारौ आंटौ[8] ॥ 3

ऐक कहै[9] हम तिन परि मरिहैं ।
जो कबीर कौ ऊपरि करिहैं[10] ॥
अैसैं रोस करत ही आऐ ।
हुते नग्र मैं सब उठि धाऐ ॥ 4

---

4. In text *f* pada *a* is somewhat different.

5. Text *a* does not distinguish clearly the letters इ ('i') and द्र ('dra'), but the difference is clear in other manuscripts. See also 3.8d.

6. Texts *f, g* invert the last two padas. Text *f* also inserts padas 3ab before padas 2cd. In texts *f, g* padas 2cd are similar to each other and somewhat different than those of texts *a, b, c, d, e*.

7. Text *a*: तातै मिटहै. Texts *b, c, d, e, g*: तातैं मिटै.

8. The last two padas of this verse are not in text *f*.

9. Texts *a, b*: कहैं. Texts *c, d, e, f, g*: कहै.

10. After first two padas texts *f, g* insert two padas not found in the other texts.

गुपती चक्र लीऐ सन्यासी ।
कौतिग देषन उमही कासी ॥
चहुं दिस बाषर छेकी[11] जाई ।
तब कबीर सनमुष भयौ आई ॥ 5

आदर करि नीकां बैसारे ।
कैसैं मया करी पग धारे ॥
बांभन क्रोध करैं दुरकारैं ।
निकरि[12] नग्र तैं[13] नहि तर मारैं[14] ॥ 6

कौंन चूक तैं मारौ मोही ।
रांम नांम चित राष्यौ पोई[15] ॥
कै मैं बाट तुम्हारी मारी ।
कै मैं तकी पराई नारी[16] ॥ 7

---

11. Text *d*: बैसे.

12. Texts *d, f*: निकसि. Text *g*: निंकसि.

13. Texts *b, d, e*: महि.

14. In texts *f, g,* this verse is followed by two padas not found in the texts *a-e*.

15. This second pada is different in texts *f, g*.

16. The last two padas are somewhat different in texts *f, g*.

कै मैं घर काहू कौ फोरचौ ।
    मांनस मारचौ कै धन[17] चोरचौ ॥
भगति[18] करी तैं हमैं न बुलाऐ ।
    सुद्र लोग सब[19] आंनि जिमाऐ ॥ 8

अब तौ हमैं रसोई दे रे ।
    नहीं तौ हम तुम लागनि है रे[20] ॥
ठीगा ठीगी जबही दषी ।
    कछु न कह्यौ कबीर बमेषी[21] ॥ 9

अब तौ नाज नहीं घर मांहीं ।
    ले आंऊं तुम बैठौ छांहीं[22] ॥
इतनी कहि कबीर टरि गइऊं ।
    केसौ कै मनि संसौ भइऊं ॥ 10

---

17. Text *d* has धन नहीं instead of कै धन.

18. Text *d*: महोछा.

19. Texts *d, f, g*: तैं. For सुद्र see note on 3.2b.

20. Text *a*: हे रे. Texts *b, c, e, g*: है रे. Text *d*: होइ रे.

21. Texts *a, c* give बमेषी. Text *b*: बेमेकी. Texts *d, f*: वबेकी. Text *e*: बवेकी. Text *g*: बंमेकी. All are variants of विवेकी.

22. In text *a* the letter छ sometimes looks very much like ब. Here the reading छ is confirmed by all the other texts.

तब हरि कारी[23] कबीर की करा[24] ।
    आंनि दरब गैब[25] का धरा ॥
सोई दरब बनीयां कूं दीन्हां ।
    भांति भांति का सौदा कीन्हां ॥ 11

मैदा चावर[26] षांड बहुता[27] ।
    सकल रसोई घृत संजुगता[28] ॥
जनां च्यारि मजूर तहां घाल्या ।
    सोई सौंज ले घर कूं चाल्या ॥ 12

बांभन देषि भयौ सुष भारी ।
    कोई न जांनैं चिरत मुरारी ॥
तिन[29] की महमां बहुत बढाई ।
    जनैं जनैं कूं सेर अढाई[30] ॥ 13

---

23. This verb form presents a particularly wide range of variants in the different manuscripts. Text *a*: कारी. Texts *b, c*: कीनी. Texts *d*: करी. Text *e*: कीन्हीं. Text *f*: करचा. Text *g*: करि. Metrically करी is best.

24. Text *c*: कला. Texts *a, b, d, e, g*: करा.

25. Text *d* alone: गांठी.

26. Text *d*: चांमर appears to be a mistake. Texts *a, b, e*: चावर. Texts *c, f*: चावल. Text *g*: चांवर.

27. The reading बहूता of texts *b, d, g* completes the meter.

28. The reading संजूता of texts *d, g* fulfills the rhyme requirements better.

29. Text *d*: जिन. Texts *a, b, e*: तिन. Text *c*: तनि. Text *g*: जंन. Text *f* is not clearly legible.

30. Texts *f, g* invert the order of verses 12 and 13. In text *g*, the following verse (Callewaert's numbers 3.14) contains four additional padas (two of which are "indented") very similar to those of this verse.

ऐेक कहैं जुलहै निध पाई ।
सो दिवांन[31] सूं कहीऐ जाई ॥
ऐेक कहैं नीकौ रे नीकौ ।
भली करी उदार[32] है जी कौ ॥ 14

बीरा पांन देत सुष पावै ।
तब कबीर सब कै मनि भावै ॥
मिटचौ क्रोध स्वारथ जब भईया ।
धनि धनि करि अपनैं घर गईया ॥ 15

॥ साचौ भगत कबीर है,
कासी प्रगटचौ आइ ।
जो या[33] की निद्य करै,
सोई नरकां जाइ ॥ doha

31. Texts *f, g*: राजा.

32. Texts *b, d*: उधार.

33. Texts *b, c, d, e*: वा. Texts *f, g*: कोई.

Section Four

जहां कबीर तहां हरि गइऊ ।
अनपहचांने[1] बांभन भइऊ ॥
बैठौ कहा करे[2] रे भाई ।
काहे न तूं कबीर कै[3] जाई ॥ 1

सब काहू कूं देत रसोई ।
जौ पैं झोली वोडै[4] कोई[5] ॥
मैदा चावल सेर अढाई ।
घृत सहत अरु षांड चढाई ॥ 2

---

1. Text *e* has अन यह बामे. One suspects that here R. K. Varma misread the manuscript since प and य are often not distinguished while बा and चा and मे and ने are easily confused.

2. Text *a* has a कै written in the margin, making the word look like ककैरै. This कै really goes in front of or instead of घरि (last pada).

3. Text *a* alone adds घरि after the कै. In text *a*, the कै is written in the margin (see previous note). A mark over the घ of घरि shows that the कै should be inserted there. Given the other readings the घरि should be dropped.

4. Texts *a, b*: वोडै. Text *c*: वोटि. Texts *d, g*: मांडै. Text *e*: कोरनी दौडै. Text *f*: जाइर मांगै. वोडै is correct.

5. Texts *f, g* here insert two padas of the next verse (4.3ab).

बांभन अरु संन्यास्यां लीन्ही ।
    या देषौ हम ही कूं दीन्हीं[6] ॥
यतनी सुनत भयौ सुष भारी ।
    केसौ राषी बात[7] हमारी ॥ 3

तब कबीर अपनैं घरि आयौ ।
    हरि कौ चिरत[8] न काहू पायौ ॥
बहुत सौंज देषी घर मांही ।
    अजहूं बांभन ले ले जांही[9] ॥ 4

धनि धनि बोलै सब कोई ।
    दास कबीर रह मुह गोई ॥
धनि सम्रथ हरि करता[10] मेरौ ।
    हूं तौ[11] सदा हरि जी कौ[12] चेरौ[13] ॥ 5

---

6. In texts *f, g,* these two padas precede the previous two (4.2cd).

7. Text *b:* कांनि. Texts *a, c, d, e, f, g*: बात.

8. Texts *b, e*: किरत. Texts *a, c, f*: चिरत. Text *d*: चरत. Text g: चरित. The reading चिरत is apparently a variant of Sanskrit चरित. Nonetheless the reading किरत (Sanskrit कृत) is also suggested by its presence in texts *b, e.* In sense, किरत is perhaps to be preferred although the difference in sense is in fact slight.

9. Text *c* omits the second two padas.

10. Text *d*: करता हरि.

11. Text *d*: होता. Texts *a, b, e*: हूं तौ. Text *c*: हौं तो. Text *f*: हौं तौ.

12. Text *b*: जी को. Texts *c, d*: ही कौ. Text *e*: ही कै. Texts *f, g*: तुम्हारौ.

13. Texts *f, g* contain many differences from the rest, particularly pada *c.* After this verse, these texts add a verse not found in texts *a-e.* It is the same as *Kabir Granthavali, sākhī* 38.1.

हरि बिन कौंन बडाई दैहै ।
    हरि बिन कूंन अपनौ करि लैहै ॥
तब कबीर कै तरली[14] लागी ।
    भई परतीति[15] भरम गयौ[16] भागी ॥ 6

प्रेम सहत हरि[17] के गुन गावै ।
    लोक दूरि तैं दरसन[18] आवै ॥
सोनौ रूपौ कपरा देही ।
    दास कबीर कछु नही लेही ॥ 7

छाजन[19] भोजन इतनौ लेही ।
    भाव सहत जौ हरिजन देही ॥
राजा परजा कौ हठ त्यागै ।
    त्यूं त्यूं अधिक जात्रा लागै ॥ 8

---

14. Texts *a, c, d*: कै तरली. Text *b*: कै तली. Text *e*: के उतर ली. Text *f*: कै तारी. Text *g*: की ताली.

15. Text *d*: प्रीति.

16. Text *d*: सब.

17. Text *a*: गोबिंद. Texts *b, c, d, e, f, g*: हरि.

18. Text *a*: दरस. Texts *b, c, d, e*: दरसन. Text *g*: दरसंनि. This pada is not found in text *f*.

19. In text *a*, here as elsewhere, the छा looks somewhat like a बा.

दिन दिन भीर होत अधिकाई ।
सुमिरन करत चित चलि जाई ॥
तब कबीर ऐक बुधि बिचारी ।
लोक बड़ाई धरूं उतारी ॥ 9

प्रात समैं गनिका कै[20] गइऊ ।
लीन्हीं संग अचंभौ भयऊ ॥
गरै बांह गनिका कै घाली ।
गनिका[21] मिलि कबीर संगि चाली ॥ 10

भरि[22] करई[23] चरनौदिक लीन्हौ ।
मद कै धोषै करि करि पीन्हौ ॥
जाइ बजार मांहि नीसरचौ[24] ।
मांनूं ग्यांन[25] सबै बीसरचौ[26] ॥ 11

---

20. Text *a* has कै घरि. The घरि is dropped in all other texts, and adds too many syllables to the meter.

21. Text *e*: गविश.

22. Texts *a*: भर. Texts *b, c, d, e, g*: भरि.

23. Text *e*: कर नीई.

24. Text *e*: नीगस्यौ.

25. Text *c* adds ध्यांन after ग्यांन.

26. This verse is not found in text *f*.

हासी करै नग्र कौ लोगू[27] ।
हरिजन कै मनि उपज्यौ सोगू ॥
बांभन बनीयां बहुत बिगोवै[28] ।
हरिजन[29] देषि देषि मुह गोवै ॥ 12

भगति कीया[30] चाहै सब कोई ।
नीच जाति तैं[31] कैसैं होई ॥
दिन दस भगति कबीरै कीन्हीं ।
अब[32] देषौ गनिका संगि लीन्हीं[33] ॥ 13

---

27. Texts *a, b*: लौगू. Text *c*: लोगूं. Texts *d, e, f, g*: लोगू. This minor change is suggested by the other readings and the rhyme.

28. From the third pada of this verse to the fourth pada of verse 5.3, the manuscript text *c* was unavailable to me.

29. Text *a*: हरि हरिजन. This is apparently a copyist's error.

30. Texts *a, e*: कीया. Text *b*: कीयौ. Text *d*: कियौ. Text *f*: करण. Text *g*: चरन.

31. Text *d*: सैं. Texts *a, b*: तैं. Text *e*: तै. Text *f*: पै. Text *g*: पैं.

32. Text *e*: सब.

33. Texts *f, g* invert the order of the two half-verses.

चलत चलत कबीर गयौ जहां[34] ।
    नगर कौ राजा बैठौ तहां[35] ॥
और दिनां आंगै ह्वै लेतौ[36] ।
    टारि[37] सिंघासन आसन[38] देतौ ॥ 14

ता दिन आदर कछु न कीन्हौ ।
    सभा कै पीछैं[39] बैठन[40] दीन्हौ ॥
सब कै मनि अचिरज सो भयऊ[41] ।
    अैसौ भगत बिगरि कयौं गयऊ ॥ 15

भयौ अचंभौ नगर मैं,
    सब कौ करै बिचार ।
निंदैं बिंदै का भयौ,
    सिर परि सिरजनहार[42] ॥ doha

---

34. Text *d*: तांहां. Text *f*: तहां.

35. Text *d*: जाहां नगर कौ राजा बैठौ ताहां. Texts *e, f*: जहां.

36. The readings of this pada in texts *f, g* are quite different from the rest.

37. Text *d*: डारि.

38. The word आसन is missing from text *a*. This seems to be simply a copyist's error.

39. Texts *b, e*: बाहरि. Text *d*: ठौर. Text *f*: पीछै. Texts *a, g*: पीछैं.

40. Text *a* alone inserts a कूं after बैठन. This is unnecessary and metrically inferior.

41. Text *d*: सब ही कैं मनि अचिरज भयेऊ.

42. Text *a* alone omits the सिर of सिरजनहार.

Section Five

तिहि औसर कबीर जल ढारचौ ।
हरि कौ पंडौ जरत[1] उबारचौ ॥
तब अैसैं[2] पूछैं नरपती ।
कहौ कबीर आपनी गती ॥ 1

कहा ढचर करि तुम[3] दिषरायौ ।
ता कौ मरम न हम ही[4] पायौ ॥
कहै कबीर सुनौ हो राई ।
कह्यां सुन्यां तैं[5] को पतिआई ॥ 2

जगंननाथ[6] कौ पंडौ जरीयौ ।
पातौ फूटि पाव परि परीयौ [7]॥
सो जल सींच लेइ मैं राष्यौ[8] ।
इहां उहां सब देष्यौं आंष्यौ ॥ 3

---

1. Text *e* adds तनु after जरत.

2. Text *d*: सब संसा.

3. Texts *a, b*: ढचर करि तुम. Text RPP #37981: ढचर तुम करि. Text *d*: चरित तुम करि. Text *e*: पाखंड करि तुम. Text *f*: चिरत तैं करि. Text *g*: चरित तैं करि.

4. Texts *a, b, e*: न हम ही. Text *d*: हम नहीं. Texts *f, g*: न काहू.

5. Text *e* omits तैं.

6. Text *b*: जंगनाथ. Text *d*: जब जगंनाथ. Texts *e, f, g*: जगनाथ.

7. Text *e*: या तौंकू दिया पानी परीया.

8. Text *d*: जल सीचत सोई मैं राष्यौ. Text *e*: सो जल सेय सीच में राख्यौ.

तब राजा सब कौ[9] मुष चाहै ।
साची कहै[10] क हम कूं बाहै ॥
भगत ऐक अैसैं समझावै ।
राजा परजा कै मनि भावै ॥ 4

छाक्यौ अरु[11] अणछाकयौ[12] बोलै ।
कबीर कहै सो कैसैं डोलै ॥
राजा पाती तुरत लिषाई ।
घरी महूरति भूलि न जाई[13] ॥ 5

जगंनाथ द्वै जना चलाया[14] ।
जन[15] कबीर अपनैं घरि आया ॥
दिन दस जनां पहूंत जाई[16] ।
दाधा[17] पंडा लीयां बुलाई ॥ 6

---

9. Text *d* omits कौ.

10. Text *d*: साची कै.

11. Text *a* has रु only instead of अरु. Text *b*: अर. Texts *c, d, e*: अरु.

12. Text *e*: छादयो अरु अणछादयों.

13. Text *c* omits this pada.

14. Only texts *a, b* (?) give this reading. Text *e* differs only in giving है for द्वै, probably R. K. Varma's mistake. This pada is missing in text *c*. Text *d* gives: जब जगंनाथ कौं नफर चलाया. More or less the same reading as this is given in texts *f, g*. The word नफर (man) is unusual.

15. Text *d*: तब.

16. I have used text *b* for this pada. Texts *c, e* are virtually identical. Text *a* gives: दिन दस जगंनाथ पहुंथा जाई. The reading जगंनाथ yields an acceptable sense but is metrically inferior, and is found in none of the other texts. Text *d* has: दिना दसानै पहुता.

17. Text *e*: दाघा, probably R. K. Varma's mistake.

कहौ[18] पंडा अपना सतभाऊं ।
    कैसें जरचौ तुम्हारौ पाऊं ॥
पंडौ कहै पसावत जरिऊ[19] ।
    पातौ फटि पाव परि परऊ ॥ 7

तबै कबीर जल लै धायौ[20] ।
    कृपा करि पग आंनि बुझायौ ॥
इतनी बात सुनि पूछै संसौ ।
    कौंन कबीर हुतौ सौ केसौ ॥ 8

जाति जुलाहौ कासी बासू ।
    सब को जांनैं[21] हरि कौ दासू ॥
जगंनाथ कै दरसन आवै ।
    हरिष हरिष हरि का गुण गावै[22] ॥ 9

---

18. Text *a*: कहुं. Texts *b, c, d, e, f*: कहौ. Text *g*: कहि.

19. Text *d*: पंडौ कहै पांव तब जरीयौ. Text *e* has य साचत for पसावत, probably R. K. Varma's mistake. Note the reading of text *f*: भात पसावत.

20. Text *a*: ध्यायौ. Texts *b, c, d, e*: धायौ. Text *e*: धायो. Text *f*: आया. Text *g*: आवा.

21. Text *e*: मानैं.

22. Text *a* alone omits the word हरि, probably a copyist's mistake. The last two padas are inverted and have a somewhat different reading in texts *f, g*.

सो कबीर हम देष्यौ[23] जबही ।
    पाव जलत जल ढारयौ तबही[24] ॥
तबही दूत मनि आंनंद[25] कीनौ ।
    पलटि पयांनौं घर कूं दीनौ ॥ 10

दिन दस मांहि कासी चलि आया ।
    लोक नगर का बूझन ध्याया[26] ॥
दूत कह्यौ राजा सूं भेदू ।
    हम पंडै कौ कीयौ न षेदू ॥ 11

पंडै हम सूं कही जु साषी ।
    सो हम तुम सूं कछू न राषी ॥
तब राजा मनि बिलषौ[27] भयऊ ।
    मंत्री आइ बिसर जन गयऊ[28] ॥ 12

---

23. Text *d*: देष्यौ हम.

24. Text *d*: जबही.

25. Text *a*: आंनिद. Texts *b, c, f, g*: आंनंद. Texts *d, e*: आनंद.

26. Text *b*: बूझैन ध्यायौ. Text *c*: बूझन धायौ. Text *d*: पूछन ध्याया. Text *f*: पूछण धायौ. Text *g*: बूझन धाया. All these variants are in fact much the same in sense. Text *e* gives a virtual repeat of pada 5.10d, an obvious error.

27. Text *e*: मिलखो, a mistake.

28. This pada is somewhat of a puzzle. The principal problem is बिसर जन. This can be equivalent to बिसर कर जनु (roughly "as if being forgotten"), or विसर्जन (roughly "[being] dismissed"). Neither reading seems very satisfactory. The readings are varied:

वैं महंत हम मरम न जांनैं ।
    सब सोहै सो[29] लीला ठांनैं ॥
राजा[30] रांनी बूझ्यौ जाई ।
    भई जु कथा कही समझाई ॥ 13

रांनी कहै बार जिन करिहु ।
    धाइ चरन कबीर कै परहु ॥
राजा बोलै डरपै[31] भारी[32] ।
    श्राप देत कौ लेइ उबारी ॥ 14

Text *a*: मित्र आदि (?हि) बिसर जिन गयऊ.
Text *b*: मित्र आहि बिसर्पुनि गयउ.
Text *c*: मित्र आई बिसर जन गऐऊ.
Text *d*: मंत्री आइ बिसर जन गयौ.
Text *e*: मित्र आ बिसर जन गइऊ.
Text *f*: आया मंत्री बिसर जन रहीया.
Text *g*: आया मंत्री बिसर जंन गया.
In sense, the forms of मित्र seem inferior to those of मंत्री.

Texts *f*, *g* here add two padas that are in fact roughly equivalent to 5.15ab.

29. Text *e*: सब.

30. Text *d*: तब राजा.

31. This is the reading of texts *a*, *d*. The other texts used for this edition have verb endings more clearly indicating the first person. Text *b*: डरपू. Texts *c*, *f*, *g*: डरपौं. Text *e*: डरपूं.

32. Here भारी is equivalent to बहुत.

अब कबीर कूं[33] मिलीयै जाई ।
नांहीं तर कछु नांहि भलाई[34] ॥
कौंन भेट ले मिलीऐ जाई ।
दरब[35] देषै तौ उठै रिसाई ॥ 15

कांध कुढारी[36] घालि[37] कैं,
मांथै तिणकौ[38] भार ।
कुटंब सहत राजा चल्यौ,
कासी कौतिगहार[39] ॥ doha

---

33. Text *d*: सौं.

34. In texts *f, g* this pada and the previous one appear after verse 5.12.

35. Text *e*: इब. It seems that R. K. Varma probably misread the similar letter इ for द्र. See above, notes on verses 3.2 and 3.8.

36. Texts *a, b* (?): कुढारी. Texts *c, d, f, g*: कुहाडी. Text *e*: कुठारी.

37. Texts *a, b, c, e*: घालि. Text *d*: मेलि. Texts *f, g*: मेल्हि.

38. Texts *a, b, c, d*: तिणकौ. Text *f*: लकरिन. Text *g*: लकडा.

39. This phrase is a difficult one because of what seems to be a mistake common to several mansucripts. Text *a* has: कासी कौ गतिहार. Text *b* has: कासी को गतिहार. Text *e* has: कासी कौ गत्यहार. The apparently correct readings appear only in two of the texts used for this edition, text *c* (कासी कोतिगहार) and text *d* (सब जग कौतिगहार). In other words, the evidently mistaken readings invert the syllables ति (or त्य) and ग. The correct readings are confirmed in the manuscripts RPP #37981 (सब जुग कौतिगहार) RPP #35150 (सब जग कौतिकहार). Texts *f, g* give: सब जग देषणहार. Both देषणहार and कौतिगहार seem to mean "onlooker" or "spectator."

This verse may be compared to Tulasi-das's, *Ram-charit-manas* 6.29.4.

Section Six

बरसिंघदे[1] बाघेलौ राजा ।
  कबीर कारण षोई लाजा ॥
दूरि ही तैं कबीर उठि ध्यायौ ।
  राजा देषि प्रेम ह्वै आयौ ॥ 1

डारि डारि माथै का बोझू ।
  मेरै मन मैं नहीं किरौधू[2] ॥
मेरै बैर न मेरै भाऊ ।
  मेरै रंक न मेरै राऊ[3] ॥ 2

राजा जाइ[4] डंडवत[5] कीन्हां ।
  अंकमाल[6] कबीर भरि लीन्हां ॥
ऐक पाव राजा गहि रहीयौ[7] ।
  दूजौ पाव कुटंब सब लहीयौ[8] ॥ 3

---

1. Texts *a, b* (?): बरसंगदे. Texts *c, e, f*: बरसिंघदे. Texts *d, g*: बरसिघदेव.

2. Texts *b, c*: क्रोधू. Texts *d, g*: रोसू. Text *e*: किरोधू. The extra matra in texts *a, e* seems to be intended to complete the meter. The "normal" form of the word is, of course, क्रोध.

3. The second two padas are not found in texts *d, f, g*.

4. Text *d*: आइ. Texts *a, c, e, g*: जाइ. Text *b*: जाय.

5. After this word, texts *b, e, g* add जु. Text *c* adds बरत instead.

6. Text *a* alone: अंकमाला. Text *f* adds तब before अंकमाल.

7. Text *c*: लीयौ. Texts *a, b, d, e*: रहीयौ. Texts *f, g*: रहीया.

8. Text *c*: गहीयौ. Texts *f, g*: गहीया. Texts *a, b, d, e*: लहीयौ.

बकसौ स्वांमी चूक हमारी ।
तुम बिन कौंन करै रषवारी ॥
हम हि पीठि जिनि देहु गुसांई ।
बार बार कहा कहूं[9] बनाई[10] ॥ 4

कहै कबीर भली तुम्ह कीन्हीं ।
हम कूं आइ बडाई दीन्हीं ॥
बडौ जु औरै देइ बडाई ।
बडौ जु बांटि बांटि धन षाई ॥ 5

बडौ जु साच झूठ पहिचांनैं ।
मूरिष कहा बडाई जांनैं ॥
राजा कै मनि आंनंद भइऊ ।
दरसन पाइ अपनैं घरि गइऊ ॥ 6

9. Texts *d, g*: कहू कहा. Texts *a, c*: कहा कहूं. Text *b*: का कहूं. Text *d*: कहा मुंहूं.

10. The last two padas are not found in text *f*.

कबीरा[11] अपनौ नांव मिटावै ।
ज्युं कुलवंती ग्रभ दुरावै ॥
दिन दिन प्रगट होत है सोई ।
करनी कैसैं छांनी होई[12] ॥ 7

जे को[13] अपनी करै बडाई ।
सुष न पावै जरि जरि जाई ॥
अपनां कुच अपनैं कर मरदै ।
कैसैं कांमनि टुटै[14] दरदै[15] ॥ 8

---

11. The long final रा is also found in texts *b, e*. Since it adds one matra too many to the meter, it was probably meant merely to indicate the natural *sandhi* between कबीर and अपनौ.

12. Texts *f, g* invert the last two padas. The reading of pada *c* in text *f* (i.e. pada *d* in that text) is different from the others.

13. In terms of the meter this को, found in texts *a* and *e*, is better than the कोई found in texts *b, d, f*. Text *c* has no word. Text *g* gives कोउ. The meaning is कोई.

14. Text *b*: टूटैं. Text *d*: मैटै. Text *e*: ढूढै. Text *g*: मेटै.

15. The last two padas are not found in text *f*. The last pada is not found in text *c*.

अैसैं[16] सब संसार भुलांनां ।
हरि सुमिरचा तिन मारग जांनां[17] ॥
बहुरि कबीर कूं[18] चढी बडाई ।
दुनीयां दरसन देषन धाई[19] ॥ 9

बिगरे कारिज रांम संवांरै[20] ।
भौजल डुबत[21] रांम ही तारै[22] ॥
काजी मुलां करै उपाधी ।
बांभन बनीयां अति अपराधी[23] ॥ 10

16. Text *e* alone जैसे.

17. Texts *f, g* are mutually different and both different from the rest.

18. Texts *d, g*: हि. Texts *a, b, c, e*: कूं.

19. Texts *d, g*: आई. Texts *a, b, c*: धाई. Text *e*: ध्याई. The last two padas are not found in text *f*.

20. Texts *b, c, d, e*: सुधारै. Texts *a, f*: संवारै. Text *g*: संवारै.

21. Texts *b* (?), *c, e*: डूबत. Texts *d, g*: बूडत. Text *f*: बुडत.

22. Texts *a, c*: रांम हीतारै. Text *b*: रांम ही तारैं. Text *d*: रांम उधारै. Text *e*: राम उबारे. Text *f*: पारि उतरै. Text *g*: रांम उबारै.

23. The last two padas are not found in text *f*.

बैर करै अरु मारन[24] तकवै ।
समझि समझि अरु[25] मन मैं झषवै ॥
ऐसैं करत बहुत दिन[26] बीते ।
बाद करत कबीर दिन[27] जीते ॥ 11

अरु कबीर[28] की माता षोटी ।
भगति न भावै पकरै चोटी[29] ॥
बहू[30] सहत करै दिन रारी ।
धनि कबीर सो[31] लेह सहारी[32] ॥ 12

---

24. Text *b*: मन मैं. Text *e*: मन में. Texts *a, b, g*: मारन. Text *d*: मरन.

25. This अरु is not found in text *d*.

26. Text *b* alone: सबै देन.

27. Text *d* alone जन. Text RPP #37981 has the interesting variant: नित. This verse is not found in text *f*.

28. Text *d* alone has only वीर.

29. Text *a* alone चौटी.

30. Texts *a, c*: बहु. Texts *b, d, g*: बहू. Text *e*: बहुत. Text RPP #37981: बैर.

31. Texts *d, g* alone: जो.

32. This verse is placed after 15b in texts *f, g*. There is no equivalent to pada *c* in text *f*, which substitutes a pada, and which refers to presumably the same woman as कबीर की नारी.

बाहिर बैरी अरु घर मांहीं ।
रहै कबीर रांम की छांहीं ॥
भगत[33] कौ बैरी सब संसारू ।
आदि अंति हरि राषनहारू ॥ 13

ऐक समैं अैसी हाइ आई ।
विधि[34] संजोग[35] न मेट्यौ जाई ॥
स्याह सिकंदर[36] कासी आया ।
काजी मुलां कै मन भाया ॥ 14

चले फिरादी बार न लाई ।
बांभन बंनीयां मिलीया जाई[37] ॥
अरु कबीर की माता दौरी ।
समझै नही भई मति बौरी[38] ॥ 15

---

33. Text *e* alone: भगति.

34. Text *a*: बिध. Texts *b* (?), *d, e*: विधि. Texts *c, f, g*: बिधि.

35. Text *c* alone: सजो.

36. Text *a*: सिकदर. Texts *b* (?), *d, e, f, g*: सिकंदर. Text *c*: सिंकसदर. Texts *d, f* give साह instead of स्याह. Text *g* has साहि.

37. Here texts *f, g* insert four padas. The first has no equivalent. The second is equivalent to 12d, the third to 12a, the fourth to 12b. Text *g* then adds six indented padas equivalent to 12c, 12d, 13a, 13b, 13c, 13d respectively.

38. Text *e* alone: सब के तही भई मति बौरी.

सब मिलि आतुर जाइ पुकारचा ।
जांन क उन का मांनस मारचा[39] ॥
कबीर की रछ्या करै भगवंतू ।
सो जस गावै दास अनंतूं ॥ 16

स्याहि सिकंदर तूं जीवौ,[40]
मेटि हमारी पीर ।
अैसी काहू[41] ना करी,
जैसी करी कबीर ॥ doha

Section Seven

कहै सिकंदर क्या है भाई ।
गांव प्रगना लीया छिनांई[1] ॥
गांव प्रगनां नाहीं लीया ।
जुलहै ऐक अमारग कीया[2] ॥ 1

---

39. Text *d* alone has: जाणि क मारचौ उन्ह का परवारा. Text *d* here also adds the following two padas:
सव ही मिलि मिलि करत फिरादी ।
हम कूं निंदै इक अपराधी.

40. Text *b*: जीवैं. Texts *c, e*: जीवै. Texts *d, f*: बडौ. Text *g*: बडा.

41. Texts *a, b, c, e*: काहू. Texts *d, f, g*: कोई.

1. Text *d*: छिडाई. Text *f*: छुडाई. Texts *a, b, c*: छिनंई. Texts *e, g*: छिनाई.

2. Text *d*: अचंभा कीया. Texts *f, g* here substitute a different pada.

मुसलमांन की छोडी[3] रीती ।
अरु हींदू की भांनैं छीती ॥
निंदै तीरथ निंदै बेदू ।
निंदै नवग्रह सूरज चंदू[4] ॥ 2

निंदै संकर निंदै माई ।
निंदै सारद गणपति राई[5] ॥
निंदै ग्यारस होम सराध्य ।
निंदै बांभन जग[6] आराध्य[7] ॥ 3

निंदै मातपिता की सेवा ।
बहन भांणजी अरु सब देवा ॥
निंदैं सकल धरम की आसा[8] ।
षट दरसन अरु बारह मासा[9] ॥ 4

---

3. Texts *d, g*: छांडी. Texts *a, b, c, e*: छोडी.

4. This verse is not found in text *f*.

5. Text *c* here inserts an extra pada equivalent to pada 7.4a, which also appears in its correct place.

6. Text *a* alone has जुग.

7. Text *g* here substitutes two different padas. In text *f*, the same padas appear after verse 7.4d.

8. Texts *d*: बाता. Text *f*: मंतु. Texts *a, b, c, e, g*: आसा.

9. Text *c* inverts the first and second halves of this verse. In texts *f, g,* the last two padas are somewhat different from each other and very different from the other texts.

अैसी बिधि[10] सब लोक बिगारा ।
    हींदू मुसलमांन तैं[11] न्यारा ॥
ता तैं हमैं न मांनैं कोई ।
    जब लग जुल्हा कासी[12] होई[13] ॥ 5

ऐसी बिपति निवारि हमारी ।
    तूं हीं बाप तूं हीं महतारी[14] ॥
सुनंत सिकंदर उठ्यौ रिसाई ।
    छरीदार द्वै दीयै पठाई[15] ॥ 6

आंनूं बेगि बार जिन होई[16] ।
    ताहि मारूं बीनती करै सोई[17] ॥
जाइ पयादै बात सुनाई[18] ।
    स्याह सिकंदर बुलवै[19] भाई ॥ 7

---

10. Text *d* alone: हीं.

11. Text *e* alone: सूं.

12. Text *d* alone: का मिष.

13. Text *f* adds a verse here. The first two padas are also found in a different place in text *g* (padas 7.2cd in that edition).

14. Text *d* substitutes this pada: बडौ पातसाह तूं हितकारी. Text *f* has a similar reading.

15. Text *e* alone: हुकम सुनाई.

16. Text *d*: लाई. Text *f*: कीजे. Texts *a, b, c, e, g*: होई.

17. Text *d* alone: जो बीनती कराई. Text *f* substitutes a somewhat different pada.

18. Texts *f, g* substitute a somewhat different pada.

19. Text *d*: बोलै. Texts *a, b*: बुलवै. Texts *c, e*: बुलावै. Text *f*: तोहि बुलावै. Text *g*: बोले.

हमैं सिकंदर काहे[20] जांनैं ।
कौंनैं कह्यौ कैसैं पहिचांनैं ॥
तेरी माइ उपजाई रारी ।
काजी बांभन सहंत पुकारी[21] ॥ 8

समझि कबीर चल्यौ मन मांहीं ।
जो न चलूं तौ बल[22] ले जांहीं ॥
सब संतन कूं दीया प्रमोधू ।
तुम जिन करौ हमारौ सोधू ॥ 9

---

20. Text *d*: कैसै. Texts *a, b, c, e*: काहे. Text *f*: कहै क्यौं. Text *g*: कैसैं.

21. Text *f* here adds six padas. Text *g* adds more or less the same padas "indenting" the first two and last two. Pada four is different and does not rhyme.

22. Text *d* alone: बहुरचौ for तौ बल. For बल, text *b* has बले and texts *c, e, f, g* have बलि.

अति[23] आतुर[24] करि[25] असुर[26] पठाया ।
तौ लूं दोइ जनां औरूं आया[27] ॥
ले[28] कबीर षरौ[29] तहां[30] कीन्हौं ।
जहां[31] सिकंदर डेरौ दीन्हौं[32] ॥ 10

देह सांवरी मनमथ लाजै ।
ता परि माला तिलक बिराजै[33] ॥
मुदित बचन अरु नृमल नैंनां ।
मुष तैं निकसै सीतल बैंनां[34] ॥ 11

---

23. Text *a* alone has अंति.

24. Text *c* alone omits आतुर.

25. Texts *a, d, e*: करि. Text *b*: होइ. Texts *c, f, g*: ह्वै.

26. Text *a* alone has आसुर.

27. Text *f* here substitutes a somewhat different pada and adds four padas more.

28. Texts *b, c, e* add a र not found in texts *a, d, g*.

29. Text *g* alone has ले उभा. Dictionaries give ऊभा meaning खड़ा.

30. Text *d* alone has जब.

31. Texts *a, c, g*: जहां. Text *b*: जहा. Text *d*: तांहा. Text *e*: तहां.

32. Text *f* omits the final two padas. After the final pada, text *g* adds two padas equivalent to the final two of the four padas added in text *f* after 7.10b.

33. Texts *f, g* have somewhat different readings for this pada.

34. Texts *f, g* substitute a different reading for this pada.

तब काजी बौलै[35] समझाई[36] ।
    करि तसलीम दिवांनैं भाई[37] ॥
हूं तसलीम कहा करि जांनूं ।
    तूं जिन काजी होइ दिवांनूं[38] ॥ 12

कहै सिकंदर ऐसी बाता ।
    हूं तौहि देषूं दोजिग जाता ॥
राह छाडि तैं[39] गही कुराहा ।
    क्यूं बे जुल्हा कौंनैं बाहा ॥ 13

अपनी राह चल्यां गति होई ।
    हींदू तुरक बूझि लै दोई[40] ॥
कबीर बोलै बचन बसेषू ।
    सकल सभा मृतक सी देषू ॥ 14

---

35. Texts *b, c*: बोलै. Text *d*: ले (only). Text *e*: बोले. Text *f*: कहै. Text *g*: कहि.

36. Text *a* alone: स्मझाई.

37. Text *f* has a somewhat different reading in this pada.

38. Text *d* alone: अयानौ.

39. Texts *a, b, c, e*: तैं. Text *d*: कै. Text *f*: अर. Text *g*: करि.

40. Text *f* substitutes a somewhat different pada.

दोजिग परिहैं तुरक अरु हींदू ।
काजी मुलां अरुबड[41] भूंदू ॥
हम तौ भगति मुक्ति मैं आऐ ।
गुर परसाद रांम गुण गाऐ ॥ 15

रांम भरौसै गिनैं न काहू ।
सब मिलि राजा रंक रिसाऊ ॥ 16

राषणहारा रांम है,
मारि न सकै कोइ ।
पातिस्याह हूं[42] नां डरूं,
करता करै स होइ ॥ doha

41. Texts *a, c*: अरुबड. Texts *b, e*: अरबड. Text *d*: ऐ दोई. Text *f*: भूले दोऊ (omiting भूंदू). Text *g*: ये बड.

42. Texts *a, c, e, f*: हूं. Text *b*: सूं. Text *d*: हौं. Text *g*: मैं.

Section Eight

काढि कतेब दिषावै काजी ।
बिचि बिचि बांभन दैहैं भांजी ॥
माला तिलक दूरि करि डारौ[1] ।
पीछैं सूं[2] पथरूं करि मारौ ॥ 1

•

तिह बरज्यां[3] सुनौ सब कोई[4] ।
मुसलमांन जौ काफर होई[5] ॥
कहै कबीर समझि किन करिहू ।
तुमही[6] काफर तुमही मरिहू ॥ 2

कौंन कतेब जौ गाइ कटाई ।
बकरी मुरगी किन फरमाई[7] ॥
जितनां देषूं आत्म घाती ।
तितनां[8] की जम तोड़ै छाती ॥ 3

---

1. Texts *f, g* have different readings for this pada.

2. Text *d*: सात. In somewhat different readings text *f* has सात and text *g* सत.

3. Text *d*: हैत वरवा.

4. Texts *f, g* give a different reading for this pada.

5. Text *a* alone: होइ.

6. Text *a* alone: तुम्ही.

7. This pada is the same as *Bijak, ramainī* 49.3a.

8. Texts *d, f, g*: तिन. Texts *a, b, c, e*: तितनां.

राजा परजा नरक पडांही ।
    रांम कहै[9] तिन कूं भै नांहीं ॥
सुनंत सिकंदर कोप[10] करांहीं ।
    जांनूं घृत घालि आहूत[11] बरांहीं[12] ॥ 4

जांनूं कारै की पूंछ मरोरी ।
    जांनूं[13] सोवती सीहनी टंटोरी[14] ॥
जांनूं बैसंदर मेल्ह्यौ होरी ।
    जांनूं चीता की[15] आंषि जु[16] छोरी ॥ 5

---

9. Text *d* alone: भजै.

10. Text *d* alone here adds हि.

11. Text *d* alone here adds ज्यूं.

12. In texts *f, g,* the reading of the last two padas is somewhat different.

13. Text *a* alone here adds अब.

14. Text *f* gives a different reading of this pada.

15. Text *d*: मानौ चिते षां.

16. Text *a* alone: ज.

गाफिल संक न मांनैं मोरी ।
    अब देषूं साची करमाति[17] तोरी[18] ॥
बांध्यौ पग मेल्ह्यौ जंजीरू[19] ।
    ले बोरचौ[20] गंगा कै नीरू[21] ॥ 6

हुकम करत कबीर गहि लीन्हौं ।
    मंझि धार गंगा कै दीन्हौं ॥
छूटि[22] जंजीर परचौ[23] जल मांहीं ।
    लागौ तिरन बूडि गयौ[24] नांही ॥ 7

---

17. Text *a* alone: करमात.

18. Text *f* gives a somewhat different reading and adds an extra pada.

19. Texts *f, g* give somewhat different readings of this pada.

20. Text *a*: बोरौ. Texts *b, e*: बोरचौ. Text *c*: बौरचौ. Text *d*: वोलौ. Text *f*: डारचौ. Text *g*: डारौं.

21. Texts *b, c*: जीरूं. Text *d*: तीरी. Text *e*: तीरू. Texts *f, g*: तीरा.

22. Text *a*: छूठि. Text *b*: छूटे. Texts *c, d, e*: छूटि. Texts *f, g*: टूटि.

23. Text *d*: तिरचौ. The other texts give variants of परचौ.

24. Texts *a, b, d*: बूडि गयौ. Text *c*: डूबि गयौ. Text *e*: बूढ़ि गयो. Text *f*: सो बूडा. Text *g*: बूडिगा.

क्रोध भरचौ असुर[25] यूं भाषै ।
जल मैं रह्यौ अबै को राषै ॥
बहौरचौं बांधि[26] मदिर मैं डारचौ ।
आसि पासि[27] ले पावक जारचौ[28] ॥ 8

भयौ हुतासन जैसौ[29] नीरू ।
हरि हरि सुमिरै दास कबीरू ॥
कबीर की करुनां हरि चीन्हीं[30] ।
पहुप ब्रषा गण[31] गंध्रप कीन्हीं ॥ 9

---

25. Texts *a, b*: क्रोध भरचौ असुर. Text *c*: क्रोध भयौ अश्वर. Text *d*: क्रोध हि भरचौ असुर. Text *e*: क्रोध भरचो असूर. Text *f*: उपज्यौ क्रोध असुर. Text *g*: क्रोध भयौ अस्वर.

26. Texts *a, b, c, e*: बांधि. Text *d*: लै. Texts *f, g*: कबीर.

27. Text *a* alone: आस पास.

28. Texts *a, c, e*: ले पावक जारचौ. Texts *b, d*: पावक परजारचौ. Texts *f, g*: पावक परजारचा.

29. Text *a* alone: तैसौ. The other texts have variants of जैसौ.

30. Text *d*: कबीर जी की करुनां हरि जी कीन्हीं.

31. Texts *a, g*: ग्रण. Texts *b, c, d, e*: गंण. Text *d*: दींनीं. The other texts have variants of कीन्हीं. The last two padas are not found in text *f*.

जरि गयौ मंदिर षेह उडांनी ।
सही करामात सुर नर जांनीं[32] ॥
अधिक रूप नाराइन दीन्हौं ।
देह उबटि[33] जल मंजन कीन्हौं[34] ॥ 10

जै जै कार भयौ जग मांही ।
काजी[35] बांभन बहुत रिसांई ॥
नाटक चेटक जुल्हा जांनैं ।
साह सिकंदर तूं जिन[36] मांनैं ॥ 11

इतनी सुनि मन उपज्यौ रोसा ।
अब कबीर तोहि[37] कौंन भरोसा[38] ॥
माता हस्ती असुर बुलाया ।
अपनी छांह बेधता आया ॥ 12

32. Text *f* here substitutes a different pada.

33. Text *d*: दे उबारि.

34. Texts *f, g* here substitute a different pada.

35. Text *b* alone: कासी.

36. Text *a*: जि. Texts *b, c, e*: जिन. Text *d*: मति. Text *f*: जनि. Text *g*: जिंनिं.

37. Text *a* alone: तौहि.

38. The first two padas are not found in text *f*.

संक न करै महावत केरी ।
सब हस्तन मैं लीयौ निवेरी ॥
सोनैं सांकल बांध्यौ राषै ।
दांनौं कूंची दूरि तैं[39] नांषै ॥ 13

सोनै आंकस दांत मढाया[40] ।
बिचि बिचि हीरा[41] मोती लाया ॥
नगर मांहि जौ छूटन पावै ।
मांनस[42] मारै कोट ढहावै[43] ॥ 14

39. Text *e*: कूंभी दूरि सूं.

40. Text *a* alone makes the first syllable of this word मा.

41. What survives of the manuscript RPP #8561 (text *h*) of 1754 V. S. begins here.

42. In texts *b, d, e,* the word तौ precedes मांनस. In text *c,* तो does the same. This तौ/तो is not found in texts *a, f, g, h*.

43. Text *h*: काट गढ ढावै.

रिण मैं रावत मारचा बांका ।
भाट बिडद[44] बोलत है ता का[45] ॥
भैरूं काल मथो[46] हर थूपा ।
तेल सिंदूरि[47] पूजै धूपा[48] ॥ 15

षूनी बहौत नांव रिण जीतू ।
पंथ चलै तब[49] गावै गीतू[50] ॥
सदा सिंगार[51] घटा चौरासी ।
इंद्र लोक मांनूं[52] उपमां जैसी ॥ 16

44. Text *h* alone here adds ढढ.

45. Texts *f, g* here add two padas not found in the other texts.

46. Text *e* alone has भयौ, possibly a transcription error of R. K. Varma. The other texts have variants of मथो.

47. Texts *c, d, e, f, g h* add a न at the end of सिंदूर (and its various variants).

48. Texts *a, b, c, e* make the rhyme थूपा . . . धूपा. Texts *d, f, h* make the rhyme थापा . . . धापा.

49. Texts *a, b, c, d, e*: तब. Texts *f, h*: जौ.

50. Texts *f, g* place these padas after 8.15b.

51. Text *a* alone has घा instead of गा in this word.

52. Text *b*: मांनु. Text *c*: जांनूं. Text *d*: मनौ. Text *e*: जानूं. Text *f*: नही. Text *g*: मानौं (at beginning of pada). Text *h*: जानू.

सो कबीर कूं आंनि झुकाया[53] ।
पीछैं भागा आगा नहीं आया[54] ॥ 17

काल रूप गज आईया,
सब कौ[55] चाल्या भागि ।
दास कबीर न डरपई,
रह्या रांम ल्यौ[56] लागि ॥ doha

53. Texts *a, b, c, e*: झुकाया. Text *d*: ढुकायौ. Texts *f, g*: ढुकावा. Text *h*: झुकायो.

54. Text *h* has नायो for नहीं आया (and variants). Text *d* alone adds, before these two padas, the following two padas:

अैसौ हाथी कहूं न देषा ।
सो कवीर सूं करिहै धेषा ।

Texts *f, g* add, after the two padas common to all texts, the following two padas:

तब रजि रहचौ रोस धरि अैसैं ।
जन कबीर आगैं सिध बैसैं ॥

55. Texts *b, e, f, g*: कीई. Texts *c, d, h*: को.

56. Text *b*: चरण चित.

Section Nine

सिंघ रूप केसौ डरपावै ।
ता तैं हस्ती[1] निकटि न आवै ॥
पीलवांन कूं दरसन दीन्हौ ।
मोरि गयंद षरौ तहां कीन्हौ[2] ॥ 1

पीछैं स्याह सिकंदर दीठा ।
कबीर आगैं सिंघ बैईठा ॥
पीलवांन हाथी करि न्यारा ।
भई करामात अब की बारा[3] ॥ 2

साचा रांम कबीर तुम्हारा ।
अब कै राष्यौ जीव हमारा[4] ॥
काजी मुलां मरम न जांनैं ॥
सिरजनहार तुम्हारी मांनैं[5] ॥ 3

---

1. Text *a*: हसती. Texts *b, c, e, h*: हस्ती. Texts *d, f, g*: हाथी.

2. Text *b*: तहां कीनूं. Text *c*: तहां कीनौं. Text *d*: करि लीनूं. Text *e*: तहा कीनों. Text *f*: करि लीना. Text *g*: तब कींनां.

3. Text *f* here substitutes a different pada.

4. Texts *f, g* invert the first two padas.

5. Padas *c, d* are not found in text *f*.

देषि दीनता कहै कबीरू ।
    चरन सरन राषै रुघबीरू[6] ॥
जौ न सिकंदर अब कै डरता[7] ।
    तौ हरि निहचै परलै करता[8] ॥ 4

नां कबीर कै दुषन[9] आई[10] ।
    ता तैं असुर सझा नहीं[11] पाई ॥
जे को[12] आगैं औगुन ठानैं ।
    ता कौ साध भलौ करि मांनैं[13] ॥ 5

---

6. Texts *a, c*: रुघबीरू. Text *b*: रुघबीरूं. Text *d*: हरिबीरू. Texts *e, f, h*: रघुबीरू. Text *g*: रघुबीर. Texts *f, g* give a somewhat different reading for pada *b*.

7. Texts *f, g* give a different reading for this pada.

8. Text *f* gives a different reading for this pada. Texts *f, g* here add four padas, roughly equivalent to verse 9.6 padas *c, d, a, b*.

9. Texts *a, b, c*: दुषन. Texts *d, e*: दूषन. Texts *f, g*: दूषणि. Test *h*: दूषनि. The syllable दू is better for the meter.

10. Text *d*: पाई.

11. Text *a*: सु सझ नही. Text *b*: सझा नहा. Text *c*: सझ्या(?) नही. Text *d*: न सज्या. Text *e*: सका नहीं. Text *f*: सजा नही. Text *g*: स जाहि. Text *h*: सजा नहि. The word सझा and its variants seems to be equivalent to modern सज्जा.

12. Texts *a, e*: जे को. Texts *b, c*: जे कोई. Text *d*: कोई जो. Text *f*: जै कोई. Text *g*: जौ कोई. Text *h*: जै कोउ.

13. Text *g* here adds four padas.

जौ हरि ऊपरि राषै भाऊ[14] ।
ता कौ काज न बिगरै काऊ ॥
जौ जन देषै हरि कौ कीयौ ।
सो जन हरि[15] अपनौ करि लीयौ ॥ 6

तब[16] केसौ अदृष्टि ह्वै जाई ।
असुर गहे कबीर के पाई ॥
मांगौ सोनां मांगौ रूपा ।
मांगौ कपरा अधिक अनूंपा ॥ 7

मांगौ गांव प्रगनां घोरा ।
तुम कौं दीजै सो[17] सब थोरा ॥
कहै कबीर न मांगूं[18] माया ।
राजा रंक सबै इन[19] षाया ॥ 8

14. The corresponding pada in texts *f, g* is different from this reading and different in each as well.

15. Texts *a, c, f*: सो जन हरि. Text *b*: सौ तौ हरि. Text *d, h*: सो निज हरि. Text *e*: सो हरिजन. Text *g*: ते हरि निंज.

16. Text *b* alone: जब.

17. Texts *a, e*: जौ. Texts *b, d, f, g, h*: सो. Text *c*: सौ.

18. Texts *a, b, e*: मांगूं. Texts *c, f, g*: न भांगौं. Text *d*: मांगौ नही. Text *h*: न मागौ.

19. Texts *a, d, e*: इन. Texts *b, c*: यन. Text *f*: ईनि. Text *g*: इंनि. Text *h*: षनि.

जो मांगै सो भगत[20] न होई ।
मन दिढ राषै निज जन सोई ॥
हाथ जोरि कैं माथा नाया[21] ।
जन कबीर अपनैं घर आया[22] ॥ 9

जहां जहां[23] कष्ट तहां हरि तूठा ।
काजी बांभन होइ गया झूठा[24] ॥
अपनैं घरि आईयो कबीरू ।
गुर परसादैं[25] अमर सरीरू ॥ 10

तब कबीर की[26] लागी जाता ।
मिलैं संत जन बूझैं बाता ॥
हसि हसि[27] बोलै दास कबीरू ।
चरन सरन राषै रुघबीरू ॥ 11

---

20. Text *a* alone: दास. The other texts all give भगत or भक्त.

21. Texts *a, b, d*: नाया. Text *c*: न्हाया. Text *e*: लाया. Text *g*: नायौ. Text *f* substitutes a different pada.

22. Texts *a, b, d, e, h*: आया. Text *c*: उठि आया. Text *f*: बैसौ. Text *g*: आयौ.

23. Text *a* alone has only one जहां. The other texts all have two (with variant spellings).

24. Text *f* places the first two padas after verse 9.12b instead of here. Text *g* "indents" these padas here and repeats roughly the same padas after 9.12b.

25. Texts *a, c*: परसदैं. Text *b*: परसादै. Text *d*: प्रसाद तै. Text *e*: प्रसादूं. Texts *f, g*: प्रसादि.

26. Text *a* alone: कै.

27. Texts *a, g*: हरि हरि. Texts *b, c, d, e*: हसि हसि. Text *f*: हस्य हस्य.

पातिसाह जब[28] कसणी दीन्ही ।
मेरै मन संक्या नही कीन्ही[29] ॥
जिन कै भगतन कौ बल होई ।
तिन कूं मारि न सकै[30] कोई ॥ 12

कोटि पाप हरि भगति[31] नसावै ।
भगतन पीछैं[32] हरि चलि आवै ॥
जे हरि भगतन तैं रहैं न्यारे ।
तिन के रांम नही[33] रषवारे ॥ 13

28. Text *d* alone: जे.

29. Texts *f, g* here add two padas roughly the same as verse 9.10ab.

30. Text *d* alone: सकै नहीं.

31. Texts *a, b, d, e*: भगति. Texts *c, g*: भक्त. Text *f*: भगत.

32. Text *a*: पाछैं. Texts *b, c, f*: पीछैं. Texts *d, g*: पीछै. Text *e*: पीछें.

33. Texts *a, b, c*: रांम नही. Text *d*: नहीं रांम. Text *e*: राम नहीं. Text *f*: ताही हरि. Text *g*: नांहीं हरि.

जो भगतन की निंद्या करही ।
    कूंभी[34] नरक पाप ते परही[35] ॥
जे भगतन तैं[36] करैं भरांती ।
    तिन कैं गलि जम दैहै[37] कांती ॥ 14

सकल जीव मैं देषूं[38] रांमूं ।
    हरि भगति बिनां सरै नहीं कांमूं[39] ॥
गुर गोबिंद भगति हम[40] चीन्हां ।
    ता तैं[41] मेरा कछू न कीन्हां[42] ॥ 15

---

34. Texts *a, b, c*: कूंभी. Texts *d, g*: कूंभीपाक. Text *e*: कुंभी.

35. Text *a*: परिही. Texts *b, c, e*: परही. Texts *d, g*: परहीं. Text *f* omits these first two padas.

36. Texts *a, c*: तैं. Texts *b, g*: सूं. Text *d*: सौं. Text *e*: ते. Text *f*: स्यौं.

37. Texts *a, b*: जम दैहै. Text *c*: जम दैहैं. Text *d*: जम मेल्हैगा (without गलि). Text *e*: जमु देहैं. Texts *f, g* give different readings for this last pada.

38. Texts *a, b, g*: देषूं. Texts *c, d, e*: देषै.

39. Text *d*: हरि भगतन बिन कोऊ कांमूं. Text *f* omits these first two padas.

40. Texts *a, e*: भगति हम. Text *b*: भगोत हम. Text *c*: भक्ति ही हम. Text *d*: भगत मै. Text *f*: भगतन मैं. Text *g*: भक्ति मैं.

41. Text *e*: पै. The other texts all give variants of तैं.

42. Texts *f, g* here add two padas each. The padas of each text are different.

जल बोरचौ पावक जरचौ,[43]
बिनस्यौ नहीं सरीर ।
गज तोरत हरि राषीयौ,
निरभै भयौ[44] कबीर ॥ doha

Section Ten

इह प्रकार कबीर उबारा ।
जहां तहां हरि भया रषवारा[1] ।
बहुरि सिमट[2] मत बांभनां कीन्हौं ।
जुलहै हमैं बहुत दुष दीन्हौं ॥ 1

परपंच ऐक कीयौ अनहोतौ ।
छल बल तकवै अपनी वो तौ ॥
बांभन चहूं कौ मुड मुडायौ ।
माला तिलक सांग पहरायौ ॥ 2

---

43. Text *d*: धरचौ. The other texts all give variants of जरचौ.

44. Texts *a, b, c, e*: भयौ. Texts *d, f, g*: दास.

1. The first two padas are not found in text *f*.

2. Texts *b, e*: समटि. Text *c*: स. Text *d*: संकटि. Text *f*: मिलि. Text *g*: सिंकदरि. Text RPP 37981: सकल.

तिनह सीष दे गुपत चलाया ।
चहुं देस का भगत बुलाया ॥
दीज्यौ दल कबीर कै नांऊं ।
असी[3] कोस लग जितनां गांऊं ॥ 3

माघ मास पहलै पषवारै ।
नौमी कै दिन चलैं सवारै ॥
झूठौ[4] दल दीन्हौं सब काहूं ।
बेगि बसंत पंचमी आहू ॥ 4

दास कबीर महोछा थाटा ।
सब संतन की जोवै बाटा ॥
मांथै मांनि मांनि[5] दल लीनौ ।
पाषंड भेष न काहू चीनौ[6] ॥ 5

---

3. Texts *a, c*: अैसी. Texts *b, d, e, g*: असी. Text *f*: सौ सौ.

4. Text *e* alone: कूवौ. This is an obvious misreading based on the similarities in the old script between झ and क and between व and ठ.

5. Text *e* omits one मांनि.

6. Text *f* gives a different reading for this pada.

अैसो परपंच कीयौ बांभनां ।
घरि आऐ तब हरिषि मनां[7] ॥
ता पीछैं हरि जन चलि आऐ ।
जांनूं पावस[8] रुति बादल धाऐ[9] ॥ 6

बीसक पंडित लेषन लेही ।
बीसक बैठे सीषन[10] देही ॥
बीस दिनां नहीं आवै अंता ।
सो जस गावै दास अनंता[11] ॥ 7

सनमुष चलै न[12] गिनती होई ।
गंगा तीर मिलै सब कोई[13] ॥
सुनत कबीर गुपत ह्वै रहीयौ ।
सब संतन कौ आंवन भईयौ[14] ॥ 8

---

7. Text *f* gives a different reading of this pada.

8. Texts *a, g*: पावक. Texts *b, c, d, e* give पावस.

9. The last two padas are not found in text *f*. Text *e* reads छाऐ for धाऐ.

10. Text *e* wrongly separates this as सीख न.

11. Texts *f, g* here add two padas (indented in *g*) and a complete doha.

12. Text *d* alone omits न.

13. These two padas are not found in text *f*.

14. Text *a*: भयौ. Text *b*: भइयौ. Texts *c, e*: भईयौ. From the point of view of the meter, भइयौ is best. For the rhyme, भईयौ is best. Texts *d, g* have variants of a different reading for this pada. Text *d*: सुनमुष जाइ कछू बात न कह्यौ. Text *f* omits this verse and the next and substitutes two other verses (135, 136).

तब केसौ आपन पर लीनी ।
    कोटि कला कबीर की चीन्ही[15] ॥
डेरै डेरै आदर लीयौ[16] ।
    जो जिस मांग्यौ सो तिस दीयौ ॥ 9

कहीं कहीं नाचै अरु गावै ।
    हरि का चिरत न कोऊ पावै ॥
दिनां पांच लग लीला कीन्ही ।
    ता पीछैं पहरांवंन दीन्हीं[17] ॥ 10

सब कूं बिद्या[18] दई करि भाऊ ।
    कृपावंत भयौ त्रिभवन राऊ[19] ॥
मांही मिलि कबीर सुष देष्यौ ।
    जीवंन जनम सुफल करि लेष्यौ ॥ 11

---

15. Text *d*: कींन्हीं. The other texts have variants of चीन्ही.

16. Text *d*: कीयौ. Text *g*: कीनां. The other texts have variants of लीयौ.

17. Texts *f, g* here add two padas, indented in *g*.

18. Texts *a, c, g*: बिद्या. Texts *b, d, e*: बिदा. The latter is in fact a better reading both for meter and sense.

19. The first two padas are not found in text *f*. Text *g* indents these two padas.

रांम कबीर सदा बनि आई ।
तीजै बांभन रहे षिसाई[20] ॥
बरस एक बीच्यौ[21] है जबही ।
हरि[22] अपछरा पठाई तबही ॥ 12

देषौ जाइ[23] कबीर बर तेरा ।
बसै बनारसि निरंजन केरा[24] ॥
छल बल करि लीज्यौ अंग लाई ।
बार बार भगवंत[25] सिषाई[26] ॥ 13

आंनि अपछरा दई दिषाई ।
जांनि[27] सुषदेव पैं रंभा आई[28] ॥
जा कै रूप न पूजै कोई ।
मधुरे बचन सुनावै सोइ ॥ 14

---

20. Texts *f, g* here add two padas and a complete doha. Text *g* "indents" all of this.

21. Texts *a, b, e*: बीच्यौ. Text *c*: कबीर च्यौ. Text *d*: बीत्यौ. Texts *f, g*: भयौ.

22. Text *f* alone: इंद्र.

23. Text *a* alone देषौं. Although a mark in the text indicates something should be inserted, in text *a* alone जाइ (and its variants) is missing.

24. Texts *a, b, c, e*: निरंजन केरा. Text *d*: निज जन मोरा. Text *g*: निज जंन मोरा. Text *f* omits the first two padas.

25. Text *a*: भगव. Texts *b, c, d, e*: भगवंत. Text *f*: यौं इंद्र. Text *g*: भगवंति.

26. Texts *f, g* invert the order of the last two padas.

27. Texts *a, b*: जांनि. Text *c*: जांनौं. Text *d*: जाणौ.

28. Texts *f, g* give a somewhat different reading for this pada.

चंचल चपल दृष्टि जब करही ।
    मांनूं बन[29] बिडरी हिरनी फिरही[30] ॥
चितवत चित सबन कौ हरहीं ।
    मांनस कहा ब्रह्मा तप टरही ॥ 15

पांचूं इंद्री बसि करी,
    चीन्हि लीया निज तंत ।
कबीर हरि[31] का भांवंता,
    गावै दास अनंत ॥ doha

Section Eleven

धनि कबीर जु मन नही[1] राषै ।
    हरि के चरन कवल रस चाषै[2] ॥
कांम चेष्टा ले ले बोलै ।
    कबीर का मन कैसैं डोलै[3] ॥ 1

---

29. Texts *a, b, c*: बन. Text *d* omits this word. Text *e*: अनि.

30. Texts *f, g* substitute a different pada for this one.

31. Text *c* alone: ता.

1. Texts *a, b, c*: मन नही. Text *d*: मन महीं. Text *e*: तुम निबहीं. Text *f*: मन दिढ. Text *g*: मंन दिढ.

2. Text *g*: चित भाषै. The other texts all have variants of रस चाषै.

3. Text *a* only: कैसैं डोलैं. Texts *b, c*: कैसैं डोलै. Text *d*: निमिष न ड़ोलै. Text *e*: कैसे डोलै. Text *f*: निमष न डोलै. Text *g*: कबहूं न डोलै. Text *h*: नै कब डोलै.

हम सूं तुम सूं कौंन संगाता ।
जल महि अगनि न लागै माता ॥
जौ पै तूं रुघनाथ पठाई[4] ।
दैन महात्म हम कूं आई ॥ 2

मधिम नांम कमीन[5] हमारा ।
जहां जाहू तहां राज कंवांरा[6] ॥
गोरा मेद कपूर जुबादी ॥
अग्र क चोवा अरु फूलवादी[7] ॥ 3

सकल भोग राजा कै कीजै ।
पाथर कैसें पांनी भीजै ॥
नीची दृष्टि कबीर तुमारी ।
देषौ मेरौ रूप निहारी ॥ 4

4. Text *e* has for this pada: जो पैं सुरूं घन चमडाई.

5. Texts *a, e, h*: कमीन. Text *b*: कमीनि. Text *c*: कधामीन (?). Texts *d, g*: कबीर. For नांम कमीन text *f* has जाति मैं जनम.

6. Text *d*: तुमारा. The other texts have variants of कंवांरा.

7. Texts *f, g* give a considerably different reading for the last two padas.

कष्ट कीऐ[8] काहू नहीं पाई ।
सो हूं[9] तुमारै[10] सहजैं आई ॥
काती[11] कलंजर[12] माघ पिरागू ।
नैंमषर जौ कीजै फागू ॥ 5

गंगा जाइ दसहरा करही ।
कासी करवत ले ले मरही ॥
जा लग परसै[13] देव केदारू ।
सो हम तुमरै[14] सहज भरतारू[15] ॥ 6

---

8. Texts *a, b, c*: कीऐ. Text *d*: कीयै. Text *e*: कीए. Text *f*: कीयां. Text *g*: करचां. Text *h*: क कीये.

9. Texts *a, b, e*: हूं. Text *c*: हुं. Text *d*: हम. Texts *f, g*: हंम. Text *h*: हौ.

10. Text *a* alone: तुरै. The other texts all have variants of तुमारै.

11. Texts *a, b, c, e*: कासी. Texts *d, h*: काती. Texts *f, g*: काग.

12. Texts *a, b, c, d, e*: कलंजर. Texts *f, g*: काज जल. Text *h*: फल जनू.

13. Texts *a, e*: परसै. Text *b*: परसैं. Text *c*: पर्सैं. Texts *d, g*: बसै. Text *h*: वसै.

14. Text *a* alone: सो हम तुमरै. Texts *b, c*: सो तुमारै. Text *d*: सोऊ मेरे. Text *e*: सो तुम्हारें. Text *g*: सो हम तुमरै.

15. Text *f* omits the last two padas.

ऐक[16] तीरथ कोटिक न्हांहीं ।
    एक धूंवां घोटि घोटि मरि जांहीं ॥
ऐक तौ जाइ हिवालै सीझैं ।
    तौ न ताहि[17] अपछरा[18] रीझैं ॥ 7

जब लग लीया न सुष हमारा[19] ।
    तब लग झूठा जन्म तुम्हारा ॥
इतनी मांनौ बात हमारी ।
    बहुत नहीं तौ[20] राषौ दिन च्यारी ॥ 8

तब कबीर बोलै समझाई[21] ।
    हूं तौहि पूछूं सुनि री माई ॥
सुरग लोक तैं कैसैं आई[22] ।
    कैसैं करी हमारी चाही[23] ॥ 9

---

16. Texts *a, b, c, d, e*: ऐक. Text *f*: येक. Text *g*: एकज. Text *h*: ईक तौ.

17. Texts *a, e*: तउ न ताहि. Text *b*: तौ कुन ताहि. Texts *c, d*: तऊ न ताहि. Text *f*: तिन सौं नही. Text *g*: तिनिं सौं नही. Text *h* gives for the whole pada: ता उपर अपछरा नहि रीझै.

18. Text *a* alone has अपरा.

19. Text *a* alone: हरा.

20. This तौ is found only in texts *a, f*. It adds two extra matras to the meter.

21. Text *a* alone: स्मझाई.

22. Texts *a, b, c*: तैं कैसैं आई. Text *d*: कैसैं कै आई. Text *e*: तें कैसी आई. Text *f*: मैं किहि दुषि आई. Text *g*: तैं किहि दुषि आई. Text *h*: तै कैसे आ.

23. Texts *f, g* substitute two different final padas. Text *f* omits the next two verses, substituting two-and-one-half different verses.

ढिग बैठी तुम लाजन मरिहूं ।
  नीच देषि मन संक न करिहूं ॥
बकसि बकसि हूं करूं निहोरा ।
  तुम्हारा ष्याल मरन होइ मोरा[24] ॥ 10

कौंन कौन कौ[25] कह्यौ करांऊं ।
  अब ही रोम रोम[26] बंटि जांऊं ॥
तेरै हाथ न लांऊं मांई ।
  साहिब मेरा रांम[27] रिसाई[28] ॥ 11

नैंन बैंन बिष लगै[29] तुम्हारा ।
  हरि सूं[30] बांध्यां प्रांन हमारा ॥
जिन जिन करी तुमारी आसा ।
  ता कूं निहचै नरके निवासा[31] ॥ 12

---

24. Text *g* omits the final two padas and substitutes two full verses similar to the verses found in text *f*.

25. Text *h* alone omits कौ (and variants).

26. Text *d* alone: अब टूंक टूंक मै.

27. Texts *a, b*: रांम. Text *c*: षरारि. Text *d*: षरा. Texts *e, h*: राम.

28. Texts *f, g* omit the final two padas.

29. Texts *a, b*(?): लैगै. Texts *c, d, e, h*: लगै.

30. Text *a*: सु. Texts *b, c, e*: सूं. Texts *d, h*: सौ.

31. Texts *f, g* omit this verse, but padas similar to *a* and *b* are found in the verses added in these texts after 11.10b.

जो नर[32] तुम सूं प्रीति बढावै ।
ते परचौ बहांवनि पार न पावै ॥
घरि बालक कूवैट[33] पनिहारी ।
न्यौलीयौ चल्यौ सरप कूं मारी ॥ 13

सिर घट ले ता ही परि डारचा ।
बहुरि दांत जीभ[34] सूं मारचा ॥
ऐसा मनि पछितावा होई ।
तेरा संग करै जे कोई ॥ 14

हुंतौ पिटारै मांहीं कारौ ।
मूंसैं जांन्यौं मिष्टि अहारौ[35] ॥
काटि पिटारौ मांही भयऊ ।
निगलि[36] भवंग छेद होइ गयऊ[37] ॥ 15

---

32. Texts *a, g*: जन. Texts *b, c, d, e, h*: नर.

33. Texts *b, d, e, f, g*: कूवै. Text *c*: कूंवै. Text *h*: कुवटै.

34. Text *a* alone: जींभ.

35. Text *d* alone: हमारौ. The other texts give variants of अहारौ.

36. Texts *a, b, c, e*: निगलि. Texts *d, h*: निकसि. Texts *f, g*: निगल्यौ.

37. Text *b* alone omits गयऊ (and variants).

ऐसी गति ता ही की होई ।
तोरौ संग करै जे कोइ[38] ॥
छौडौ माता आस हमारी ।
सुरग लोक कहा परी उजारी[39] ॥ 16

बहुत जतन करि पचि रही,
भया कबीर अडोल[40] ।
गई अपछरा घरि आपणैं,
रह्या भगत का बोल ॥ doha

38. The first two padas are similar to 11.14cd.

39. Text *f* here adds a full chaupai; the first pada of which is similar to the first quarter of the following doha.

40. Text *g* adds here two "indented" padas of a chaupai and one-half of a doha. These padas of the chaupai are the same as the padas cd of the chaupai added after 11.16 in text *f*. The indented half-doha of text *g* is almost the same as the first-half of the doha in text *f*.

Section Twelve

हरि[1] सूं कह्यौ अपछरा जाई[2] ।
कबीर आगैं कछू न[3] बसाई[4] ॥
सकल अंग मांहि मोहन चाहा ।
अंति ऊंडौ नहीं पांऊं थाहा ॥ 1

जौ रवि पछिम उदै करांहीं ।
परबत टारि आघा सिरांही[5] ॥
धू दिषन[6] जो देय पयांनां ।
तउ न होइ कबीर[7] अयांनां ॥ 2

---

1. Text *f* alone: इंद्र.

2. Text *a* alone: अपछराई.

3. Text *b* alone has कहा in place of कछू न (and variants).

4. Text *a* alone: बैसाई.

5. This is reading of text *a* alone. Text *b*: अघास सिरांही. Text *c*: आघास सिराही. Text *d*: आघासरकाई. Text *e*: अघास सरांही. Text *f*: अरु अगनि सिरांही. Text *g*: अरु अग्नि सिराई. Text *h*: अघा अह रीई.

6. This is variant of text *a* alone. Text *b*: दषिन. Text *c*: द . . . न. Texts *d, h*: दछिन. Text *e*: दक्खन. Texts *f, g*: पछिम.

7. Texts *a, g*: न होइ कबीर. Text *b*: न कबीरा होय. Text *c*: न कबीरा होई. Text *d*: न कबीरौ होइ. Text *e*: न कबीरा होइ. Text *f*: कबीर न होई.

माया का सुष तिन भरि लेषै[8] ।
जोग जुगति गोरष बसेषै ॥
तब केसौ अपनौ करि लीन्हौ ।
दर्सन आइ कबीर कूं दीन्हौ ॥ 3

संष चकर गदा पद्म बिराजै ।
कौस्तक मणि पीतांबर साजै[9] ॥
भृगु लता गरुडासन सोहै ।
माथै मुकट देष मन[10] मोहै[11] ॥ 4

श्रवन कुंडल नैंन बिसाला ।
चत्र[12] भुजा बैजंती माला ॥
नष सष सुंदर स्याम सरीरा ।
कुंद कली दसनां वल हीरा ॥ 5

---

8. Text *e* alone: देखै.

9. Texts *a, b, c, e*: साजै. Texts *d, h*: छाजै.

10. Texts *a, b, c, e*: मन. Texts *d, h*: जग.

11. This verse and the next verse and one-half are not found in texts *f, g*. Text *f* substitutes two full chaupais (166, 167), followed by two chaupai padas, followed by what is roughly a doha (168), followed by two chaupai padas. The doha is virtually identical to *Kabir Grathavali, sākhī* 5.1. Text *g* includes the same verses, some padas being indented.

12. Texts *a, b, c*: चत्र. Text *d*: चक्र. Text *e*: छत्र. Text *h*: चतुर.

गज मोतिन की दुलरी कंठा ।
ऐसी भांति बसै[13] बैकूंठा ॥
देषत सीतल भयौ सरीरू ।
चरन कंवल गहि रह्यौ कबीरू ॥ 6

हरि संपति की रति[14] उपजावै ।
तीन लोक कौ सुषद[15] सुनावै ॥
मांगि मांगि मांगै द्यौं सोई ।
जौ तेरै मनि इछा[16] होई[17] ॥ 7

कहै तौ पहुमी कौ पति करिहूं ।
मांथै छत्र अटल करि धरिहूं ॥
कहै तौ इंद्र लोक बैसारूं ।
राषूं सदा कब हु नहीं[18] टारूं ॥ 8

---

13. Text *a*: बैसै. Texts *b*, *c*, *e*: बसै. Texts *d*, *h*: रहै.

14. Texts *a*, *b*(?): हरि संगति की रति. Texts *c*, *e*, *h*: हरि संपति की रति. Text *d*: हरि संपति की रुचि. Text *f*: रांम प्रीति करि रुचि. Text *g*: हरि माया की रुचि.

15. Texts *a*, *b*, *c*, *e*: सुषद. Texts *d*, *g*: सुष हि. Text *f*: सुष ही. Text *h*: सुष.

16. The readings of texts *a*, *b* are not completely clear. Text *c*: यंछ्या. Texts *d*, *g*: इंछा. Text *e*: अंछराप्छाय. Text *h*: इछा.

17. The final two padas are not found in text *f*.

18. texts *d*, *h* put the न before कब. Texts *f*, *g* give a somewhat different reading of this pada.

कहै तौ करामात द्यौं सारी[19] ।
जरंत गडंत उडंत बुडकारी[20] ॥
कहै तौ साचा सबद फुरांऊं ।
याह रहन[21] दे और सुनांऊं ॥ 9

ऐक सरीर चलै[22] छिटकाई ।
दूजी देही लेहु उठाई[23] ॥
अठ सिधि नौ निधि हूं देऊं[24] ।
कंवला सहत चरन हूं[25] सेऊं ॥ 10

---

19. Texts *a, g, h*: सारी. Texts *b, e*: च्यारी. Texts *c, d*: चारी. Text *f*: बहुते री.

20. With minor variants this is the reading in texts *a, c, e*. Text *b* has बूंडंत कारी in place of बुडकारी. Text *d*: जरंत बुडंत उडंत उकारी. Text *f*: गड़ंत उडंत बुड़ंत जलकारी. Text *g*: गडंत वुडंत उडंत जलकारी. Text *h*: जरंत गडंत बुडत उडत कारी.

21. Text *a*: याह रन. Texts *b, c*: या रहन. Text *d*: याह रहण. Text *e*: याह रहन. Text *f*: इहै रहन. Text *g*: वहै रहन. Text *h*: इहै रहण.

22. Texts *a, g*: चलै. Text *b*: चलौ. Texts *c, e*: चलो. Text *d*: चलहु. Text *h*: चल्यौ.

23. Text *h* alone: तुबाई. These first two padas are not in text *f*.

24. This reading, with minor variants, is given for this pada in texts *a, b, c, d, e*. Text *h*: कहैत अठ सिधि नौ निधि देउ. Texts *f, g* are similar to *h*.

25. Text *a*: नित. Texts *b, c, d, e, f, g*: हूं. Text *h*: हौ.

कहै कबीर सुनौ सुनौ सुषदाई ।
    कछू न मांगैं त्रिभुवन राई[26] ॥
अलप बुधि हूं मांगि न जांनूं ।
    सुष सागर कैसैं पहचांनूं ॥ 11

चीटी क्यूं प्रबत ही उठावै ।
    जंगम[27] क्यूं चंद्रमां छिपावै ॥
मोर न उडि आकासैं जाई ।
    अंजुली कैसैं समद समाई ॥ 12

बालक हाथ सरप कूं नांवै ।
    माता सूं पकरन नहीं पावै[28] ॥
भिष्टा अंग लगावै जबही ।
    जननी सावधांन होइ तबही[29] ॥ 13

---

26. Text *d* alone दाइक.

27. Texts *a, b*(?), *c, e*: जंगम. Text *d*: जगन. Text *f*: जीगरा. Text *g*: जिगनां. Text *h*: जौगना.

28. Texts *a, c, e, h*: पावै. Text *b*: आवै. For this pada text *d* gives: माता वाही दूरि रहावै. Texts *f, g* give a somewhat different reading for both the first two padas.

29. Text *d* alone: जबही. The last two padas are not found in texts *d, f*.

गुड दे लीन्हीं मोहर छिनाई[30] ।
    मत मूरष घर देइ लगाई ॥
सुभ असुभ न जांनूं बोली ।
    ऐसी मेरी मति है भोली[31] ॥ 14

इतनी सुनि केसौ सुष पायौं ।
    धनि[32] कबीर जौ मन न डुलायौ ॥
तब हरि च्यारचौं कर माथै दीन्हां ।
    अजर अमर अबिनासी कीन्हां[33] ॥ 15

दे प्रसाद सबै दुष टारचा[34] ।
त्रिभुवन पति बैकूंठ पधारचा[35] ॥ 16

---

30. Text *a* as above. Text *b*: लीनी मोहौरि छिपांई. Text *c*: लीनी मोहर छिनाई. Text *d*: मोहर लीजै छिनाई. Text *e*: मोहर छिनाई. Text *f*: मुहरन लेहु छूडाई. Text *g*: मुहरौ लेइ छिनांई. Text *h*: लीजै मुहर छिनाई.

31. Text *g* inverts the last two padas. Text *f* omits the third pada. Texts *f* and *g* (indented) here add two padas not found in the other texts. Text *g* inverts the order of *f* for these two padas.

32. Text *a*: धन. Texts *b, c, d, e, h*: धनि. Text *g*: धंनि.

33. Text *g* inverts the order of the two half-verses. The readings of texts *f* and *g* are considerably different.

34. Text *a*: हारचा. Texts *b, c, f, g, h*: टारचा. Text *d*: टारे. Text *e*: टारय.

35. Text *d* completes this half-verse adding the following two padas before the padas given above:

निरगुन सरगुन एक है,[36]
सब घटि रह्या समाइ ।
दरीया केरी लहर ज्यूं,
रूपै धरै मिलि जाइ ॥ doha

Section Thirteen

बालपनौ धोषा मैं गयौ[1] ।
बीस बरस तैं चेतन भयौ ॥
बरस सौउ लग कीन्ही भगती ।
ता पीछैं पाई[2] है मुक्ती ॥ 1

सांची भगति कबीर तुह्मारे ।
मोह माया सूं रहै नियारे ।

Texts *f, g* give a considerably different reading for the two padas of the corrected text. These two texts also add here two additional padas (indented in *g*) not found in the other texts.

36. With minor variants (text *a* has नृगुन) this is the reading of the first thirteen *mātrās* in texts *a, b, c, d, e.* Text *f* has: निरगुंन गुंन अलिपत रहै. Text *g* has: निरगुन ब्रह्म अलेष है. Text *h* has: निरगुन एक है.

1. The pada is the same, apart from minor variants, in all texts except text *f*. Text *f*: बारा बरस बालापनि गाईया.

2. Text *d*: कीन्ही. The other texts all have पाई or पइ.

मरना कै मिसि लीला थाटी ।
    सोधि लई मगहर की पाटी[3] ॥
कासी मुक्ति कहैं सब कोई ।
    मगहर मरै सो रासिब होई ॥ 2

कासी काटै सब का पापू ।
    हूं राषूं हरि कौ परतापू ॥
हीन्दू तुरकां पाड़ी आंटी ।
    तुम जालीज्यौ तुम दीज्यौ[4] माटी ॥ 3

बोझ बतीस[5] का फूल मंगाया ।
    तलैं उपरैं[6] सैंन कराया[7] ॥
सब संतन मिलि नाचैं गावैं ।
    ताल पषावज संष बजावैं[8] ॥ 4

---

3. Texts *a, b, d, e, g, h*: पाटी. Text *c*: माटी. Text *f*: बाटी.

4. Text *a* alone: दीज्यो.

5. Text *d* alone: तीन.

6. Text *d* alone here adds: दे.

7. Text *f* omits the first two padas and substitutes a complete verse. Text *g* inserts (indented) the second two padas of the substitute verse after 13.4b.

8. Here text *f* adds four padas, the last two of which are repeats of the last two padas of this verse. The first two of the added four padas are also found (indented) in text *g*.

अमर भयौ छूट्यौ न सरीरू ।
    भयौ[9] सैंदही दास कबीरू ॥
भगतन मांझ अचंभौ भईया ।
    फूल देषि अपनैं घर गईया ॥ 5

एक सुनि सुनि नाज न षांई ।
    एक लोग बहुत पछितांही ॥
कबीर बिना कासी अंधियारा ।
    ज्यूं चंदा बिन दीसैं[10] तारा[11] ॥ 6

ज्यूं बरात मैं दुल्हा नांहीं ।
    ज्यूं घृत बिनां जिवनांर नसाही[12] ॥
ज्यूं बसतर बिन देह मलीनां ।
    यूं कबीर बिन कासी हीनां[13] ॥ 7

---

9. Texts *a, b, c, e*: भयौ. Text *d*: गयौ. Text *g*: गया. Text *h*: गयो. Text *f* has a slightly different reading of this pada.

10. Text *h* alone here adds: सव.

11. Texts *f, g* give somewhat different readings for some of the padas. Texts *f*, and *g* (indented) here add two padas.

12. Text *h*: भोजन कछु नाही. Texts *b, c, d, e* have readings virtually the same as that of text *a* given above. Texts *f, g* have somewhat different readings of this pada, both using the word भोजन.

13. Texts *f, g* omit the final two padas and here add fourteen padas (indented in *g*) not found in the other texts.

जहां जहां कबीर चलि जाई ।
तहां तहां चौगनी बडाई ॥
स्यौ[14] बिरंच आगैं ह्वै लेही ।
सुरपति टारि सिंघास्न[15] देही[16] ॥ 8

बिष्न[17] कहै बैकूंठ तुम्हारौ ।
बसौ[18] सदा यहु भाव हमारौ[19] ॥
सिध सनेह करैं बहौतेरा ।
सौंपन करै भंडार कुमेरा ॥ 9

---

14. Texts *a, b, c, g, h*: स्यौ. Text *d*: सिब. Text *e*: ह्यौ. Text *f*: सिव.

15. Text *c* alone: दुलीचा. The other texts have variants of सिंघासंन.

16. The readings of the last two padas are somewhat different in texts *f, g*.

17. Text *a*: बिष्म. Text *b*: बिष्नं. Text *c*: बिष्न. Text *d*: not clear. Text *e*: विष्णु. Text *g*: बिसन. Text *h*: बिलु. Text *f* has बैठौ यौ in place of बिष्न कहै. In texts *a, c* the half ष looks a bit like a half घ. A similar half ष is found in verse 1.2.

18. Texts *a, b, c, e*: बसौ. Text *d*: वसौ. Texts *g, h*: रहौ.

19. Text *f* omits this pada.

सनकादिक मिलि बैठें संगा ।
    नारद सूं अति बाढचौ रंगा[20] ॥
कहौं कहां लग सब सुष जेता ।
    भयौ अब्यापी[21] देह समेता ॥ 10

हरि अपनां गुन आपै गावै ।
    जन कूं जस दे प्रीति बढावै[22] ॥
भगतन कै संग लागौ डोलै ।
    भगवंत भगतन कै घटि बोलै[23] ॥ 11

20. Text *f* omits the first two padas. They are indented in text *g*.

21. Owing to the similarity of the signs for य and प in several manuscripts, it is possible that the word is अब्यायी. Since all the manuscripts used for this edition have अब्यापी (or अब्यायी), this reading must be accepted. The sense of the verse; however, seems to call for ब्यापी or बियापी; the latter being the reading given in two of Callewaert's manuscripts and used by him in his edition (text *g*).

22. The first two padas are omitted in text *f* and indented in text *g*. Nonetheless, they are nearly the same as the two extra padas added immediately after the end of this verse.

23. With minor variants, this pada is as given above in texts *a, b, c*. Text *d*: भगतन कैं घटि बैठौ बोलै. Text *h*: भगतनि कै संग बैठौ बोलै. Text *f*: अरु भगतनि कै घटि ह्वै बोलै. Text *g*: अर भगतन कै घटि घटि बोलौं.

इतनी कथा कहूं हूं[24] तेरी ।
गावत सुनत मुक्ति ह्वै चेरी[25] ॥
नरनारी जे गावै कोई ।
सहज भाइ[26] सुष पावै सोई[27] ॥ 12

नासै रोग स त्रष्यौ[28] जांहीं ।
ग्यांन भगति उपजै मन मांहीं ॥
बिद्या हींन जो बिद्या पावै ।
कबीर का गुन रूचि रुचि[29] गावै[30] ॥ 13

कबीर है[31] करता की करा ।
भगति करन पहौमी अवतरा ॥
नृगुन ब्रह्म कबीर बिचारा ।
तातैं उतरयौ भवजल पारा ॥ 14

---

24. Texts *a, b, c* are as above (with minor variants). Text *d*: कहूं कहूं हरि. Text *h*: कथा कहौ हरि.

25. Texts *a, b, c*: चेरी. Texts *d, h*: मेरी. The first two padas are not found in texts *f, g*.

26. Text *a*: भाइ. Text *b*: सुभाइ. Text *c*: सुभाई. Texts *d, h*: सब.

27. Texts *f, g* give considerably different readings of this pada.

28. Texts *a, b, h*: स त्रष्यौ. Text *c*: छ त्रष्यौ. Text *d*: सब त्रिषा. Texts *f, g* have somewhat different readings for this pada.

29. Texts *a, g*: रूचि. Texts *b, d*: करि. Text *c* omits the word. Text *h*: कै.

30. Text *f* omits the final two padas. In text *g*, they are indented.

31. Texts *a, c, d, f, h*: है. Text *b*: हैं. Text *g*: कहै.

सुरगुन भक्ति न सांसौ[32] भागै ।
जब[33] लग चित न नृगुन[34] लागै ॥
हरि केता गुन बरनूं तेरा ।
गावत बित्त रहै[35] मन मेरा[36] ॥ 15

जो[37] गिरपति जारि बारि मसि कीजै ।
भार अठारा लेषन लीजै[38] ॥
सात समद की कीजै दोती ।
बसुधा जे कागद की होती[39] ॥ 16

सारद लिषत न आवै अंतूं ।
का कहि गावै दास अनंतूं[40] ॥ 17

32. Text *d*: सांसौ न. The other texts have variants of न सांसौ.

33. Text *d* alone: तव.

34. This is the reading (with variants) of texts *a, g*. Texts *b, c, d, h* give (with variants): नृगुन चित न (text *b*).

35. The reading बित्त रहै (with variants) is given in texts *a, b, c, g*. Text *d*: चक्र तरहै. Text *h*: चक्रि तरहै.

36. Text *f* omits this verse. In text *g*, it is indented.

37. The word जो is found in texts *a, b*(?), *c*. It is not found in texts *d, f, g, h*. The meter is better without it.

38. Texts *a, b, c, f, h*: लीजै. Texts *d, g*: कीजै.

39. Texts *f, g* invert the order of the last two padas.

40. These two padas are somewhat different in texts *f, g*.

दास अनंत कहा[41] कहै,
हरि की[42] कथा अपार[43] ।
कछु ऐक कही कबीर की,
सतगुर कै उपगार ॥ doha

41. Texts *a, b, h*: कहा. Text *c*: का. Text *d*: कथा.

42. Texts *a, b, c, h*: की. Text *d*: गुन.

43. Texts *f, g* give a somewhat different reading for the first half of this doha.

APPENDIX A

THE 1693 V. S. MANUSCRIPT (RPP 11583) OF ANANTA-DAS'S *KABIR PARACHAI*

कवीर जी की परचई । ग्रंथ लिषतं च ॥

रांमांनंद कौ सिष कवीर ।
मति कौ संत भगति दिढ धीर ।
पैहली तौ दासातन कीन्हौ
बहुतक सुष भ[ग][1]तन कौं दीनौं ॥ 1 [1. doha b]

कपरा बुनै बेचि ले आवै ।
अरध पछेवरी षाई षूलावै ।
येक दिना हरि परचौ लीहौ ।
आई चौहटै दरसन दीन्हौ ॥ 2 [2.2]

1. This letter is missing from this text.

यौ हंम सुन्या कबीरा दासा
तातैं हम आये तुम पासा ।
भगति रूप कीये तन षीना
बस्तीर मांग ह्वै ह्वै लीनी ॥ 3 [2.3]

आधी फारि देन जब लागौ ।
सगली देह भगत ह्वै नागौ
दीन्ही तुरत बार नही लाई ।
तव कबीर घर कौं नही जाई ॥ 4 [2.4]

हाटि बाटि कहैं रहे लुकाई
घर कै काहू सुधि न पाई ।
द्यौस तीनि के मांनस भूषे ।
बालक रोवैं बहुत बिदूषे ॥ 5 [2.5]

हरि बिणजारे का रूप बणाया ।
घरि बैठा बालदि लै आया
बहुत सौंज ले आंनि उतारी ।
बरजत ही बाषरि मैं डारी ॥ 6 [2.6]

माता माल धरौ घर माहै ।
बाहरि तैं कोइ ले जाही ।
माता कहै कवन कौ माला ।
महा कठिन कबीर की चाला ॥ 7 [-]

घर मैं धरौ कबीर की माता ।
देहै रांम तुमारौ दाता ।
को है रांम कहा कौ दाता ।
सुनैं कबीर करै अपघाता ॥ 8 [2.7]

दन्हौ लेई न का पैं मांगै ।
मसाकति करै रांम स्यों लागैं ।
जेता बीचै तेता करई ।
उदिम करै यै उदर भरई 9 [-]

तु को बीर कहां तैं आया
को बिनजारौ काहि पठायौ ।
सो हूं हरि भगतन कौ दासा
सदा रहौं संतन कै पासा ॥ 10 [2.8ab, -]

सुनि री माता बात हमारी
कासी नाथ बिस्व अधिकारी ।
ता कै दरसन राजा आया ।
तहि कबीर कू माल चढायौ ॥ 11 [2.9]

दरब न लेई बेटा तोरा
तब राजा उठि कीया निहोरा ।
तुम्ह नही लेहू संतन मुषि दीजे
साहिब जांणि मांनि यहु लीजे ॥ 12 [2.10ab, -]

र तव राजा सब सौंज मंगाई
सो कवीर घरि देन पठाई
घरी येक लैं सोई आवै ।
लोग नगर कै दरसन पावै ॥ 13 [2.11]

ईतनी बात सुनी है जबही ।
माता कौ मन मांन्यौं तबही ।
तब केसौ अदृष्टि ह्वै गयौ ।
अपणौ भेद कछू नही कह्यौ ॥ 14 [-, 2.12ab]

सेवग लैन कबीर ही धाये ।
नीठि नीठि करि घरि लै आये ।
स्वांमी तुम कौं भेट जुअ आई ।
कै षरचौ कै धरौ उठाइ ॥ 15 [2.12cd, 2.13ab]

जब जाई देषी अपना नैंनां ।
तब पतीये पर के बैना ।
कबीर उवाच ।
कौंणै दई कहा तै आई ।
तब माता सब कथा सुणांई ॥ 16 [2.13cd, 2.14ab]

तब कबीर अंतरि गति जांणी ।
क्रिपा करी सो सारंगप्रांनी
ठाकुर मेरौ अैसा करी ।
अब जन काहे कौं डरई ॥ 17 [2.14cd, 2.15ab]

तनना बुनना त्यागि करि ।
    रह्यौं रांम चित लाइ
अब गोब्यंद कृपा करी ।
    पचि पचि मरै बलाई ॥ 18 [2. doha]

तब कबीर कै मनि उपजी अैसी ।
    सौज सकल षरचन की बैठी ।
ठौर ठौर तैं भगत बुलाउ ।
    जा की है सब ताहि चढांउ ॥ 1 [-]

तब भ[ग][2]त बुलाई महोचौ कीन्हौ ।
    कछू न राष्यौ सगलौ दीनौ
कोपे बांभण अर सन्यासी ।
    निद्या करैं कबीर की हासी ॥ [2] [3.1]

[राज]ा आांन्यं दीयौ सोई द्रबु ।
    दे घाल्यौं सुद्रन कौ सर्बु
कछू न राषी बात हमारी ।
    नग्र [मा]झ तैं देहू निकारी ।
विप्र कहीं तै घटि करि जांन्यां ।
    राजा परजा जुगि जुगि मान्यां ॥ 3 [3.2ab,-, 3.2dc]

2. This letter is missing from the text.

येक कहै तिन परि हंम मरिहै ।
जे कबीर कौ उपर करिहै ।
कै हंम कै यौ अैसी आई ।
लुटि लेहु घर मारौ जाई ।
अैसें क्रध करत सब आये
हुते नगर मैं सब उठि धाये ॥ 4 [3.4ab,-, 3.4cd]

गुपती चक्र लीया सन्यासी ।
तमासा देषै सब कासी
चहुं दिसि बाषरि रोकी जाई ।
तब कबीर सनमुष होई आये ॥ 23 [3.5]

आदर करि आगैं बैठारे ।
क्रिपा करी कहौ क्यौं पग धारे ।
बाभन करोध करै द्वावारै ।
निकसि नगर तैं ना तो हि मारैं ॥ 24 [3.6]

जरैं सिन्यासी अति बिन आगी ।
मारै बेगि जाई गौ भागी ।
कौंन चूक तैं मारौ मोही ।
बिगरी बात कहौ किन सोइ ॥ 25 [-, 3.7a,-]

कै मै बाट बिरांणी मारी
    कै मै तकी पराई नारी ।
कै मैं घर काहु का [फो] रचा ।
    मांनस मारि नही घ[र] का [ह] का चोरचा ॥ 26 [3.7cd, 3.8ab]

[भग] ति करी तैं हंमह न बुलाये ।
    सुद्र लोक तैं आणि जिवाये ।
अबही रसोई हंमैह [-] देगा ।
    नही तर हंम तु[-] वैर ब[-]गा ॥ [27] [3.8cd, 3.9ab]

[ठीं]गा ठींगी [ज]बही देषी
    क्रोध न करै कबीर वबेकी ।
अब ईतना नाज नही घर मांहै ।
    लै आंउ तुम [बै]ठौ छाही ॥ 28 [3.9cd, 3.10ab]

संकोच करि कबीर टरि गयौ ।
    केसौ कै मनि बिसंभौ भयौ ।
तब हरि करचा कबीर का आकारा ।
    माथैं द्रब गैब का धारा ॥ 29 [3.10cd, 3.11ab]

सोइ द्रब बनीयां कै दीन्हा ।
    भांति भांति कौ सौदौ लीन्हां
देषि बिप्र सुष उपज्या भारी ।
    कोई न जांनौ चिरत मुरारी ॥ 30 [3.11cd, 3.13ab]

[ज]न की मैंहमा बहुत बढाइ ।
    जनां जनां कौं सेर अढाई
मैंद चावल षांड बहुता ।
    सकल रसोई घृत सहेता ॥ 31 [3.13cd, 3.12ab]

जना च्यारि मंजुर ले घाल्या ।
    सकल सौंज ले घर कौं चाल्या ।
येक कहै जुलहै निधि पाई ।
    सो राजा स्यों कहीये [-] ई ॥ 32 [3.12cd, 3.14ab]

ऐक कहै नीकौ रे नीकौ
    बहुत उ[दा][3]र है जीव कौ ।
बीरा पांन की देत वहुत सुष पायौ ।
    तब कबीर सब कै मनि भायौ
गयौ करोध तब स्वारथ भयौ ।
    धनि धनि सब करता घरि गया । [-] [3.14cd, 3.15]

साचौ भगत कबीर है
    कासीं प्रगट्यो आइ ।
जे कोइ [निद्या] करै
    सोई नरका जाइ ॥ 33 [3. doha]

---

3. This letter is missing from the text.

जहां कबी[र][4] तहां हरि गया ।
अनपहैचानत बाभन भया ।
बैठौ कहा करै रे भाई ।
काहे न तु कबीर के जाई ॥ 34 [4.1]

सब काहु कौं दैत रसोई ।
जौ परि जाइ र मांगै कोई ।
बांभन और स्यन्यासी लीन्ही ।
या देषौ मोहु कौं दीन्हा ॥ 35 [4.2ab, 4.3ab]

मैंदा चावल सेर अढाई ।
घृत सहत अरु दई मिठा ।
इतनी सुनत भयौ सुष भारी ।
केसौ राषी बात हंमारी ॥ 36 [4:2cd, 4.3cd]

तब कबीर घर कौं उठि आयौ
हरि कौ चिरत काहु नही पायौ ।
सकल सौंज [देषी] घर मांहै ।
अजहु बाभण ले ले जांही ॥ 37 [4.4]

धन्य धन्य करै सब कोई ।
तब कबीर महु रष्यौ गोई ।
धन्य धन्य प्रभु ठाकर मेरा ।
हौं तौ सदा तुम्हारौ चेरा ॥ 38 [4.5]

---

4. This letter is missing from the text.

नां कुछ कीया न करि सक्या
न कछुरणैं जोगि सरीर ।
जो कछु कीया स हरि कीया
तातैं भया कबीर कबीर[5] ॥ 39 [-]

हरि विन कौंन वडाइ देई
हरि बिन कौंन अपनौं करि लेई ।
[ब]हु[रि] कबीर कै तारी लागी
भई प्रतीति भर्म गयौ भागी ॥ 40 [4.6]

पेम सहैति हरि के गुन गावै
सोना रूप कपरा देई ।
दास कबीर कछू नही लेई ।
छाजन भोजन ईतनौ लेई ।
भाव सहै जोर हरि जन देई ।
राजा परजा कौ हठ करि त्यागै ।
ता तै अधिक जात्रा लागै ॥ 41 [4.7, 4.8]

निस दिन भीर होत अधिकाई ।
सुमिरण करत चित चलि जाई ।
तब कबीर [ये]क बुधि बिचारी ।
लोक बडाई धरी उतारी ॥ 42 [4.9]

---

5. This verse is the same as *Kabīragranthavali, sakhi* 38.1. In the second pada, the reading should be करणैं.

प्रात समैं ग[नि]का कै गईया ।
        लीन्ही संगि अचंभा भया ।
गलै वांह गनिका कै घाली ।
        गनिका मिलि कबीर संगि चाली ॥ [43] [4.10]

हासी करैं नगर कौ लोगू ।
        भगतन कै मनि उपज्यौ सोगु ।
बांभन बणीयां बहुत बिगोवै ।
        हरि जन देषि देषि मुह गोवै ॥ 44 [4.12]

दिन दस भगति कबीर कीन्ही ।
        अब देषौ गनिका संगि लीन्ही ।
भगति करण चाहैं सब कोई ।
        नीच जाति पै भागति न होई ॥ 45 [4.13cdab]

चलत चलत कबीर गयौ तहां
        नगर कौ राजा बैठौ जहां
और बेर आदर अति करतां
        बै[स]ण कौ सिघासन देतौ । [-] [4.14]

ता दिन आदर कछू न कीन्हा ।
        सब कै पीछै बैठन दीन्हा ।
राजा मनि अचिरज भया ।
        ऐसौ भगत बिगरि क्यों गयौ ॥ 47 [4.15]

भयौ अंचंभौ नगर मैं ।
    सब कोई करै बिचार ।
निद्या बिंद्या क्या भया ।
    सिर परि सिरजनहार ॥ 48 ॥ 3 ॥ [4. doha]

जैंह औसरि कबीर जरि डारचा ।
    हरि का पंडा जरत उबारचा ।
सांसौ बुझै नगर कौ पती
    कहै कबीर जा अपणी गती ॥ 49 [5.1]

कौंण चिरत तैं करि दिषलाया ।
    ता का भेद न काहु पाया ।
कहै कबीर सुणौ हो राई ।
    कहैं सुनैं तौ को पतिआई ॥ 50 [5.2]

जगनाथ का पंडा जरीया ।
    पाता फूटि पाव परि परीया ।
सो जल सीचि लीयौ मैं राषी ।
    हरि कृपा तै देष्यौ आंषी ॥ 51 [5.3]

तब राजा सब कौ मुष चाहै ।
    साची कहै क हम ही बाहै ।
भगत येक अैसैं समझावै ।
    राजा परजा कै मनि भावै ॥ 52 [5.4]

छाकि छाकि छाक्यौ सौ बोलै ।
    कबीर कौ मन निमष न डोलै ।
राजा पत्री तुरत लिषाई ।
    घरी महूरत भूलि न जाई ॥ 53 [5.5]

जगनाथ कौं नफर चलायौ ।
    कबीर अपणै घरि उठि धायौ ।
दिन दस मैं जो पहुतौ जाई ।
    दाधा पंडा लीया बुलाई ॥ [-] [5.6]

कहौ पंडा मन का सतभाउ ।
    कहिं बिधि जरचा तुमारा पाउ ।
भात पसावत पंडा जरचा
    पाता फूटि पावन परि परचा ॥ 55 [5.7]

तब कबीर पां[नी] ले आया ।
    दया करी तिहि आंनि बुझाया ।
इतनी बात सुनि बूझै सांसा ।
    कौंन कबीर कहौ धौं कै [सा] ॥ 56 [5.8]

जाति जुलाहा कासी बासा ।
    सब कोई जांनैं हरि कौ दासा ।
पेम सहित हरि के गुन गावै
    लोक दुरि के दरसन आवै ॥ 57 [5.9abdc]

सो कबीर हम देष्या तबही ।
    पाव जरत जर आन्यौ जबही ।
तब दूतनि मनि आंनंद कीयौ
    उलटि पयांनौं घर कौं दीयौ ॥ 58 [5.10]

दिन दस मै कासी चलि आया ।
    लोग नगर को पूछण धायौ ।
दूत कहै राजा स्यौ भेदू ।
    हंम पांडे स्यौं कीयौ न षेदू ॥ 59 [5.11]

जो पांडे हम स्यौ नृप भाषी ।
    सो हंम तुम स्यौ कछू न राषी ।
राजा का मन बिलषा भया ।
    आया मंत्री बिसरजन रहीया ॥ 60 [5.12]

अब कबीर कौं मिलिये जाई ।
    नातर कछू न होई भलाई ।
कबीर साधू का हम मरम न जांनां ।
    सो हंम उतर तम स्यौ ठांनां ॥ 61 [5.15ab, 5.13ab]

राजा रांनी तुरत बुलाई ।
    भई कथा सो कहि कमझाई ।
रानी कहै बिलंम न कीजे ।
    येक बेर कबीर के पाई परीजे ॥ 62 [5.13cd, 5.14ab]

राजा बोलै डरपौं भारी ।
देई सराप कै ले उबारी ।
कौंण भेट ले मिलिये जाई ।
दरब देष ता उठै रिसाई ॥ 63 [5.14cd, 5.15cd]

कंधि कुहाड़ी मेल्हि करि ।
सिरि लकरिन का भार
कंटुब [सहैत] राज चल्यौ
सब जग देषणहार ॥ 64 ॥ 4 ॥ [5. doha]

बरसिंघ दे बाघेलौ राजा ।
साध जांणि सब षोई लाजा ।
देषि कबीर सांमहां उठि धाया ।
हिरदै उमगि प्रेम होई आया ॥ 65 [6.1]

डारि डारि माथा का भारू ।
हमारै रोस न येक लगारू ।
भारा रारि नृप डंडवत कीना ।
तब अंकमाल भरि लीना ॥ 66 [6.2ab, 6.3ab]

येक पव राजा गहि रहीया ।
दूजा पाव कटूंब सब गहीया ।
बकसौ स्वामी चूक हमारी
तुम बिन कौंन करै रषवारी ॥ 67 [6.3cd, 6.4ab]

कहै कबीर भली तुम कीन्ही ।
    हंम कौं आनि बड़ाई दीनी ।
बडे और कौं देहि बडाई ।
    कै सो बडा बांटि धन षाई ॥ 68 [6.5]

साचा [झू]ठ कौ बडा पहिवांनै ।
    मुरिष कहा बडाई जांनै ।
तब राजा मनि आंनंद भया ।
    दरसन पाई अपनैं घ[रि] गया ॥ 69 [6.6]

बहुरि कबीर अपनौं नाउ मिटावै ।
    ज्यौं कुलउती गृभ द्वरवै ।
करनी कैसैं छांनी होई ।
    उग्या अरक छिपै नही सोई ॥ 70 [6.7abdc]

जौ कोई अपनी करत वडाई ।
    बडौ न होई हीनता जाई ।
अैसी बिधि सब लोग भुलांणां ।
    हरि जन हरि भजि हरि ही समांनां ॥ 71 [6.8ab, 6.9ab]

विगरच कारिज रांम संवांरै ।
    भौजल बुडत पारि उतारै ।
येक समैं अैसी मनि आई ।
    बिधि संजोग न मेट्या जाई ॥ 72 [6.10ab, 6.14ab]

साह सिकंदर कासी आयौ ।
काजी मुलां कै मनि भायौ ।
चले फिरादि मिले सब कोई ।
ईनि बांभन बनियां की मति षोई ॥ 73 [6.14cd, 6.15ab]

घर मैं बुरी कबीर की नारी ।
धनि कबीर सो लेइ सुधारी ।
और कबीर की माता षोटी ।
भगति न भावै पकरै चोटी ॥ 74 [-, 12dab]

तब कबीर की माता दौरी
समझाई समझै नही बौरी ।
अति आतुर ह्वै जाइ पुकारी ।
मानहु उन के मांनस मारी ॥ 75 [6.15cd, 6.16ab]

कबीर की राक्ष्या करै गोब्यंदु ।
सो जस गावै दास अनंदु ॥ [6.16cd]

साह सिकंदर तु बडौ
मेटि हमारी पीर
अैसी कोई ना करी ।
तैसी करी कबीर ॥ 76 ॥ 5 ॥ [6. doha]

कहै सिकंदर क्या है भाई ।
        गांव पड़िगना लीया छुडाई ।
गांव पड़िगनां नाही लीनां ।
        हंम कौं कबीर बहुत दुष दीना ॥ 77 [7.1abc,-]

नीदै संकर नीदै माई ।
        नीदै सारद गंणपति राई ।
नीदै मात पिता की सेवा ।
        बहनि भांनिजी सब ही देवा ॥ 77 [= 78] [7.3ab, 7.4ab]

नीदै छह दरसन का मंतु ।
        नीदै तीरथ अनंतु ।
नीदै माला तिलक जनेउ तारा ।
        सालिगरांम अरू दस औतारा ॥ 79 [-]

ये सब झूठा कहै कबीरा ।
        हींदू तुरक दहु नहीं नीरा ।
अैसी बिधि सब लोक बिगारचा ।
        हींदु तुरक यैक ठा बैठारचा ॥ 80 [-, 7.5ab]

जब लग जुलहा कासी होई ।
        तब लग हमैं न मांनै कोई ।
अैसी बात तुं निवारि हंमारी ।
        बडौ पातिसाहं तू अधिकारी ॥ 81 [7.5dc, 7.6a,-]

सुनत सिकंदर उठ्यौ रिसाई ।
छरीदार दोइ दीये पठाई ।
आंनौं बेगि बार नही कीजे ।
बीनती करै सजा ताहि दीजे ॥ 82 [7.6cd, 7.7a,-]

छरीदार जाई षबरि सुनावै
साह सिकंदर तोहि बुलावै ।
मोहि सिकंदर कहै कयौं जांनै ।
कहा कहौ कैसै पहिचांनैं ॥ 83 [7.7cd, 7.8ab]

तेरी मा उप्रजारी रारी ।
काजी बांभण सहैति पुकारी ।
प[ति] साह कबीर दुष दीनां ।
सब मात मेटि वेक मत लीनां ॥ 84 [7.8cd,-]

मुसलमांन की छाडी राहा ।
हीदू तुरक की करणी नही चाहा ।
ज्यौं जानैं त्यों ही लै आहूं ।
हम कौ हूकम कीयौ पतिसाहू ॥ 85 [-]

समझि कबीर चले मन माहैं ।
जौ न चलै तौ बलि लै जांही
सब संतन कौ दे परमोधू ।
तुम जिनि करौ हमारौ षोधू ॥ 86 [7.9]

अति आतुरि ह्वै असुर पठाया ।
जन द्वै बारि लैन जब आया ।
येक बेर बेगि लै आई ।
पातिसाह कौं षबरि सुनाई ॥ 87 [7.10ab,-]

साह सिकंदर बैठौ आई ।
पकरि कबीर कौं आगै लै जाई ।
दे सांवर मनमथ लाजै ।
सिर परि तुलछी तिलक बिराजै ॥ 88 [-, 7.11ab]

मुदित बचन अरु न्रमल नैंनैना ।
जब बेलै तब अंमृत बैना ।
काजी मुलां कहै समझाई ।
करि तसलीम सीस फुनि नांई ॥ 89 [7.11cd, 7.12ab]

हौं तसलीम कहा करि जांनौ ।
तू काजी कछू भयौ दिवांनौं ।
कहै सिंकंदर अैसी बाता ।
हौं तूहि देषौं दोजिग जाता ॥ 90 [7.12cd, 7.13ab]

राह छांडि अर गही कुराहा ।
कैहै बे जुलहा तु किन बाहा ।
अपनी राह चलत गति होई
बेद पुराण पुछि मंत दोई ॥ 91 [7.13cd, 7.14a,-]

कबीर बोलै ग्यान बसेषौ
सकल सभा मृतक समि लेषै ।
दोजिग परै तुरक अरु हीदू
काजी बांभण भूले दोऊ ॥ 92 [7.14cd, 7.15a,-]

हौं तौ भाव भगति मै आयै ।
गुर परसादि रांम गुण गाये ।
रांम भरोसै गिणौ न काउ
सब मिलि राजा रांक रिसाउ । [7.15cd, 7.16ab]

राषणहारा रांम है ।
मारि न सकै कोइ ।
पातिसाह हूं ना डरूं ।
करता करै स होई ॥ 94 ॥ 6 ॥ [7. doha]

काढि कतेब सुनावै काजी
बिचि विचि बांभण दैहैं भाजी ।
देषौ धरम तुमारौ या कौ ।
सात पथरी या यौ करि मारौ ॥ 95 [8.1]

तब रहै रवा जानै सब कोई ।
मुसलमांन काफर नही होई ।
कहै कबीर समझि कि न करहु ।
तुम ही काफिर तुम ही मरहु ॥ 96 [-, 8.2bcd]

कौंण कतेब जु गाइ कटाई ।
    बकरी मुरगी किनि फुरमाई ।
जेते देषौं आतम घाती
    तिनकी जम तोड़ैगा छाती ॥ 97 [8.3]

राजा परजा नरकि पराइ ।
    रांम कहै तिनकौं डर नांही ।
सुनत सिंकंदर उठे रिसाई ।
    जानौं घृत आहुति लगाई ॥ 98 [8.4]

ज्यौ कारे कौ पुछ दबायौ ।
    जानौ तुपक पलीतौ लायौ
ज्यौ बैसांदर दीन्हौ होई ।
    गाफिल संक न मांनैं मोरी ॥ 99 [8.5abc, 8.6a]

करामाति सो मोहि दिषावै
    राषणहारा सो बेगि वुलावो ।
हाथ बांधि गहि मेल्रा जंजीरा ।
    लै डारचौ गंगा की तीरा ॥ 100 [-, 8.6cd]

हुकम करत कबीर गही लीना ।
    मांझ धार गंगा मैं दीनां ।
टूटि जंजीर परचा जल मांहैं ।
    लागा तीर सो बूडा नाही ॥ 101 [8.7]

उपज्यौ क्रोध असुर यौ भाषै ।
    जल तैं उबरचा अब को राषै ।
बहुरि कबीर मंदिर मैं डारचा ।
    आसि पासि पावक परजारचा ॥ 102 [8.8]

भया हुतासन जैसा नीरा
    हरि हरि सुमरै दास कबीरा ।
जरि गया मंदिर षेह उडांणी ।
    कबीर नै राषै सारंगप्राणी ॥ 103 [8.9ab, 8.10a,-]

अधिक रूप नारांईन दीनां
    पावक जरत राषि हरि लीना ।
जै जै कार भया जग मांहै ।
    काजी बांभण बहुत रिसांही ॥ 104 [8.10c,-, 8.11ab]

नाटिक चेटक जुलहा जांनैं ।
    साह सिकंदर तू जनि मांनैं ।
तब मातौ हाथी असुर बुलायौ
    अपनी छांह बेधतौ आयौ ॥ 105 [8.11cd, 8.12cd]

संक न करै महावत केरी ।
    सब हाथनि मैं लीयौ नबेरी ।
सोनैं सांकर बांध्यौ राषै ।
    दांनां कुची दुरि तैं नांषै ॥ 106 [8.13]

सोनैं आंकुस दांत मढाये ।
बिचि बिचि हीरा मोती लाये ।
नगर माहि जौ छुटन पावै ।
मांनस मारै कोट ढहावै ॥ 107 [8.14]

रिण मै रावत मारे बंके ।
भाट बिड़द बोलत है ताके ।
कुजरि बहुत नांव रिण जीतु ।
पंथि चलै जौ गावै गीतु ॥ 108 [8.15ab, 8.16ab]

भौर काल मथा हर थापा ।
तेल सिदुरन धूपनि धूपनि धाप ।
सकल सिगार घंटा चौरासी ।
इंद्र लोक नही उपैं जासी ॥ 109 [8.15cd, 8.16cd]

सो कबीर कूं आणि ढुकावा ।
पीछैं चलै न आगैं आवा
तब रजि रह्यौ रोस धरि अैसैं ।
जन कबीर आगैं सिध बैसैं ॥ 110 [8.17ab,-]

काल रूप गज कोपीया ।
सब कोई चाल्या भागि ।
दास कबीर न डरपई ।
रह्यौ रांम स्यौ लागि ॥ 111 [8. doha]

स्यंघ रूप [केसौं] डरपावै ।
    ता तैं हाथी निकट न आवै ।
पीलवान कौं दरसन दीनां
    मोडि गईद षड़ा करि लीना ॥ 112 [9.1]

पीछैं साह सिकंदर दीठा ।
    कबीर आगैं सिंघ बईठा ।
पीलवांन हसती करि न्यारा ।
    देष्या कबीर रांम तुमारा ॥ 113 [9.2abc,-]

अब कै राषौ जीव हंमारा ।
    साचा रांम कबीर तुमारा ।
देषि दीनता कहै कवीरा
    जिनि डरपौ राषै रघुबीरा ॥ 114 [9.3ba, 9.4ab]

अब जौ निमष येक नही डरता ।
    संत वैर हरि परलै करता
जो जन देषै हरि की काया ।
    सो जन हरि अपना करि लाया ॥ 115 [-, 9.4d, 9.6cd]

मंन वच क्रम जो हरि का होई ।
    ता को काज न बिगरै कोई ।
कबीर कै दूषणि नही आई ।
    ता तैं असुरि सजा नही पाई ॥ 116 [-, 9.6b, 9.5ab]

जै कोई आगैं औगंन जांनै ।
ताऊ साध भलौ करि मांनैं ।
काजी बांभन मरम न जांनैं ।
सिरजनहार तुम्हारी मांनैं ॥ 117 [9.5cd, 9.3cd]

जो भगतन की निद्या करई ।
कूभी नरक मांझ सो परई ।
तब केसौ अद्रिष्टि ह्वै गईया
गहे असुर तब कबीर के पाई ॥ 118 [-, 9.7ab]

मागौ सोना मांगै रूपा ।
मांगौ कपरा अधिक अनूपा ।
मांगौ गांव परिगना घोरा ।
तुम कौं दीजे सो सब थोरा ॥ 119 [9.7cd, 9.8ab]

कहै कबीर न मांगौं माया ।
राजा परजा सब ईनि बाह्य ।
माया मांगै भगत न होई ।
मन दिढि राषै निज जन सोई ॥ 120 [9.8cd, 9.9ab]

मसतग नाई कह्यौ तब अैसैं ।
जाऊ कबीर अपनैं घरि बैसौ ।
घरि आये तब दास कबीरा ।
गुर प्रसादि भया अमर सरीरा ॥ 121 [-, 9.9d, 9.10cd]

बुहरि कबीर की लागी जाता ।
　　सब संतनि मिलि पुछी बाता ।
हस्य हस्य बोलै दास कबीरा ।
　　चरण सरण राषै रघुबीरा ॥ 122 [9.11]

पातिसाह जब कसनी दीनी
　　तब मेरै मंनि संक न कीनी ।
जहां जहां कष्ट तहां हरि तूठा ।
　　काजी बांभन है गया झूठा ॥ 123 [9.12ab, 9.10ab]

भगत भगवंत कौं बल जहां होई ।
　　ता कौं मारि न सकै कोई ।
कोटि पाप हरि भगत नसावै ।
　　भगतन पीछैं हरि चलि आवै ॥ 124 [9.12cd, 9.13ab]

जो भगतन स्यौं होई नीयारा ।
　　ता का ताही हरि रषवारा ।
जो भगतन स्यौं करै भरांती ।
　　सो जीव होई सदा नरक पांती ॥ 125 [9.13cd, 9.14c,-]

गुर गोब्यंद भगतन मैं चीन्ह ।
　　ता तैं मेरा कछु न कीना ।
भगत भगवंत भये दोन्यों सहाई ।
　　ताती बाव निकट नही आई ॥ 126 [9.15cd,-]

जल बोवत पवक जरत
    बिनसत नही सरीरा ।
गज तौरत हरि राषीया ।
    निृभै दास कबीरा ॥ 127 ॥ 8 ॥ [9. doha]

बहूरचौ मिलि बांभना मतौं कीनौं ।
    जुलहै हंम कौं बहुत दुष दीनौं ।
परपच ऐक कीया अनहौंता
    छल बल ताकै अपनी वोता ॥ 128 [10.1cd, 10.2ab]

बाभन चौह का मुड मुडाया ।
    माल दई अरु तिलक मनाया ।
सीष दई अरु गुपत चलाया ।
    चहुं देस के भगत बुलाया ॥ 129 [10.2cd, 10.3ab]

दल सब दीयौ कबीर कै नांउ ।
    सौ सौ कोस तहां चलि आवो ।
माघ मांस पैहैलै पषवारै
    ऐकादसी पधारौ द्वारै ॥ 130 [10.3cd, 10.4a,-]

दास कबीर महोछै थाटा ।
    सब संतन की चाहै बाटा ।
माथै मानि मानि दल लीन्हा ।
    संतनि सकल पयाना दीन्हा । [10.5abc,-]

अैसौ कपट बाभना कीन्हौ ।
केसौ सबै साच करि लीन्हौ ।
बीसक बाभन लेषनि लेही ।
और बीसक सिषावनि दैहै ॥ 132 [10.6a,-, 10.7ab]

दिना बीस लौ न ावै अंतू ।
सो जस गावै दास अनंतू ।
जा की वोर [आ]प है रांमू ।
ता कौ कौंन बिगारै कांमू ॥ 133 [10.7cd,-]

करी कुटिलतादि जन मिल्य ।
मन मैं बाध्यौ बंध ।
रांम सहाई कबीर की ।
अजहू न जाणै अंध ॥ 134 [-]

भगत सकल जस गावत आवै ।
कहां कबीर दरस हंम पावै ।
द्वारौ छोडि कबी[र][6] तब गयौ ।
केसौ रूप कबीर कौ भयौ ॥ 135 [-]

भगत भगत कौ साम्हौ आयौ ।
करि अस्तुति र डेरौ द्यायौ ।
ज्यूं ज्यूं कहै त्यूं त्यूं करही ।
जन जन आगै बिग पति करई ॥ 136 [-]

6. This letter is missing in the manuscript.

कही कोई नाचै कही कोइ गावै ।
　　हरि का भेद कोई नही पावै ।
दिना पंच लौं लीला कीनी ।
　　ता पीछै पहरांवनी दीनी ॥ 137 [10.10]

महिमा अधिक महोचै राषी ।
　　धनि धनि कबीर सब कोई भाषै ।
माहि हूवो कबीर सुष देषै ।
　　जीवनि जन्म सुफल करि लेषै ॥ 138 [-, 10.11cd]

राम कबीर ऐसी बनि आई ।
　　ता तैं बाभन रहे षिसाई ।
जिन का काज आप हरि करीया ।
　　तिन परि दोष और क्या सरिया ॥ 139 [10.12ab,-]

बाभन सब अचिरज भयौ ।
　　रह्यौ महोछै रंग
गाई बछ ज्यूं कबीर कै ।
　　सदा रहै ह[रि] संग ॥ 140 [-]

बरस येक भयौ है जबही ।
    इंद्र अपछरा पठई तबही ।
बार बार यौं इंद्र सिषाई ।
    छलबल करि लीज्यौ अंगि लाई ॥
आन्य अपछरा [-]ई दिषाई ।
    सुरग लोक तैं रंभा आई[7] ॥ 142[10.12cd, 10.13dc, 10.14ab]

जा कै रूपि न पुजै कोई ।
    मधुरे वचन सुनावै सोई ।
चंचल चपल दिष्टि जब करही ।
    मन संकोचन ब्रह्मा डरई ॥ 143 [10.14cd, 10.15ab]

पांचौं ईंद्री बसि करी
    चीन्हि लीया निज संत ।
कबीर हरि का भांवता ।
    यौं गावै दास अनंत ॥ 144 [10. doha]

धनि कबीर जिनि मन दिढि राष्यौ ।
    हरि कौ चरणं कंवल रस चाष्यौ ।
कांम चेष्टा अति ले बोलै ।
    कबीर कौ मन निमष न डोलै ॥ 145 [11.1]

---

7. The copyist apparently omitted two padas that are in fact found in other manuscripts. They come after the first two padas.

हंम ही तुम ही नही सगाई ।
जल मैं अग्नि न लागै माई ।
जौ पैं तुम रघुनाथि पठाई ।
दीने महातुम हंम कौं आई ॥ 146 [11.2]

मधिम जाति मैं जनम हंमारा ।
जहां जाव तहां राज कुवांरा
अगर कपुर चंदन कस्तूरी ।
सकल भोग राजन कै पुरी ॥ 147 [11.3]

बहत भोग राजन कै कीजै ।
हंमारै आई कहौ का कीजै ।
जाति जुलाहा नांव कबीर ।
हमै तुमैं नही कछु सारा ॥ 148 [11.4a,-]

माता हंम स्यौं बाद न कीजे ।
पाथर पांन्यौ कैसैं भीजै ।
पानी मौंहौ अगिन्य न लागै ।
माता हम बलिक हूं तुम आगै ॥ 149 [-, 11.4b,-]

नीची दृष्टि कबीर तुम्हारी ।
हंम दिस देषौ रूप निहारी ।
कसट कीयां किनहूं नही नही पाई ।
सो हंम सहजि तुम्हारै आई ॥ 150 [11.4cd, 11.5ab]

काग काज जल माघ पियागा ।
    नीबषा[स्य] कजै फल लागा ।
येक गंगा जाई दसहैरा करइ ।
    येक कासी करवत ले ले मरई ॥ 151 [11.5cd, 11.6ab]

येक तीरथ जाई जाई न्हांवै ।
    धूम घोटि केई मरि जावै ।
केई जाई हीवालै सीझै ।
    तिन सौं नही अपछरा रीझै ॥ 152 [11.7]

जब लग नही लह्या सुष हंमारा ।
    तब लग झुठा ग्यांन तुम्हारा ।
इतनी बीनती मांनि हंमारी ।
    बहुत नही तौ राषी दिन च्यारी ॥ 153 [11.8]

तबै कबीर कहै समझाई ।
    हौं तोहि पूछौ सुनि री माई ।
सुरग लोक मैं किहि दुषि आई ।
    सो हंम आगैं कहि समझाई ॥ 154 [11.9]

कहत मोहनी काज न कोई ।
    तुम ही [भर]तार करन हंम आई ।
जाति जुलाहां संगि न काजू ।
    छि[ढे]ग बैठे तैं मरिये लाजू ॥ 155 [-, 11.10a]

नीच देषि तोहि संक न आवै ।
नैन बैन बिष लागै माई ।
चितहि चपलता अधिक तुमारी ।
कांम रूप भरि जोति निहारा ॥ 156 [11.10b,-]

हरि सौं लागा प्रांण हमारा ।
नाही कछु तुमारा चारा ।
कौंन कौंन कौ कह्यौ कराई ।
अब तौ रोम रोम बंटि जाई ॥ 157 [-, 11.11ab]

घरि बालक कूवै पणिहारी ।
चाल्यौ न्यौल सर्प कौं मारी ।
सिर तैं गागरि उपरि डारी ।
पीछैं जीभ दांत स्यौं मारी ॥ 158 [11.13cd, 11.14ab]

अैसी गति ताहू की होई ।
तुम सौं प्रीति करै जौ कोई ।
हुतौ पिटारा भीतरि कारा ।
मूंसौं जानैं मिट अहारा ।
काटि पिटारा भीतरि धावा ।
निगल्यौ भू[वं]ग छेद ह्वै आवा ॥ 159 [11.14cd, 11.15]

अैसी गति ताहूं की होई ।
तुम सौं प्रीति करै जौ कोई ।
छाडौ माता आस हंमारी ।
सुरग लोक का परी उजारी ॥ 160 [11.16]

बहुत जतन करि करि पचि हारी ।
    दास कबीर न निमष निहारी ।
नैं बैंन सब [बा]न चलाये ।
    कबीर निकटि येक नही आवै ॥ 162 [11. doha a,-]

अपछरा अपनै सब कीई ।
    भयौ कबीर अडोल ।
गई अपछरा अपनै ।
    रह्यौ भगत कौ बोल ॥ 163 [-, 11. doha bcd]

इद्र सौं कह्यौ अपछरा जाई ।
    कबीर जी आगैं कछू न बसाई ।
बहत जतन करि हंम हारी ।
    कबीर कै मनि बसै मुरारी ॥ 163[8] [12.1ab,-]

जौ रवि पछिम उदौ कराही ।
    मेर टरै अरु अगनि सीरांही
जौ धू पछिम करै पयांनां
    तउ कबीर न होई अयांनां ॥ 164 [12.2]

माया का सुष तिन भरि लेषै ।
    जोग जुगत्य गोरष बसेषै ।
तब केसौ अपना करि लीया ।
    प्रगट कबीर कौ दरसन दीया ॥ 165 [12.3]

8. The number is repeated.

बाहरि भीतरि जोति सरूपा ।
अबिनासी तत अगम अनुपा
रोमि रोमि रवि अंत प्रकासा
हिलिमिलि दामनि अनंत उजासा ॥ 166 [-]

तेज पुज सकल भरपुरा ।
हिलिमिलि षेलै दास हजुरा ।
सोभा कहौ कवन की दीजै
धरी बसत उपजै सब छीजै ॥ 167 [-]

हरि की सोभा हरि ही छाजै ।
दूजा कौंवन समीप विराजै ।
कबीर तेज अनंत की
मांनु उग्या सूरिज सेनि ।
पति संगि जागी सूदरी ।
कौतिग देष्या तेनि[9] ॥ 168 [-]

महिमा मुष तै कहत न आवै ।
मन मांहै अतिसै सुष पावै ।
देषत सीतल भया सरीरा ।
चरण कवल गहि रह्या कबीरा ॥ 169 [-, 12.6cd]

---

9. This verse is the same as *Kabir Granthavali, sākhī* 5.1.

रांम प्रीति करि रुचि उपजावै ।
तीनि लोक का सुष ही सुनावै ।
कह तौ पहमी कौ पति करौ ।
माथैं छत्र अटल करि धारैं ॥ 170 [12.7ab, 12.8ab]

कहै तौ ईंद्र लोक बैठारौं ।
राषौं अटल कदे नही टारौं ।
कहै तौ दैहु करांमंति बहुतेरी ।
गडंत उडंत बुडंत जलकारी ॥ 171 [12.8cd, 12.9ab]

बृधि सरीर आपनौ मेलै ।
नइ देह घरि घरि षेलौं ।
कहै तौ साचा सबद फुरांउ ।
इहै रहन दै और सुनांउ ॥ 172 [-, 12.9cd]

कहत अठ सिधि नव निधि दैउ
कंवला सहत चरण हूं सेउं ।
कहत कबीर सुनौ सुषदाई ।
कछू न मांगौं त्रिभुवनराई ॥ 173 [12.10cd, 12.11ab]

चीटी कैसैं मेर उठावै ।
कहां जीगरा चंद छिपावै ।
मोर न उडि आकासां जाई ।
अजरी मैं क्यूं स्मद स्माई ॥ 174 [12.12]

बालक अगनि हाथ दे जबही ।
    माता सावधान होइ तबही ।
गुड़ दे मुहरन लेहु छूडाई ।
    मूरिष मति छैरि देइ लगाई ॥ 175 [12.13ab, 12.14ab]

ऐसी मेरी मति है भोरी ।
    मांगौं कहा अलप बुधि थोरी ॥ 176
तुम सरबंगी सकल बिधि जानौं ।
    चरंण छडि मांगै स अयाना ॥ 176 [12.14d, 12.11c,-]

तब केसौ अपना करि लीया ।
    भगत जांनि अरू सर्बस दीया ।
अंग सौं अंग समरस करि लीन्हा ।
    अजर अमर अबीनासी कीना ॥ 177 [-, 12.15d]

देइ अभै पद सब सुष टारचा ।
    जन कबीर ऐसै निस्तारचा ।
निरगुंण ब्रह्म निरंजन नाथा ।
    सो कबीर कैं संगि ही साथा ॥ 178 [12.16a,-]

निरगुंन गुंन अलिपत रहै ।
    सब घटि रह्या स्माई ।
दरिया केरी लहरि ज्यूं ।
रूप धरै मीली जाई ॥ [12. doha bcd]

बारा बरस बालापनि ग[-] ईया ।
बीस बरस का चेतनि भइया ।
बरस सौ लौं कीन्ही भगती ।
ता पीछै पाइ है मुकती ॥ 180 [13.1]

मरणै कै मिसि लीला ठाटा ।
सोधि लई मगहर की बाटी ।
कासी मुकति जात सब कोई ।
मंगहर मरै स रासिब होई ॥ 181 [13.2]

जौ कासी काटै सब पापू ।
मैं राषौं हरि कौ परतापूं ।
हीदु तुरक दहू पड़ी आटी ।
तुम जारौ तुम दीज्यौ आटी ॥ 182 [13.3]

फुल बिछाइ सैन तब कीनी ।
हीदु तुरक रारि कैसी लीन्ही ।
वै कहै गाडौ वै कहैं जारै ।
अपनौ अपनौ धरम बिचारै ॥ 183 [-]

संत सकल मिलि नाचै गावै ।
तार पषावज संष बजावै ।
दहूं वोर तैं देषन आये ।
पाये फूल कबीर न पाये ॥ 184 [13.4cd,-]

संत सकल मिलि नाचै गावै ।
तार पषावज संष बजावै ।
भया अमर छूटै न सरीरा ।
सैदेही उठि गया दास कबीरा ॥ 185 [13.4cd, 13.5ab]

सेवग संतन नाज न षाई ।
कबीर बिछरचा बहुत पछिताई ।
बिन कबीर कासी अँधीयारी ।
चंद बिना नही सोहै तारा ॥ 186 [13.6]

दीपक बिना न मंदिर सोहै ।
बिन कबीर कासी मैं को है ।
दूलह बिना बरात न सोहै ।
घृत बिन भोजन का[-] होई ॥ 187 [-, 13.7ab]

इंद्र लोकि भया अधिक उछाहा ।
सुर तेतीसौ कौतिगि आया ।
पूजा अरचा अधिक बनांया ।
ये हरि दास कहां हंम पावै ॥ 188 [-]

ब्रह्मा कहै भाग बड मेरा ।
साध दरसण कौं निसदिन हेरा
ब्रह्म लोक है तुम परिवारी ।
दरसन दुलंभ भयौ करौ मनहारी ॥ 189 [-]

बिसन कहै बैकूठ ही लीजे ।
सो है कहा स तुम दीजे ।
श्री सहैत सब विभौ बिलासु ।
सो तुम आगैं करै निग्वासू ॥ 190 [-]

हरि जन हरि बिन नजरि न आंनैं ।
केवल ब्रह्म सति करि जांनैं
जहां तहां कबीर चलि जाइ ।
जहां तहां चौगनी बडाइ ॥ 191 [-, 13.8ab]

सिव बिरचि बिसन आगैं धरि लैंही ।
चुरि सिंघसन आसन दैंही ।
बैठौ यौ बैकुठ तुम्हारा ॥ 192 [13.8cd, 13.9a]

सिध सनेह करै अधिकारी ।
सोपुनि कहै कूमेर भंडारी ।
कहै कहां ल्यौं सब सुष जेता ।
भयौ [अ]ब्यापी देह सहेता ॥ 193 [13.9cd, 13.10cd]

भगत कै संगि लाग्यौ ही डोलै ।
अरु भगतनि कै घटि ह्वै बोलै ।
भगतन कौ जसु आपन गावै
जन कौं जस दे प्रीति बंधावै ॥ 194 [13.11cdab]

नर नारी जे कोई गोवै
पांवन होई परमपद पावै
नासैं भरम करंम सब जांही ।
उपज्यौ ज्ञांन भगत कै माही ॥ 195 [13.12cd, 13.13ab]

कबीर है करता की करा ।
भगति काजि पहुमि औतरचा ।
नृगुण ब्रह्म कबीर बिचारा
तातैं भौजल उतरचौ पारा ॥ 196 [13.14]

गिर परि जारि बारि मसि कीजे ।
भार अठारा लेषनि लीजै ।
बसुधा कौ सब कागद कीजे
सातौं समंद दोति मसि कीजे ॥ 197 [13.16abdc]

तउ न हरि गुण आवै अंत ।
सो जस गावै दास अनंत ।

दास अनंत कथा कही ।
अरु गुन अनत अपार ।
कछु कछु कही कबीर की
सत गुर कै उपपगार ॥ 198 [13.17ab, 13. doha]

॥ कबीर जी की परचई संपूरण समापता ॥

BIBLIOGRAPHY

Acharya, N. R. (ed.). 1959. *Panchatantra*. Bombay: Nirnaya Sagara Press.

Adi Granth. See Macauliffe; R. K. Varma 1966.

Amin, Shahid. 1988. "Gandhi as Mahatma: Gorakhpur District, Eastern UP, 1921-2." In Ranajit Guha and Gayatri Chakravorty Spivak (eds.), *Selected Subaltern Studies*. New York: Oxford University Press, pp. 288-348.

Ananta-das. *Kabir Parachai*. See R. K. Varma 1983.

Anurag Sagar. Hindi text. See Yugalananda 1953: vol. 2.

Anurag Sagar. 1984. Translation into English under the direction of *sant* Ajaib Singh Ji as *The Ocean of Love: The Anurag Sagar of Kabir*. Sanbornton, New Hampshire: Sant Bani Ashram.

'Attar, Faridu'd-Din. 1975. *Tazkiratu' l-Auliya'*. Abridged trans. by Bankey Behari. 2d ed.; Lahore: Sh. Muhammand Ashraf. First pub. 1961.

———. 1979. *Tazkiratu' l-Auliya'*. Abridged trans. by A. J. Arberry as *Muslim Saints and Mystics*. London: Routledge & Kegan Paul. First pub. 1966.

B40 Janam-Sakhi. See McLeod 1980.

Babur, Zahiru'd-din Muhammad. 1972. *Babur-Nama* (*Memoirs of Babur*). Trans. from Turki by Annette Susannah Beveridge. 2 vols. in 1. Reprint; New Delhi: Oriental Books Reprint Corporation. First pub. 1922.

Badathval, Pitambaradatta. See Barthwal, P. D.

Baghelavamshavarnan. See Kabir 1906.

Bahura, Gopalanarayan (G. N.) and Lakshminarayan Gosvami Dikshit. 1961. *Vidyabhushan-Grantha-Sangrah-Suchi*. Jodhpur: Rajasthan Prachya-vidya Pratishthan.

———. 1966. *Santa Kabir.* Ed. by Ram Kumar Varma. 5th imp.; Allahabad: Sahitya Bhavan. A devanagari edition of all of Kabir's verses in the *Guru Granth Sahib.*

———. 1969. *Kabir-granthavali.* Ed. by Mataprasad Gupta. Allahabad: Lokabharati Prakashan.

———. 1972. *Kabir-bijak.* Ed. by Shukadev Simha (Singh). Allahabad: Nilabh Prakashan.

Kabir-charitra-bodh. Hindi text. See Yugalananda: vol. 11.

Keay, F. E. 1931. *Kabir and His Followers.* Calcutta: Association Press.

Laihana Simha alias Haridas. 1962. *Kabir Kasauti.* Bombay: Shrivenkateshvar Press. Apparently written in A. D. 1885 (1942 V. S.).

Lorenzen, David N. 1972. *The Kapalikas and Kalamukhas.* Berkeley: University of California Press.

———. 1981. "The Kabir Panth: Heretics to Hindus." In David N. Lorenzen (ed.), *Religious Change and Cultural Domination.* Mexico: El Colegio de Mexico, pp. 151-71.

———. 1987a. "The Social Ideologies of Hagiography: Sankara, Tukaram and Kabir." In M. Israel and N. K. Wagle (eds.), *Religion and Society in Maharashtra.* Toronto: Centre for South Asian Studies, University of Toronto, pp. 92-114.

———. 1987b. "The Kabir Panth and Social Protest." In K. Schomer and W. H. McLeod (eds.), *The Sants: Studies in a Devotional Tradition of India.* Delhi: Motilal Banarsidass, pp. 281-303.

———. 1987c. "Traditions of Non-caste Hinduism: The Kabir Panth," *Contributions to Indian Sociology* 21:264-83.

Macauliffe, M. A. 1963. *The Sikh Religion*, 6 vols. in 3. With a translation of the *Adi Granth.* Reprint; Delhi: S. Chand and Co. First pub. 1909.

Madhava, son of Abhayachandra. 1938. *Virabhanudayakavyam.* Ed. and trans. by K. K. Lele and Anant Shastri Upadhyaya with critical analysis by Hiranand Sastri. Rewa: Rewa Durbar. See also H. Shastri.

Mahendra. 1969. *Kabir ki Bhasha.* Delhi: Shabdakar.

Mahipati. 1982. *Bhaktavijaya.* Trans. by Justin E. Abbott and Narhar R. Godbole as *Stories of Indian Saints*, 2 vols. in 1. Reprint; Delhi: Motilal Banarsidass. Trans. first pub. in 1933. Marathi text written in A.D. 1762.

Mangaladas Svami (ed.). 1962. *Shri Maharaj Haridasaji ki Vani Satippani va Apar Niranjani Mahatmaom ki Rachana ke Amshamsha.* Jaipur: Nikhil Bharatiy Niranjani Maha Sabha.

McLeod, W. H. 1966. "Guru Nanak and Kabir," *Proceedings of the First Punjab History Conference* (*November 12-14, 1965*). Patiala: Punjabi University.

———. 1976. *Guru Nanak and the Sikh Religion.* Reprint; Delhi: Oxford University Press. First pub. 1968.

———. 1980. Trans. of *The B40 Janam-Sakhi.* Amritsar: Guru Nanak Dev University.

Menariya, Omkaralal. 1974 and 1978. *Rajasthani-Hindi Hastalikhit Grantha-Suchi*, vols. 3 and 4. Jodhpur: Rajasthan Prachyavidya Pratishthan.

Muhsin Fani. 1843. *The Dabistan or School of Manners.* Trans. in two vols. by D. Shea and A. Troyer. Paris.

Munishvar Ray "Munish." 1977. *Kabir-pantha ki Jagu Shakha.* Bidupur: Kabir Math [Jagu Shakha Guru-gadi].

Nabha-das. 1969. *Shribhaktamal.* With the verse commentary of Priya-das (1712) and a modern prose commentary. 5th imp.; Lucknow: Tejakumar Press.

Nicholson, Reynold A. (R. A.). 1912. "Ibrahim b. Adham." In Carl Bezold (ed.), *Zeitschrift fur Assyriologie und Verwandte Gebiete.* Strassburg: Verlag von Karl J. Trubner, pp. 215-20.

Oberoi, Harjot S. 1987. "From Punjab to 'Khalistan': Territoriality and Meta-commentary," *Pacific Affairs* 60, 1:26-41.

Pam. Sarvajit ki Goshthi. See *Sarvajit ki Goshthi.*

Pandey, A. B. 1956. *History of the First Afghan Empire in India.* [?Delhi]: Bookland Limited.

Paramananda-das. 1956. *Kabir Manshur.* Short version. Trans. from Urdu into Hindi by Sudhadasaji Saheb "Sukavi." Baroda: Pandit Shri Motidasaji Chetanadasaji.

———. 1984. *Kabir Manshur.* Long version. Trans. from Urdu into Hindi by Madhavacharyya. New imp.; Bombay: Lakshmivenkateshvar Steam Press, 1984. The date this edition was first published is unknown.

Pritchard, James B. (ed.). 1969. *Ancient Eastern Texts Relating to the Old Testament.* 3rd ed.; Princeton: Princeton University Press.

Priya-das. See Nabha-das.

Raghav-das. 1963. *Bhaktamal.* With the verse commentary of Chatur-das (*c.* A.D. 1800) and the modern prose commentary of Narayan-das. Pushkar.

———. 1965. *Raghavadas Krit Bhaktamal.* With the verse commentary of Chatur-das (*c.* 1880 A.D.). Ed. by Agarachanda Nahata. Jodhpur:

Rajasthan Oriental Research Insitute.

Ramananda. 1955. *Ramananda ki Hindi Rachanaem.* Ed. by P. D. Badathval (Barthwal). Varanasi: Nagaripracharini Sabha.

Ramananda-das. 1974. *Shri Sadguru Kabir.* Satamalapur, Samastipur District, Bihar: Shriman Mahanta Ramavatar Sahab.

Rangaswamy, M. A. Dorai. See Dorai Rangaswamy, M. A.

Ray "Munish," Munishvar. See Munishvar Ray "Munish."

Rizvi, Saiyid Athar Abbas (S. A. A.). 1975. *Religious and Intellectual History of the Muslims in Akbar's Reign.* New Delhi: Munshiram Manoharlal.

———. 1978-1983. *A History of Sufism in India*, 2 vols. New Delhi: Munshiram Manoharlal.

Russell, R. V. and Hira Lal. 1969. *Tribes and Castes of the Central Provinces of India*, 4 vols. Ousterhout N.B.: Anthropological Publications. Reprint of 1916 edition.

Sadhusaran Gosvami. 1978. "*Kabir Bijak ki Tikaom ka Alochanatmak Adhyayan.*" In Vivek-das 1978:255-270.

Sarvajit ki Goshthi. 1930. Ed. by *baba* Lakhanadasaji as *Pam. Sarvajit ki Goshthi.* Kabir Chaura, Varanasi: the editor.

Scott, David. 1985. *Kabir's Mythology.* Delhi: Bharatiya Vidya Prakashan.

Sekkizhaar. 1985. *Periya Puranam.* Condensed English version by G. Vanmikananthan. Mylapore, Madras: Sri Ramakrishna Math.

Sen, Kshitimohan (K. M.). 1974. *Medieval Mysticism of India.* Reprint; New Delhi: Oriental Books Reprint Corp. First pub. 1929.

Sethi, V. K. 1984. *Kabir: The Weaver of God's Name.* Dera Baba Jaimal Singh, Amritsar District: Radha Soami Satsang Beas.

Shankar-das. 1955. *Shri Kabir Charitamrit.* Shivapur, Varanasi: Shri Kabir Jagu Sthan.

Shastri, Hirananda. 1925. *The Baghela Dynasty of Rewah.* Archaelogical survey of India, no. 21. Calcutta: Government of India. See also Madhava, son of Abhayachandra.

Shrikrishna Lal. "Svami Ramananda ka Jivan-charitra." In Ramananda 1955: 33-50.

Shrivastav, Badarinarayan (B. N.). 1957. *Ramananda-sampraday tatha Hindi-sahitya par usaka Prabhav.* Allahabad: Hindi Parishad.

Simha, Bhagavati Prasad (B. P.). 1957. *Ram Bhakti mem Rasik Sampraday.* Balaramapur: Avadh Sahitya Mandir.

Singh, Jodh. 1971. *Kabir*. Patiala: Punjab University.

Singh, Mohan. 1934. *Kabir: His Biography*, vol. 1 of *Kabir and the Bhagti Movement*. Lahore: Atma Ram and Sons.

Srivastava, A. L. 1964. *The Mughul Empire*. 4th ed.; Agra: Shiva Lal Agarwala and Co.

Tapasvi, Shri. 1976. *Kabir Satya Prakash Satik*. With a modern Hindi prose commentary by Charanadasaji. Limbadi, Gujarat: Kabir Ashram, the author.

Thompson, John B. 1984. *Studies in the Theory of Ideology*. Cambridge: Polity Press.

Thukral, Uma. 1979. "*Kabir Panthi Sahitya ka Alochanatmak Adhyay*," unpublished D. Phil. dissertation. Kotdwar: Gadhaval Vishvavidyalay.

———. 1989. "La doctrina del avatar en el Kabir Panth," *Estudios de Asia y Africa* 24:71-81.

Trautmann, Thomas R. (T. R.). 1969. "Length of Generation and Reign in Ancient India," *Journal of the American Oriental Society* 89:564-77.

Varma, Dhirendra. 1986. *Hindi Sahitya Kosh*. 2 vols. 2nd edition; Varanasi: Jnanamandal Limited. First published in 1963.

Varma, Ram Kumar (R. K.). 1966. *Santa Kabir*. With Kabir's works from the *Adi Granth* edited in devanagari script. 5th imp.; Allahabad: Sahitya Bhavan.

———. 1971. *Hindi Sahitya ka Alochanatmak Itihas*. 6th imp.; Allahabad: Ramanarayanalal Benimadhav.

———. 1977. *Kabir: Biography and Philosophy*. New Delhi: Prints India.

———. 1983. *Kabir: Ek Anushilan*. With the text of Ananta-das's *Kabir Parachai*. Allahabad: Sahitya Bhavan.

Vaudeville, Charlotte. 1974. *Kabir*, vol. 1. Oxford: Clarendon Press.

Venkatachari, K. K. A. 1988. Personal letter.

Vivek-das (ed). 1978. *Kabir Sahab*. Varanasi: Kabiravani Prakashan Kendra.

Westcott, G. H. 1953. *Kabir and the Kabir Panth*. Reprint; Calcutta: Susil Gupta. First pub. 1907.

Yugalananda Bihari (ed.). 1953. *Kabir Sagar*, 11 vols. Bombay: Shrivenkateshvar Steam Press. This collection seems to have been first published in the early 1930's and has been reprinted several times since.

Yugal-das. See Kabir 1906.

INDEX